90 0593197 8

Russian Masculinities in History and Culture

Also by Barbara Evans Clements

BOLSHEVIK FEMINIST: The Life of Aleksandra Kollontai

BOLSHEVIK WOMEN

DAUGHTERS OF REVOLUTION: A History of Soviet Women

RUSSIA'S WOMEN: Accommodation, Resistance, Transformation (*edited with Barbara Alpern Engel and Christine D. Worobec*)

Also by Dan Healey

HOMOSEXUAL DESIRE IN REVOLUTIONARY RUSSIA: The Regulation of Sexual and Gender Dissent

Russian Masculinities in History and Culture

Edited by

Barbara Evans Clements
Professor of History Emeritus
The University of Akron

Rebecca Friedman
Assistant Professor of History
Florida International University
North Miami
Florida

and

Dan Healey
Lecturer in History
University of Wales Swansea

First published 2002 by
PALGRAVE
Houndmills, Basingstoke, Hampshire RG21 6XS and
175 Fifth Avenue, New York, N.Y. 10010
Companies and representatives throughout the world

PALGRAVE is the new global academic imprint of St. Martin's Press LLC Scholarly and Reference Division and Palgrave Publishers Ltd (formerly Macmillan Press Ltd).

ISBN 0–333–94544–1

This book is printed on paper suitable for recycling and made from fully managed and sustained forest sources.

A catalogue record for this book is available from the British Library.

Library of Congress Cataloging-in-Publication Data

Russian masculinities in history and culture / edited by Barbara Evans Clements, Rebecca Friedman, and Dan Healey.
p. cm.
Includes bibliographical references and index.
ISBN 0–333–94544–1 (cloth)
1. Men – Russia (Federation) – Psychology. 2. Masculinity – Russia (Federation). I. Clements, Barbara Evans, 1945– . II. Friedman, Rebecca, 1968– . III. Healey, Dan, 1957–
HQ1090.7.R8 R87 2001
305.31'0947 – dc21 2001036882

Transferred to digital printing 2002

Printed and bound in Great Britain by
Antony Rowe Ltd, Chippenham and Eastbourne

University of Plymouth
Charles Seale-Hayne Library

Customer ID: *****85543

Title: The Avant-garde in Russia, 1910-1930 : new perspectives /
ID: 9009064620
Due: 18/05/2013 23:59:00 BST

Title: Russian constructivism /
ID: 9000413020
Due: 18/05/2013 23:59:00 BST

Total items: 2
Total fines: £9.70
27 Apr 2013
Checked out: 6

Thank you for using the
3M SelfCheck™ System

Contents

List of Illustrations

Notes on the Contributors

Barbara Evans Clements is Professor of History Emeritus at the University of Akron. She is the author and co-editor of several books on Russian women's history, the most recent of which is *Bolshevik Women* (1997).

Barbara Alpern Engel is Professor of History at the University of Colorado, Boulder. She has published numerous articles and books, most recently *Between the Fields and the City: Women, Work and Family in Russia, 1861–1914* (1994), and *A Revolution of their Own: Voices of Women in Soviet History*, edited with Anastasia Posadskaya-Vanderbeck (1998).

Rebecca Friedman is Assistant Professor of History at Florida International University in Miami. She received her PhD from the University of Michigan (2000) and is currently working on a monograph entitled 'In the Company of Men: On Masculinity among University Students in Nicholaevan Russia'.

Julie Gilmour is a doctoral candidate at the University of Chicago where she is completing a dissertation on Soviet sport and Soviet notions of the ideal citizen after the Second World War.

Dan Healey is lecturer in Russian history in the Department of History, University of Wales Swansea, United Kingdom. He is the author of the first book-length study of same-sex love in modern Russia, *Homosexual Desire in Revolutionary Russia: the Regulation of Sexual and Gender Dissent* (2001). He is currently working on a monograph about early Soviet forensic medicine and the limits of sexual utopianism.

Catriona Kelly is Reader in Russian at New College, University of Oxford. Her most recent publications are *Constructing Russian Culture in the Age of Revolution* (1998) and *Russian Cultural Studies: An Introduction*, edited with David Shepherd (1998); *Utopias: Russian Modernist Texts 1905–1940* (1999). *Russian Literature, Modernism, and the Visual Arts*, edited with Stephen Lovell, is forthcoming.

Nancy Shields Kollmann is Professor of History at Stanford University. She has published *Kinship and Politics: the Making of the Muscovite Polit-*

ical System, 1345–1547 (1987); *By Honor Bound: State and Society in Early Modern Russia* (1999); essays on Russia in *The New Cambridge Medieval History*, vol. 6 (2000), vol. 7 (1998) and in *Russia: a History*, ed. Gregory Freeze (1997).

Karen Petrone is Associate Professor of History at the University of Kentucky. She is the author of *Life Has Become More Joyous, Comrades: Celebrations in the Time of Stalin* (2000). Her manuscript in progress is entitled 'Masculinity and the Mobilization of the Nation: Imperial and Soviet Military and Patriotic Cultures, 1900–1953'.

Thomas G. Schrand is Associate Professor of History at Philadelphia University. His research focuses on gender and cultural history of the Stalin era and he is the author of several articles on the roles of women's labor and social activism in the Soviet industrialization campaign.

S. A. Smith is Professor of History at the University of Essex, England. His works include *Red Petrograd: Revolution in the Factories, 1917–18* (1983); *Notes of a Red Guard: the Autobiography of Eduard Dune*, edited with Diane Koenker (1993); and *A Road is Made: Communism in Shanghai, 1920–27* (2000).

Olga Vainshtein teaches theory, culture, gender studies and literature at the Russian State Humantities University in Moscow. She has written books and articles on topics as diverse as Matthew Arnold, Victorian criticism, postmodernism, Russian private life, and Russian and American fashion. Her current projects include a history of Russian dandyism.

Christine D. Worobec is Professor of History at Northern Illinois University. Her publications include *Peasant Russia: Family and Community in the Post-Emancipation Period* (1991) and *Possessed: Women, Witches, and Demons in Imperial Russia* (2001).

1
Introduction

Barbara Evans Clements

> And my men of Kursk are famed as warriors.
> They were swaddled under trumpets.
> They were brought up under helmets.
> They were fed at lance point.
> The roads are known to them.
> The ravines are familiar to them.
> Their bows are taut,
> their quivers are open,
> their sabers have been sharpened.
> They race into the prairie like gray wolves,
> seeking honor for themselves
> and glory for their prince.
>
> *The Lay of Igor's Campaign*[1]

Igor's warriors galloped across the southern plains of the Rus' lands in the twelfth century. Eight hundred years later, on the same great open landscape, millions of peasant conscripts trudged behind clanking, smoking, ponderous tanks. Igor's brightly comparisoned horses would have found no grass to eat in the wasteland that modern armies left in their wake; indeed, the vast front between German and Soviet forces was littered with the corpses of horses ground up by the war machine. And yet, the foot soldiers of the Second World War were urged into battle with songs and banners and speeches that called on the very martial ideals that had inspired the Rus' of the twelfth century. Images of medieval warriors beckoned from Soviet posters during the Second World War, and the tales of long-dead princes such as Alexander Nevskii and Ivan the Terrible were told again.

Foreign observers at the time and scholars since have interpreted the Stalin regime's appeal to ancient heroes as a desperate effort to enlist public support. In a time of utmost peril, propagandists sought to draw on any and all wellsprings of loyalty in a populace that might not rally to communist slogans, given the persecutions of the previous decade. There is probably truth to this interpretation. It seems likely as well that the medieval heroes were summoned because the values they embodied were still alive in the twentieth century, were still part of the definition of manhood and hence appealed to communist propagandists as well as to ordinary Soviet citizens. The fearsome, relentless warrior was a legend born in a distant past, but he was also an icon of European culture and hence he has remained a ready source of inspiration in wars, athletic contests, and action movies.

Exploring the creation and functioning of mythic conceptions of masculinity in Russia and uncovering more mundane, quotidian notions that have come and gone with social changes is the purpose of this collection of articles. The study of masculinity is only just beginning among Russianists and indeed among historians of other nations as well, so it is one that still requires some explanation. Why is such study important? What can it teach us that we do not already know? To answer these questions, it is necessary to survey briefly the development of the study of gender and of masculinity over the past several decades.

The study of gender

Gender is a term that is employed by social scientists to refer to the ways in which human societies distinguish between women and men. Sexual dimorphism – the physical differences between the male and female members of homo sapiens – is the physical reality on which gender ideas are based, but those ideas are social constructs. They are, in the words of Gisela Bock, 'a complex set of relations and processes' that extend their influence into every sphere of human activity.[2] 'As a *structure*,' Judith Lorber writes, 'gender divides work in the home and in economic production, legitimates those in authority, and organizes sexuality and emotional life.'[3] Gender norms are taught from infancy and in many cultures they become so internalized as to seem expressive of an essential and unchanging human nature. But in fact ideas about men and women do change, as do all social constructs. Even within individual societies, gender notions are differentiated in accord with the hierarchies of power. The lowly can and do contest norms that grant superiority to those with power over them, and the contest sometimes leads to change. 'That gender is not fixed in advance of social interaction, but is constructed in interaction, is an important theme in the modern sociology of gender,' writes R. W. Connell.[4] In short, gender ideas are complex, significant, and malleable. Because they change, they have a history.

For decades the study of gender has been the purview of anthropologists and sociologists, who perceived, if dimly sometimes, the significance of gender in human belief and behavior. Historians had not shared this perception, until scholars doing women's studies began to probe the meanings of the feminine. That inquiry produced a large body of work on ideas and practices defining women, and it also brought scholars increasingly to believe that they needed to know more about the masculine. Examining the feminine was important, particularly in view of the bias in previous scholarship toward the male, but understanding the position of women in any society also requires understanding that of men; grasping the nuances of the feminine requires grasping those of the masculine. 'Masculinity and femininity are inherently relational concepts, which have meaning in relation to each other, as a social demarcation and a cultural opposition,' Connell argues.[5] And even while establishing boundaries, notions of femininity and masculinity interact; they are, in the words of Harriet Bjerrum Nielsen and Monica Rudberg, '*conditioned by each other*'.[6] This realization has led a growing number of literary scholars, historians, and social scientists to a systematic study of constructions of masculinity, and their work to date has yielded valuable theoretical ideas.

The study of masculinity

Masculinity is most obviously a set of normative assertions about the nature of the adult male and his conduct in society. Notions about what it is to be a man are fundamental, enduring, and remarkably stable constituents of an individual's consciousness. Janet Spence has written, 'Gender is one of the earliest and most central components of the self-concept and serves as an organizing principle through which experiences and perceptions of the self and others are filtered.' Gender identity also links the individual psyche to the world it inhabits. 'My masculinity is a bond, a glue, to the patriarchal world,' Michael Kaufman has written. 'It is the thing that makes that world mine, that makes it more or less comfortable to live in. Through the incorporation of a dominant form of masculinity particular to my class, race, nationality, era, sexual orientation, and religion, I gained real benefits *and* an individual sense of self-worth.'[7]

Masculinity is also crucially involved in the establishment and maintenance of hierarchies. Kaufman continues, 'In a world dominated by men, the world of men is, by definition, a world of power. That power is a structured part of the economies and systems of political and social organization; it forms part of the core of religion, family, forms of play, and intellectual life.'[8] Power has usually been unequally distributed, of course, and, most societies, including European ones since the ancient period, have made distinctions between the types of behavior appropriate to men at different levels of the social pyramid. The masculinity of the ruling elite, the so-called 'hegemonic masculinity', defines and sanctions the character and conduct of the men at the top. Warriors such as Igor and his band were central to the hegemonic masculinity of Europe for more than two thousand years. Whether males lower down in the social hierarchy, peasants for example, were permitted to become warriors varied from time to time and society to society, but often peasants learned that only the high born, the 'nobles', possessed the innate qualities that made men valorous. The lowly did contest such notions, creating among themselves alternative conceptions of masculinity. An example from Russian history is the clever peasant of folklore who outwits his social betters to win fortune and, oftentimes, the princess as well.[9] Cleverness is a trait treated with distrust by the warrior ethos, because it is subversive and subtle rather than forthrightly aggressive.

But all men and boys in any society are also deeply influenced by the conceptions of manhood that are promoted by the powerful, and indeed certain gender values are conceived as universals. That is, most societies have a generic conception of masculinity which they apply to all men and which commonly includes requirements to be honest, physically strong, competent, dutiful to superiors, cooperative but assertive toward equals, and directive but protective toward the weak. Men of all social strata are also usually expected to provide for and defend their families. These common standards of masculinity promote social cohesion, argues David Gilmore. 'Manhood is the social barrier,' he writes, 'that societies must erect against entropy, human enemies, the forces of nature, time, and all the human weaknesses that endanger group life.'[10] The larger the society, the greater the number of distinctions raised upon the foundational, universal notions of what a man should be. Through most of European history those distinctions have been fairly elaborate and significant.

And finally, values defining European masculinity have asserted the innate superiority of the male to the female. Indeed, the Latin roots of the English word 'virtue' are *vir*, meaning male, and *virtus*, manliness. The beliefs that underlie this etymology are well known: God made the male physically and mentally stronger than the female and created the female to be man's companion and helpmeet. Maintaining control over the women in his family was therefore seen in many cultures as an important test of a man's masculinity. A man, declared the twelfth-century Rus' prince Vladimir Monomakh, should love 'his women,' but 'grant them no power over you'.[11] These rules were leavened with other gender considerations, however. A man did not have authority over women of superior social rank, and to older female kin he was enjoined to show respect. Throughout most of European history men, even kings, were supposed to honor their mothers. 'Do not forget your mother,' advised an eleventh-century Rus' collection of homilies; 'do her will and obey her with the fear of the Lord.'[12] Indeed a submissive, even reverent attitude toward one's parents was seen throughout medieval Europe as one of the primary masculine obligations.

The history of masculinity

Historians have traced in broad outline the hegemonic masculinities of the last several thousand years of European history. As summarized by Charlotte Hooper, they consist of the following:

> the Greek citizen-warrior model; the patriarchal Judeo-Christian model; the honor-patronage model; and a Protestant bourgeois rationalist model. The Greek model combined militarism with rationalism and equated manliness with citizenship in a masculine arena of free speech and politics. In contrast, the Judeo-Christian ideal of manliness emphasized a more domesticated ideal of responsibility, ownership, and the authority of the father. The honor-patronage model was an aristocratic ideal in which personal bonds between men, military heroism, and risk-taking were highly valued, with the duel as the ultimate test of masculinity. The bourgeois rationalist model idealized competitive individualism, reason, and self-control or self-denial, combining respectability as breadwinner and head of household with calculative rationality in public life.[13]

Such ideal types are necessarily more suggestive than exact, but they provide a general description from which to begin an historical discussion. Our concern in this volume will be constructions of masculinity in Russia from the Muscovite period to the 1950s, so it will be sufficient for us to employ Hooper's typology so as to sum up the general ideas about masculinity that have prevailed in Europe since the Middle Ages. Between the end of the Roman period and the twelfth century, the peoples of the continent created a dominant conception of the masculine by blending together the warrior-citizen of Greece and Rome, the Judeo-Christian pious patriarch, and the pagan warrior idealized by the Celtic, Nordic, and Slavic cultures. It was an awkward combination, for the Church advocated a far gentler character for male leaders than did the peoples it was converting to Christianity. Consequently, hegemonic masculinities in the great thousand years of the medieval period were often contested not just by the poor but also by the various elites themselves, the dialogue between the church and the warriors over the essential qualities of masculinity being only the most obvious of these disputes. Vladimir Monomakh, the twelfth-century Rus' prince, expressed these dueling conceptions perfectly in his last testament. The first two-thirds of this instruction to his sons is devoted to enjoining them to be humble, charitable managers and guardians of their households, as well as dutiful Christians. In the last third, Monomakh tells the story of his own life, a tale of battles with the enemies of the Rus' in which he stresses his physical strength, endurance, and heroism. A ferocious warrior in the field, a gentle, attentive father at home, a submissive son of the Church, these various faces of Monomakh reflect the uneasy combination of hegemonic masculine values that was typical of medieval Europe.[14]

By the fifteenth century the Christianized warrior had given way to a style of elite masculinity that has been labeled 'the honor-patronage model'. It still contained a large component of warrior values and it was still closely connected to the land-owning nobility, but it laid less stress on success in warfare and more on the social skills of the courtier. The 'honor-patronage model' in turn came under challenge in the sixteenth and seventeenth centuries from political commentators who were feeling their way toward democratic values. Beginning with contract theorists of the sixteenth century such as Philippe de Mornay, social critics proclaimed that the power to govern derived from the consent of the governed. Of course, citizens must be capable of rational, independent judgment to participate in politics, but, as John Locke declared, rationality was the birthright of all men. Eighteenth-century Enlightenment publicists in Britain and France then pushed the argument still further, contrasting decadent, effeminate nobles to an idealized middle-class man who was honest, thoughtful, and dedicated to social reform. Susan Juster has written, 'To be manly was to be open and sincere, to use language to elucidate rather than to obscure truth, to create a society where abstract reason and impartial appeals to scientific knowledge determined right from wrong.'[15] This responsible public citizen was also a kindly paterfamilias, providing for his wife and children and guiding their moral and social development.

The shift in ideals of masculinity in the early-modern period was of course very closely connected to the political and economic transformations then afoot in western and central Europe. Historians and social scientists debate the extent to which gender norms change in response to changes elsewhere in the social system, the extent to which they condition behavior and ideas and hence play a shaping rather than simply a reactionary part. Detailed study may ultimately reveal causal patterns that vary with time and place. What seems clear at this very early stage in the development of the historiography of masculinity is that the notion of what was appropriately male changed with notions of the nature of sovereignty and governance. Far more resistant to rethinking were ideas of the female. Defined as innately less rational than men, women (along with dependent men such as slaves, servants, and the poor in general) remained excluded from the circle of those entitled, even in theory, to political power and personal autonomy.[16]

In the nineteenth century the 'bourgeois-rationalist' ideal of masculinity spread across Europe, becoming ever more appealing because of its association with the successes of industrialization. It also became more democratic, for social commentators and political activists argued ever more insistently that any man, however lowly his origins, could achieve the status of self-reliant, self-disciplined citizen and provider through his own personal effort. He must be courageous and ethical to survive the corruptions of the city and also to adjust to a world of accelerating change, so he required a strong moral character, but this he could learn, along with work skills, and hone through the practice of rigorous self-discipline.[17]

The liberal individualism of the bourgeois-rationalist model is obvious, but this ideal addressed itself as well to men's relations with one another, as indeed all conceptions of masculinity must. Gender ideas, as we have seen, are important ingredients in the glue that holds societies together. To prove himself and thereby win acceptance from other men, a man must demonstrate that he has the required virtues to women and children and, most importantly, to other men. In the nineteenth century there was increasing stress on masculinity being proven in the world of work. John Tosh has written, 'The idea that what a man did in his working life was an authentic expression of his individuality was one of the most characteristic – and enduring – features of middle-class masculinity.'[18] There was as well a burgeoning assortment of organizations and places – unions, clubs, professional associations, ballparks, and taverns – that arose as centers of male sociability and display. In all these venues men arranged themselves into hierarchies, competed with one another, and established friendships and alliances. Certain cultures (the US and Britain) and social levels (the entrepreneurial and professional elites) exalted the individualism of the bourgeois ideal and tended therefore to praise a man who proved himself in an alienating world and then returned home to his family, where his deepest emotional attachments lay. Other people (working-class men and peasants generally, Europeans from the more gender-segregated cultures of the Mediterranean basin) paid more heed to the necessity for men to affiliate with one another, and hence prized kin loyalties and comradeship as expressions of masculinity. They probably also put commensurately less stress on the importance of economic success as a marker of masculine achievement, since economic success was far less possible in their milieus. Such differences between European social groups and regions remain to be studied in depth.

The masculine ideal of the nineteenth century was also defined, of course, in relation to women. The female ideal of that century is in fact rather better known than the male, thanks to the work of women's historians. She was to be, in the words of Victorian poet Coventry Patmore, 'the angel in the house', a creature less rational than the male but gifted with an innate moral sensibility that suited her for providing emotional support to her family and instruction to her children. The same qualities also enabled her to manage the chores of housewifery, which increasingly included being a knowledgeable consumer in a rapidly changing marketplace. A wife's accomplishments – devotion to her family, submission to the authority of her husband, and skill at creating a well-appointed, well-run home – also testified to her husband's mastery of the role of paterfamilias and therefore to his manliness. These ideas from the affluent middle class had enormous appeal among the less prosperous bourgeoisie and with working people as well. Trade unions all over Europe campaigned in the later decades of the nineteenth century for the so-called 'family wage', a pay packet large enough that the male worker's wife and children would not have to join the paid labor force where they would depress wages and also lower the status accorded to working men.

The successful performance of masculine virtues had always depended to some extent on women, who were both members of the audience and players in the supporting cast, but never had the importance of women to the demonstration of manliness been greater than in the nineteenth century, when democratic values and migration to the cities weakened the social power of traditional affiliations such as kinship and dependencies on class superiors. The growing significance of women, or at least of wives and daughters, to men's sense of achievement may explain, in part, the arrival of a 'crisis of masculinity' toward the end of the nineteenth century. More and more of those bourgeois 'angels' were becoming dissatisfied with the restrictions on their participation in public life, as well as with the power of husbands over wives. Feminism arose to challenge patriarchal power, with increasing success. Meanwhile, the emergence of ever larger corporations and civil-service bureaucracies meant that many middle-class and working-class men found themselves holding very routinized jobs with limited possibilities for advancement. The bourgeois-rationalist ethos promised financial success and great autonomy to the man who followed its precepts, but the chances of becoming a self-made success story seemed diminished in the cities of the industrialized world by the late nineteenth century. A sense of newly constricted opportunities and female challenges to male prerogatives brought forth profound doubts about the masculinity of middle-class men. Increasingly strident calls for elite men to engage in sports in Britain, a rising lament about the loss of virility in France, the cult of the Western hero in the US, all were among efforts made in northwestern Europe and North America to assert an aggressive and very physical masculinity in the face of unsettling social changes.[19]

This 'crisis' had manifold negative consequences. The militarism of the fin-de-siècle has been associated with the rising anxiety, as have racist attempts among the imperial powers to define British or French or German manhood in opposition to that of the men of Asia and Africa, who were derided as weak, even effeminate. It was also in the last decades of the nineteenth century that sex between men came to be seen as signifying an identity, that of the homosexual. In earlier centuries Europeans had considered sex between men as a sin to which anyone could be led; in the nineteenth century they began to see it as the fundamental character flaw of a despised and dangerous minority. Historians argue that this deeply felt need to affirm hegemonic masculinities by stigmatizing others was symptomatic of the unease gripping fin-de-siècle Europe.

These anxieties climaxed in the great catastrophe of the First World War. Scholarship on subsequent twentieth-century developments remains very rudimentary as yet, but that which has been written suggests that the century was marked by a continuing modification of the 'bourgeois-rationalist' model in the direction of ever greater stress on individualism and egalitarianism. This process accelerated in the second half of the century, after the defeat of fascism and its reactionary hyper-masculinism. Scholars argue that when feminism revived and undertook a thoroughgoing re-examination of received notions of masculinity in the second half of the twentieth century it set off a new 'masculinity crisis' akin to that of the late nineteenth century in its severity. The result was a still ongoing, often contentious debate in which Europeans, in dialogue with peoples from around the planet, struggle to affirm an ideal that preserves elements of the bourgeois-rationalist model while stripping it of its racism, sexism, and homophobia.[20]

The findings of this volume

The papers included here are pathbreaking attempts to fit Russia into these broad patterns, to determine the ways in which Russian culture across the centuries has been similar to the rest of Europe in its definitions of male character and behavior, the ways in which it has had its own particular understandings and practices. An extended discussion of conclusions suggested by this scholarship follows the papers at the end of the volume, but it behoves an introducer to provide a few suggestions at the outset as well.

The commonalities between Russian and other European ideas about men are striking, but not surprising. Russia was culturally a part of Europe; it was a Christian nation with a long history of communication with western neighbors. Consequently, even in the medieval period, Russian gender norms were similar to those that prevailed elsewhere. When, after 1650, contacts with the West grew apace, Russian understandings of masculinity were as affected by imported ideas as were Russian theories of government or styles of literature. Our volume begins with an article by Nancy Kollmann that traces the impact of western notions of romantic love on the nobility during the reign of Peter the Great (1682–1725). The ten articles that follow range in topic from education during the reign of Nicholas I (1825–55) to sports magazines in the 1950s, but all touch at least in passing on foreign influences. Rebecca Friedman finds the ideals we have labeled 'bourgeois-rationalist' being taught to university students in the 1830s; Barbara Alpern Engel uncovers them guiding the rulings of Chancellery officials on petitions for marital separation late in the century. The self-disciplined, rational, and responsible family man is arguably present as well in the Soviet period in conceptions of masculinity discussed by Catriona Kelly, Thomas Schrand, and Julie Gilmour. Meanwhile more rebellious notions of masculinity were coming to Russia too, as demonstrated by Olga Vainshtein in her discussion of dandyism and Dan Healey in his chapter on the creation of a homosexual subculture.

Nor is it surprising to discover that the enormous processes of change sweeping Russia in the nineteenth and twentieth centuries affected conceptualizations of masculinity. As in the rest of the continent, industrialization and urbanization fostered challenges to long-held patriarchal notions that had granted fathers great power over their adult sons. Christine Worobec and S. A. Smith, in studies of the late-nineteenth-century peasantry and the working class respectively, analyze the ways in which young men living in the cities came to contest the authority of their elders. Meanwhile the intelligentsia, as Catriona Kelly demonstrates, was working through new definitions of manhood that stressed a regimen of physical and psychological toughness so as to overcome the proverbial lassitude of Russia's elite and enable it to deal with a rapidly changing world. The 1917 revolution and the transition to the Soviet period created a radically altered environment, and definitions of the New Soviet Man were quick in coming, but, as Thomas Schrand argues in his examination of the 1930s, there were significant continuities between pre- and post-revolutionary notions about masculinity.

The differences between Russian ideals and those that prevailed elsewhere are somewhat less evident than the commonalities. The essays here do suggest that the existence in Russia of an intrusive government bent on engineering change did affect notions about masculinity, as it did so much else in Russian history. Friedman, Kelly, Healey, and Gilmour demonstrate that both tsarist and soviet governments were intent on civilizing what they saw as the unruly masses of men by teaching them responsibility and self-discipline. Of course this mission was also undertaken in Western Europe and North America, but by a very different mix of private and public institutions. The essays here suggest that Russian governments sought rather more forcefully than those elsewhere to employ new notions of the masculine to create loyal, obedient, cooperative subjects and therefore fostered ideas that stressed service more, individual self-development and money-making a good deal less.

And what of the persistence of traditional Russian ideals? Were they all swept away by the great upheavals of the nineteenth and twentieth centuries? Perhaps not. Smith and Gilmour point to the preservation of village values by urban men. Far from growing into the respectable, dutiful servitors envisioned by the leaders, they continued well into the twentieth century to gather in smoky taverns, to fight and carouse, to cheer on their favorite soccer teams, and generally to socialize much as had their peasant forebears. Meanwhile even the leadership harkened back on occasion to ancient masculine ideas. Karen Petrone argues that tsarist and soviet journalists reporting military engagements with the Japanese army in 1904–5 and 1938 employed very similar notions of the solitary hero sacrificing himself for the cause. In these updated tales, the warrior had exchanged his shining armor for a khaki uniform, his shield for a machine gun, but he was still leading his mates into battles that would prove their valor to the ages.

Finally, what is the value of all this study? What do definitions of the masculine teach us about a society? Has gender any explanatory power or do changes in gender ideas simply follow upon other change processes? These are perhaps ultimately unanswerable, even metaphysical questions. What is certain, and what these papers ably argue, is the centrality of conceptions of the masculine in Russia's past. Tsarist bureaucrats, Stalinist economic planners, intellectuals and social reformers from the eighteenth to the twentieth century understood that they could not change Russia unless and until they changed Russian men. Fundamental to this task was defining what Russian men were and what they should become. While reformers constructed their definitions out of borrowings and traditions, opponents of change venerated ancient ideas of the benevolent patriarch and peasant elders fought with younger men over what manhood meant. That it was men all these people were talking about was evident to them; women got scarcely a nod, except from the feminists. It is only historians who have missed the importance of masculinity to these discussions. The purpose of this volume is to begin rectifying that oversight.

Notes

1. Serge A. Zenkovsky (ed.), *Medieval Russia's Epics, Chronicles, and Tales*, revised and enlarged edition (New York: Dutton, 1974), 171–2.

2. Gisela Bock, 'Women's History and Gender History: Aspects of an International Debate', *Gender and History in Western Europe*, ed. Robert Shoemaker and Mary Vincent (London, 1998), 33.
3. Judith Lorber, *Paradoxes of Gender* (New Haven, 1994), 34. Italics in the original.
4. R. W. Connell, *Masculinities* (Berkeley, 1995), 35.
5. Ibid., 44.
6. Harriet Bjerrum Nielsen and Monica Rudberg, *Psychological Gender and Modernity* (Oslo-Copenhagen-Stockholm, 1994), 49. Italics in the original.
7. Janet T. Spence, 'Gender Identity and its Implications for Concepts of Masculinity and Femininity', *Nebraska Symposium on Motivation*, ed. T. Sondregger (Lincoln, 1985), quoted in *The Gendered Society Reader*, ed. Michael S. Kimmel and Amy Aronson (New York, 2000), 84; Michael Kaufman, 'Men, Feminism, and Men's Contradictory Experiences of Power', *Theorizing Masculinities*, ed. Harry Brod and Michael Kaufman (Thousand Oaks, Calif., 1994), 148. Italics in the original.
8. Kaufman, 'Men, Feminism, and Men's Contradictory Experiences of Power', 142.
9. For examples see *Russian Fairy Tales*, trans. Norbert Guterman (New York: Pantheon, 1973).
10. David D. Gilmore, *Manhood in the Making: Cultural Concepts of Masculinity* (New Haven, 1990), 226.
11. Quoted in Zenkovsky, *Medieval Russia's Epics, Chronicles, and Tales*, 98.
12. *The Edificatory Prose of Kievan Rus'*, trans. William R. Veder with introductions by William R. Veder and Anatolij A. Turilov (Cambridge, Mass., 1994), 71.
13. Charlotte Hooper, 'Masculinist Practices and Gender Politics: the Operation of Multiple Masculinities in International Relations', *The 'Man' Question in International Relations*, eds, Marysia Zalewski and Jane Parpart (Boulder, Col., 1998), 33.
14. Zenkovsky, *Medieval Russia's Epics, Chronicles, and Tales*, 92–100.
15. Susan Juster, 'Demagogues or Mystagogues? Gender and the Language of Prophecy in the Age of Democratic Revolutions', *American Historical Review*, 104, 5 (December 1999), 1566.
16. On early-modern political theory see Jean Bethke Elshtain, 'The Family in Political Thoughts: Democratic Politics and the Question of Authority', *Fashioning Family Theory: New Approaches*, ed. Jetse Sprey (Newbury Park, Calif., 1990), 51–66. On economic and social changes of the period see Katrina Honeyman and Jordan Goodman, 'Women's Work, Gender, Conflict, and Labour Markets in Europe, 1500–1900', *Gender and History in Western Europe*, 353–76; Michael S. Kimmel, 'The Contemporary "Crisis" of Masculinity in Historical Perspective', *The Making of Masculinities: The New Men's Studies*, ed. Harry Brod (Boston, 1987), 121–53.
17. On this ethic in Britain see James Eli Adams, *Dandies and Desert Saints: Styles of Victorian Masculinity* (Ithaca, 1995); for the US see Judy Hilkey, *Success Manuals and Manhood in Gilded Age America* (Chapel Hill, 1997); on France see Robert A. Nye, *Masculinity and Male Codes of Honor in Modern France* (New York, 1993).
18. John Tosh, 'What Should Historians Do with Masculinity? Reflections on Nineteenth-Century Britain', *Gender and History in Western Europe*, 69.

19. For Great Britain see Adams, *Dandies and Desert Saints*; for France, Nye, *Masculinity and Male Codes of Honor in Modern France*; for the US, Mark C. Carnes, *Secret Ritual and Manhood in Victorian America* (New Haven, 1989).
20. On the late twentieth century see Roger Horrocks, *Male Myths and Icons: Masculinity in Popular Culture* (New York, 1992); Nielsen and Rudberg, *Psychological Gender and Modernity.*

2
'What's Love Got to Do With It?': Changing Models of Masculinity in Muscovite and Petrine Russia

Nancy Shields Kollmann

> 'From Grand Prince Vasilii Ivanovich of all Rus', to my wife Elena. I am here, thank God, by the grace of God and his Immaculate Mother and the Miracleworker St Nikola, alive until God's will, and I am completely healthy and suffer no illness, thank God. And you should write to me about your health and do not keep me without news of your health.'
>
> 'Little mother! Since I left you, I have had no news of you, which I would like to hear, and particularly how soon you can come to Vilnius. Without you I am bored, and I expect you are, too. . . . Piter'[1]

Between 1526 and 1530, when Grand Prince Vasilii III wrote to his wife Elena Glinskaia using flowery religious language, and 1709 when Peter the Great wrote these direct lines to his consort Catherine, much had changed for men in Russia. Traditional prescriptions of behavior were being challenged by a new ethos of energetic masculinity. Such new codes do not necessarily predict actual behavior, but they shape the parameters of the acceptable and thus demarcate social boundaries. At the same time, and not coincidentally, such prescriptive visions are virtually all that survive in recorded sources; Muscovites left almost no personal testimony about how they lived their lives or how they regarded the traditional gender roles to which they were expected to conform until at least the early eighteenth century. So we shall explore here prescriptive constructions of masculinity in the Muscovite and Petrine eras, and focus on the question of love to suggest how models of masculinity were changing in early modern Russia.

Muscovite views about gender roles are less articulated than those of medieval and early modern Europe. Russians did not engage in learned discussions about the proper roles of men and women, as philosophers in classical antiquity and theologians in medieval Europe had done. Nor in Russia was there medical literature on the anatomical differences between the sexes and the correspondingly different social roles to which they destined men and women.[2] Nor did these debates travel to Russia from Byzantium or western and central Europe. Nevertheless, we can read between the lines of Muscovite sources – domestic handbooks, hagiography, chronicles, tales, court documents – to assemble a good idea of what Russians traditionally expected of men.

Masculinity in Russian sources up to the middle of the seventeenth century was grounded on the twin bulwarks of Christianity and patriarchy. Strictly speaking, the ideal of masculinity was the ascetic saint, who disdained the pleasures of the flesh, abstained from contact with society, and pursued otherworldliness through hesychast devotions. Expectations for men who lived in the world paralleled this paradigm of saintliness. Secular men were to be humble, pious and charitable, orderly and sober; their goal in life was to earn heavenly salvation. Traits that today are culturally considered 'masculine', such as assertiveness, worldly achievement or physical prowess, were not particularly associated with men in Muscovy, nor particularly esteemed for men *or* for women.[3]

Within this paradigm of piety, humility and self-abnegation, however, several 'masculinities' coexisted: men's behavior was predicated upon their social and familial role. Heads of households or men in authority were to control their dependants – wives and widowed mothers, sons and daughters, servants and, for those in political authority, subjects. Patriarchs were to be kind and merciful New Testament rulers, but also stern and disciplining Old Testament judges. A 1695 letter from a father to his children, for example, is a good illustration: he berates his son for deceiving him about his job, counsels the son not to insult his wife, inquires about the daughter-in-law's health, and requests the son to look into some financial issues.[4] Outside of the family, patriarchs were to extend hospitality and largesse to friends and strangers and treat all with Christian charity. This gendered behavior was complemented by expectations for women: that they be obedient, that they act as the moral center of the family and manager of the household, that they maintain honor and avoid shame through chastity and modesty.

For men in dependent positions by virtue of youth or social status (serfs and slaves), masculinity meant showing obedience and respect and performing one's functions in society with diligence, to the greater glory of God. The *Domostroi*, a sixteenth-century domestic handbook, advises: 'One who serves a good master should be knowledgeable, God-fearing, wise, humble, given to good deeds, farsighted. . . .'[5] For rulers, as evidenced in the many formulaic eulogies to ruling princes in Muscovite and earlier chronicles,[6] masculinity meant being a just judge, a generous giver to the poor and a valiant warrior in defense of one's realm and Christianity. For men in the political elite, masculinity meant valiantly fighting for the sake of God's Christian people and loyally serving one's prince. A eulogy to the boyar Daniil Feofanovich (d. 1392) praised him thus: '[he] was a true well-wisher of the grand prince, having served him in faith and loyalty both in the Horde and in Rus', as no one else . . . He was courageous and risked his life in foreign countries, in unknown places, in unseen lands.'[7] Chivalric exploits, heroism in battle or acts of courage were not celebrated for their own sake, but esteemed for their role in defending the faith. Thus, there were many variants of traditional Russian masculinity, all played out within the framework of Orthodoxy and patriarchy.

Russia's 'long eighteenth century' – that seminal period stretching from the late seventeenth century to at least the time of Catherine II – witnessed significant change. An implicit trend in Muscovite state-building from the mid-seventeenth century and an explicit goal for Peter the Great was to mobilize social resources, to create corporate bodies such as nobility and bourgeoisie and with them to develop a more dynamic economy and state. Italian Renaissance values of civic humanism and the theory of 'common good' penetrated Muscovy via Ukraine. Cultural contacts with Eastern Europe expanded, as did literacy, printing, and secular culture.[8] From the middle of the seventeenth century individuals influenced by such trends came to see society and state as entities to serve; they began to regard their corporate social group as a basis of identity. Such fundamental changes in social and political ethos affected expectations for men: a new masculinity demanded that men be literate and educated, that they adopt European patterns of civility and sociability and European dress, and that they pursue military valor and engagement with public life. Less self-evident but equally far-reaching were changes in the realm of love and marriage.

Surely men and women felt passionate, affective love in Muscovite Russia; that much is certain from the church's frequent condemnations of adultery and premarital sex and from the occasional criminal case that exposed illicit relationships. Popular attitudes towards love were earthy and sensual; love charms to win a lover, to excite passion in a spouse, or to jinx an enemy's sexuality were among the most common type of folk charm (*zagovor*). Examples are as old as fourteenth-century

Novgorodian birchbark documents, but became common primarily in the more prolific seventeenth-century sources, where they are associated with all social groups.[9] But these folk attitudes sharply contrasted with the prescriptions of dominant Christian morality, which condemned charms as devilish sorcery and the intents expressed in them as well, particularly for sexual relations outside of marriage.

Official morality subordinated emotional and sexual enjoyment to more pragmatic goals for marriage, goals associated with reproduction and social control. We can read this functionally, arguing that emotional love and sexuality threaten social stability. After all, first marriages were arranged by parents and the union was primarily an economic or political relationship. Social practices such as arranged marriages and patriarchal authority in the household subordinate emotion to utility; not surprisingly, in many traditional societies, including Russia, folk custom regarded emotional love and sexuality with distrust and suspicion. So the embrace of sexual satisfaction and emotional connection expressed in love charms lived in tension with prescribed morals and their broader social acceptance.[10]

According to the dominant morality, Muscovites were not to expect emotional or erotic satisfaction in marriage. These pleasures became normative goals in fact only after complex transformations in the early modern era. The Protestant Reformation promoted the concept of companionate marriage based on confession, and from the sixteenth century onward practices of private life and individual self-development were affected by a whole range of social and economic changes, such as those involved in the development of printing, literacy, social mobility, Renaissance humanism, and the scientific revolution. When Enlightenment and Romantic thinking codified the concept of marriage as an emotionally fulfilling partnership, it culminated these complex processes.[11] Until these transformations traditional morality often presented far more ambivalent attitudes toward emotional attachment. In medieval Europe and premodern Russia, notions about love, sexuality and marriage go back to a common Biblical heritage. But in medieval Europe prescriptive writers used chivalric literature and secular romances such as 'Tristan and Isolde' to legitimize affective and erotic attachments within a paradigm of Christian devotion. Premodern Russian writings never developed this genre nor its set of ideas.

Russian Orthodox teaching clung stringently to a traditional Biblical view of love in marriage as analogous to 'the spiritual love of the union between Christ and his church and between God and his children'.[12] Both western and eastern Christian churches regarded sexuality as an elemental force best kept under tight control. They preferred the ideal of chastity, even within marriage, and struggled with the tension between that ideal and the recognition of the inevitability of sexual desire and the need for reproduction. In the West medieval churchmen developed the concept of 'conjugal debt', grudgingly acknowledging the necessity of procreative sexuality within marriage and denying spouses the option of abstaining from marital relations. Russian Orthodoxy preached chastity within marriage, and spouses were discouraged from non-procreative sexual activity. As Levin notes, 'A man who truly loved and honored his wife would not want to expose her to the Satanic dangers of sexual intercourse.'[13]

Thus, the sixteenth-century handbook, the *Domostroi*, preached regular sexual abstinence: 'Love your wife and live with her within the law, according to the Lord's commandments. On Sunday, Wednesday, and Friday, on the Lord's holy days, and during Lent, live in chastity, in fasting, in prayer and repentance.'[14] Accordingly, even though husbands were told to 'love' their wives, that love was not expected to be sexual or affective. Rather, it entailed respect, mutual cooperation and patriarchal discipline. Husbands were to manage the household in consultation with wives: 'Every day in the evening, when they have said their prayers, and again in the morning . . . the husband and wife should discuss how to assign work to their household. . . .' The husband should be a spiritual guide: 'A wife should ask her husband every day about matters of piety, so she will know how to save her soul. . . .' And a disciplinarian: 'the husband should punish his wife. Beat her when you are alone together; then forgive her and remonstrate with her.'[15] The *Domostroi*'s ideal of marriage and love combined piety with hierarchy and service.

Pictorial representations of married couples, uncommon in Muscovite sources, support this image. One example is the 1668 icon by Semen Ushakov dedicated to the Mother of God and depicting the 'tree' of the Russian state (see Fig. 1). Although innovative in the use of secular figures at all, the icon's presentation conforms to traditional stereotypes, depicting Tsar Aleksei Mikhailovich, his wife Mariia Miloslavskaia and their two sons not in individualized portraits but in dress, visage and pose as iconic embodiments of piety and devotion to the church.[16]

Descriptions of relationships between spouses are as rare in Russian didactic literature as pictorial images and those that have survived tend to be formulaic.[17] Didactic works modeled traditional prescriptions: the early seventeenth-century 'Life' of Iulianna Osor'ina, for example, depicts her piety, humility and charity and praises her for breaking off

Figure 1 The Tree of the Russian State – Praise to the Vladimir Mother of God

sexual relations with her spouse after their children were grown. She is not alone in hagiography in being praised for chastity within marriage.[18] The closest that traditional Muscovite sources come to appreciation of affective love within marriage is the 'saint's life' of Peter and Fevroniia. Here elements of folk belief and Christianity intermingle: Fevroniia essentially manipulates Prince Peter into marrying her with her skillful use of medicinal herbs, and the tale praises her wiles and the couple's piety ('They ruled in their town respecting all commandments and precepts of God irreproachably, praying constantly and bestowing mercy on all people under their authority, like a doting father and mother'). Their relationship is not described as affectionate or sexual; the couple was childless. But their death scene highlights the strength of their personal bond: 'They prayed to God that they might die at the same time. And they wrote in their wills that they both should be buried in one tomb, and they ordered made two graves from one stone with only a thin partition separating them.'

And so Peter and Fevroniia took monastic vows and soon died at the same time and day. Against their wishes, however, they were buried in separate churches. Miraculously, their bodies soon appeared side by side in the tomb that they had prepared for themselves, and subsequently the tomb became an object of veneration, symbolic of a marriage based on mutual devotion.[19]

In texts other than prescriptive literary sources, we find these patriarchal values acted out. Rituals in elite families may be more symbolic of ideals than representative of 'lived experience', but they certainly conform to traditional morality. Elite women lived in a degree of seclusion, occupying separate parts of palaces and elite homes and being shrouded or confined to carriages in public. But the regime was not completely strict: at formal events such as weddings, men and women socialized in the same room, sitting at separate sides of the table. At home husbands accorded their wives and daughters respect and honor. Foreigners, for example, record family rituals that express honor to the hostess in elite families, such as elaborate ceremonies of welcoming. A court bureaucrat, Grigorii Kotoshikhin, noted the honor accorded to women as well as men in the ruling family in funeral and nameday celebrations.[20] In wills, men instruct their sons to honor their mothers, as this Muscovite grand prince does: 'and you, my sons, live as one and respect and obey your mother.'[21]

In public, men went to court vigorously to defend their honor and that of their women. Again, we should not mistake the evidence of these sources for authentic 'lived experience'. 'Honor' was an idealized construction; it represented an ideal to which people strove rather than the way they lived on a daily basis. But the fact that individuals in all social ranks litigated vigorously over honor suggests broad social acceptance of the dominant morality. The insults to which men reacted expand slightly our view of ideal masculinity: men protested when they were accused of criminal behavior, when their social status was denigrated, when their religious or filial piety was insulted, or when they were accused of sexual indiscretion. But one of the most frequent insults that men protested took the form of slurs on their wives and daughters, especially sexual aspersions. Women's honor was part of collective family honor and masculinity entailed defending and honoring women.[22]

The rare pieces of personal correspondence between spouses that survive from pre-Petrine Russia present a '*Domostroi*' model of marriage as a working partnership. In the 1680s, for example, D. V. Mikhailkov wrote to his wife from his posting on military campaign. Affectionate greetings were limited to formal, although probably sincere, inquiries about her health; the letters depict a trusting, working relationship between the husband as head of the household and the wife as its administrator. In his letters, Mikhailkov instructs his wife what provisions to send him, from which estates to gather them, and even what sorts of warm socks and clothes he needs.[23] In an undated late seventeenth-century letter the wife of a provincial servitor reveals the hardships of rural life, describing her 'sadnesses' from poverty and hunger, imploring her husband, who is away on service, to help. In a happier letter of the same period, a husband greets his wife 'with love', sends his blessings to his daughter, and writes about a death in the family.[24]

Even the more fully documented ruling family does not provide sources in the Muscovite period that do other than affirm the prescriptive ideals we have surveyed.[25] The correspondence of Muscovite rulers with their wives conforms to traditional roles and attitudes towards affective love. Thus we cannot say how strongly tsars and tsaritsas cared for each other. Correspondence with family members (very rarely, however, with wives) survives from Vasilii III (ruled 1505–33), Mikhail Fedorovich (1613–45) and Aleksei Mikhailovich (1645–76). In all cases the primary purpose of writing was to inquire about health or to inform about well-being ('arrived safely at destination'), and the language was formal and somewhat distancing.[26] Aleksei Mikhailovich's active correspondence with family members, recently examined by Isolde Thyrêt, is a good example of traditional expectations of spouses' relations and male and female roles in the context of sovereign power.[27] The tsar requested that his sisters and wife pray for his military and political projects and confided in them about the progress of battle and the ins and outs of court politics. As Thyrêt insightfully argues, Aleksei Mikhailovich depended upon his female kin to perform functions of spiritual intercession essential to his role as God's appointed on earth. He occasionally breaks through the stilted language to express a personal voice, as, for example, when he sent birthday greetings to his mother: 'We celebrated the holyday of the holy martyr Irina, your birthday, according to the liturgy, and we banqueted with joy, only we regretted that we could not see you face to face, but in spirit we are always inseparable.'[28] But such personal touches are the exception. The expression of personal feeling was clearly not a part of the genre and its absence tells us more about attitudes towards the public expression of love than the reality of it. These attitudes supported mutual respect for the sake of the collective family unity, not passionate, personal attachment.

Men and women in Muscovy led parallel lives; in marriage they were supposed to give one another respect and cooperation. The goal of marriage was to preserve the stability, resources and reputation of the family unit and to reproduce it. Affective love and sexual passion were not legitimized as ideals of male or female behavior, since they did not support and perhaps threatened those goals. Both may have flourished in some marriages, but in social life, especially in public, men and women were expected to subordinate these emotions, as well as any others not conducive to community stability, to the needs of the collective.

From the middle of the seventeenth century, however, boundaries were being transgressed. In old genres that had previously excluded the affective, and in new genres, Muscovites were revealing more emotion, and ideals of the masculine and feminine were thereby being contested. The 1680s' letters of Regent Sofiia to V. V. Golitsyn (considered by some to be her lover) contain warm, personal expressions, but are equally full of religious and formulaic rhetoric. They mark at best a transitional stage in the expression of personal affection.[29] More decidedly marking a shift in attitudes in the late seventeenth and early eighteenth centuries is the new genre of secular tales based on European picaresque novels. Here one sees attitudes common to the love charms of folk culture disseminated more broadly. These stories – some traditional morality tales, others often ribald and wickedly funny – depict relationships between men and women as earthy and emotional. Some, such as the tale of Savva Grudtsyn, follow the traditional morality of sin and redemption tales, but include graphic details of sexual liaisons. Others are satirical and subversive, celebrating individuals' sexuality and willfulness. The tale of Frol Skobeev, for example, turns traditional marriage teachings upside down, inasmuch as his marriage is accomplished by ravishing a young girl, who then welcomes his advances and proceeds to help him blackmail her father into supporting this ne'er-do-well in various schemes through life.[30]

An example of old genres with new content in the Petrine era was a primer and handbook of etiquette called the 'Honorable Mirror for Youth,' published in 1717 and based on European texts. Providing an alternative to the *Domostroi*, it prescribes ethical values more conducive to the formation of affinitive relations within marriage. Its prescriptions to women are traditional, emphasizing modesty, humility, piety, domestic skills and chastity. But those for men combine traditional values (piety and respect for elders) with new Petrine ones, such as industriousness, literacy and education, good manners and proper etiquette at social occasions. This source does not explicitly advocate emotional openness and affection in marriage, but its emphasis on the here and now, on the empowered individual making his way in life, paves the way.[31]

In the cultural transformations that began in the 1680s and accelerated throughout Peter's reign, new moral standards were being promoted in place of the dominant Muscovite ideal. The new morality was more secular, more oriented towards the individual and more activist. Discipline, service and obedience were important parts of the Petrine ethic, but so also were the concepts of agency and voluntarism. Not coincidentally, the cultural transformations of Peter's time included a significant revision of ideals of masculinity and attitudes towards love.

In everything he did publicy and privately, Peter the Great accelerated trends already under way or introduced new elements that moved moral standards towards the self. Although he was a believer, Peter downplayed piety, substituted the here and now for otherworldly salvation, and threw humility out the window. The Petrine man was to be physically dynamic, handy at mechanical and military skills, courageous in battle. Rejecting Muscovite notions that military valor was expected only of the elite and was associated with a Christian's duty to defend Orthodoxy, Peter secularized and universalized warrior virtues. His regime associated them with foreign, classical gods and counted them as an intrinsic attribute of all men. But the Petrine man, in addition to being physically adept and brave, was also to be cultured and refined. He should be educated in the secular sciences, in the humanities and European languages; he should know current European etiquette and dress in European style. He was to attend 'assemblies' where, clean shaven and dressed in the required European waistcoat and brocade vest, he would have the opportunity to chat with friends 'not only for entertainment, but also for affairs', to dance with the ladies, to play cards and other table games.[32] Women were to emerge from seclusion, adopt western dress and hairstyles, cultivate in themselves social graces and European education. For noblemen, education in practical skills such as mathematics and navigation were made requirements for marriage. The Petrine vision at its root emphasized individuals, and by his own example the Great Reformer demonstrated that the new masculine assertiveness, industriousness and secular self-definition also included emotional commitment.

Peter did so in the realm of symbolism, aggressively using classical models drawn from Europe to promote different ideas about masculine and feminine roles and a new concept of love and marriage. Images of male classical gods and martial heroes in sculpture and engravings represented valor and worldly achievement, while idealized images of women drawn from Greek mythology represented 'man's higher faculties'. Emotional love was to be seen as symbolic of supreme beauty, the taming of the passions and the achievement of culture. Therefore, individuals were accorded more freedom to make love matches and to seek personal fulfillment in love as a way to achieve those lofty ideals. Marriage in the Petrine ideal, Richard Wortman points out, 'became the consummation of love rather than the acceptance of a hierarchy of divinely ordained paternal authority'.[33] Peter himself lived out this message about individual choice and emotional attachment in one of his less remarked but very significant areas of reform.

Peter's marital history began as a typical tale for Russian rulers, as well as for monarchs across Europe.[34] He was married in 1689 when he was almost seventeen to a woman with whom he had little in common, Evdokiia Lopukhina. The partnership was intended not to provide intimate companionship but to produce male heirs so as to perpetuate the dynasty, and it did accomplish that goal. Son Aleksei was born in 1690, and eventually Evdokiia bore two other sons, who died in infancy. But Peter also challenged traditional norms early on. He looked elsewhere for sexual fulfillment, taking mistresses in the 1690s; such behavior paralleled that of monarchs across eighteenth-century Europe, but has no recorded precedents in Muscovite times. In 1699 Peter banished his wife Evdokiia to a monastery despite her unwillingness to take the veil and without the traditional rationale – infertility – for which Muscovite tsars had in the past occasionally divorced their wives. Peter then pursued emotional attachments and by 1706 was living openly with Martha Skavronska, a lowborn German woman.

Peter resolutely promoted Catherine's status, declaring her his official consort in 1711, at which time she took the name Catherine and the Orthodox religion. He married her officially in 1712, despite the objections of the church. Peter installed Catherine in palatial settings, traveled with her on campaign and diplomatic tour and with her produced at least ten children between 1706 and 1718. Only two daughters survived to adulthood (Anna, b. 1708, Elizabeth, b. 1709); Elizabeth went on to inherit the throne (1741–62), and was succeeded by Anna's son, Peter III. With great pomp and ceremony in May 1724 Catherine received the title of Empress-consort, and when Peter died in January 1725, she was declared his successor and ruled two years in her own right.

The tale of Peter's marriage and relationship with Catherine is a fine mix of politics and romance. Clearly many of the tsar's steps to advance Catherine's status reflected his anxiety over succession: Evdokiia had produced only one surviving son, Aleksei, and, increasingly, she, Aleksei and Aleksei's son, Peter (b. 1715) served as a focus for conservative opposition. So Peter was anxious to create an alternative line of succession. The Tsar's quest for legitimate heirs would, however, have been made much easier if he had chosen a second wife from his social equals, making a match with some highborn European princess who agreed to accept Orthodoxy. As it was, Catherine's lowly birth (it was well-known in western Europe that she had been a camp follower and mistress to Peter's close friend Alexander Menshikov before taking up with the tsar), perceived irregularities in her conversion to Orthodoxy, and the birth of many of their children before marriage raised a cloud of illegitimacy. Why would Peter take so complicated a path to such sensitive and strategic ends?

The answer, it would seem, is love. Peter by all accounts was deeply in love with his wife and showed it to the whole world. His correspondence with Catherine dispenses with religious rhetoric and formalism; he speaks from the heart. Personal and tender, the letters are full of domestic detail, affectionate nicknames and comfortable joking. Throughout a reign of almost continual travel he wrote to her, as in this characteristic letter of 1712: 'Katerinushka, my dear friend, greetings! I hear that you miss me, and I also miss you. However, you can understand that affairs keep me too busy to be too bored. I don't expect to be able to leave here to come to you soon, and if your horses have arrived, then come. . . .'[35] Here Peter breaks through the formulaic rhetoric of the Muscovite epistolary genre to display openly his warm, emotional attachment to his wife.

Peter turned his devotion to Catherine to political ends in myriad ways. He commissioned many portraits of himself, her and their children, individually and as a family group. These portraits, particularly the portable enamel miniatures, demonstrated to the world the healthy Petrine line of succession and also put forward a new ideal of familial affection. A particularly touching image of 1715 commemorated the birth of his son Peter: an enamel miniature shows Peter and Catherine linked by two entwined hearts and crowned by their three surviving children, Anna, Elizabeth and baby Peter. Peter also disseminated an engraving that celebrated the birth of his son and grandson in 1715 and praised his union with Catherine.[36]

Peter's grand celebration of his wedding to Catherine in 1712 served both to challenge Muscovite tradition and to promote his new European symbolic code. He invited the diplomatic corps and the cream of the Russian elite (documenting the event in a widely disseminated engraving) and illustrated the fireworks ceremony with a scrim (later circulated as an engraving; see Fig. 2) that Wortman calls 'an allegory of marriage as love'. It featured Peter in classical garb, Catherine 'holding a burning heart', a pair of kissing doves, the slogan 'united by your love', and 'the all-seeing eye' presiding over the scene, all symbolizing the triumph of idealized love, culture and reason over disorder, passion and ignorance.[37] Peter had broadcast the message that individuals can change their destinies and seek out their own personal fulfillment. As tsar, of course, he had greater leeway to challenge convention than did his subjects, but he exercised his prerogatives to open up new visions of the purpose of life.

Figure 2 Engraving depicting fireworks on the marriage of Peter I to Catherine, 1712

Some of Peter's social reforms, while motivated by his desire to undercut the power of Moscow's hereditary elite clans, also advanced new attitudes towards love and marriage. The tsar, for example, weakened parental control over marriage choice by allowing betrothed couples to cancel arranged marriages within a specified period. Peter also made divorce more difficult to obtain, thus restricting a husband's ability to use marriage instrumentally and subtly promoting the concept of marriage as a personal, long-lasting bond.[38] He demanded that elite women should participate in public social events, further threatening parents' monopoly over their children's marriages and personal contacts. He imported western dress for men and women and encouraged the construction of West-European-style buildings that allowed men and women to live and socialize together. He encouraged secular painting styles that allowed for personalized self-representation. By the end of Peter's reign portraiture embodied the new masculinity: the many martial portraits of Peter idealized valor; other portraits celebrated western culture, military and political honors or worldly profession; others portrayed familial love, beautifully exemplified by Andrei Matveev's 1729 self-portrait with his wife (see Fig. 3).[39] At the same time,

Figure 3 A. Matveev, *Self-Portrait with Wife*, 1729

Peter cracked down on superstition, including the use of love charms; in Peter's world love was a conscious choice, not a magical force.[40] And indeed, in classical poetry of the eighteenth century (Sumarokov, Trediakovskii), affective love became a dominant motif, allegorical of personal fulfillment.

These Petrine cultural trends affected only noblemen and the highest echelons of merchant and professional elites and took generations to reach full fruition. Marriages continued to be arranged well into the nineteenth century, and noblemen served away from home many months of the year throughout their lives for most of the eighteenth century. Thus, these steps to legitimize affection within marriage in the Petrine era may not have been widely acted upon at first. But once introduced in the receptive climate of Russia's Europeanizing elites, they could not be turned back.

Changes begun in the mid-seventeenth century and epitomized by Peter I and his reforms carved out new dimensions of male behavior, challenging men not only to be educated, engaged and accomplished, but also to act on their feelings. By so publicy demonstrating his affection for his wife, Peter may have been motivated by no more than love. But simply because of who he was, his actions created policy. His advocacy of emotional voluntarism for men complemented the implicit message of so many of his other reforms. Peter's validating of personal affection, like his emphasis on manual skills, martial arts, education and European civility, imbued life with a different purpose, one focused on achievement on earth rather than salvation in heaven. It implicitly expanded personal agency. Most subversively, affirming emotional ties between husbands and wives sits in tension with respect for tradition, for it raises the possibility that attachment to a beloved could legitimately transcend loyalty to clan or family. The logical next step might be empowering individuals to question social and political structures as well. The long-term implications of the new Petrine masculinity – energetic, voluntaristic and self-determining – are profound.

Notes

1. *Pisma russkikh gosudarei (PRG) i drugikh osob tsarskogo semeistva, 1526–1658*, vol. 1 (Moscow, 1848), 3; *PRG*, 5 vols (Moscow, 1861–96), 1: no. 13, 9.
2. See essays on this topic, including Jo Ann McNamara, 'The *Herrenfrage*: the Restructuring of the Gender System, 1050–1150', and Vern L. Bullough, 'On Being a Male in the Middle Ages', *Medieval Masculinities; Regarding Men in the Middle Ages*, ed. Clare A. Lees, *Medieval Cultures*, vol. 7 (Minneapolis, 1997), 3–45.
3. See G. P. Fedotov, *The Russian Religious Mind. Vol. II: the Middle Ages: the*

Thirteenth to Fifteenth Centuries (Cambridge, Mass., 1966), esp. ch. 2, and Carolyn Johnston Pouncy, ed. and trans., *The Domostroi; Rules for Russian Households in the Time of Ivan the Terrible* (Ithaca, 1994).

4. *Gramotki XVII – nachala XVIII veka* (Moscow, 1969), no. 329, 173–4.
5. *Domostroi*, 104.
6. *Polnoe sobranie russkikh letopisei* (*PSRL*), 41 vols to date (St. Petersburg-Moscow, 1841–), 9: 251–2 (1175); *PSRL*, 2: cols 703–4 (1197); *PSRL*, 10: 64–5 (1213); *PSRL*, 10: 156 (1278); *PSRL*, 11: 108–21 (1389); *PSRL*, 13: 75–7 (1533).
7. M. D. Priselkov, comp., *Troitskaia letopis'* (Moscow-Leningrad, 1950), 411 (1392).
8. On the new civic humanism of the late seventeenth century, see my *By Honor Bound: State and Society in Early Modern Russia* (Ithaca, NY, 1999), 210–26, and Paul Bushkovitch, *Religion and Society in Russia; the Sixteenth and Seventeenth Centuries* (New York, 1992), ch. 7. On Petrine models of civic engagement, see Marc Raeff, *The Well-Ordered Police State; Social and Institutional Change through Law in the Germanies and Russia, 1600–1800* (New Haven, 1983), and Sumner Benson, 'The Role of Western Political Thought in Petrine Russia', *Canadian-American Slavic Studies*, 8, no. 2 (1974): 254–73.
9. On love charms, see W. F. Ryan, *The Bathhouse at Midnight: an Historical Survey of Magic and Divination in Russia* (University Park, Penn., 1999), 179–83; E. B. Smilianskaia, 'Sledstvennye dela 'o sueveriiakh' v Rossii pervoi poloviny XVIII v. v svete problem istorii obshchestvennogo soznaniia', *Rossica* (Prague), I, no. 1 (1996): 3–20. Texts of such charms are published by V. L. Kliaus and Smilianskaia in *Russkii eroticheskii fol'klor*, ed. A. Toporkov (Moscow, 1995), 344–70.
10. On 'illicit' sex condemned by the church, see Eve Levin, *Sex and Society in the World of the Orthodox Slavs, 900–1700* (Ithaca, NY, 1989), 179–97.
11. See Orest Ranum, 'The Refuges of Intimacy', *A History of Private Life, III: the Passions of the Renaissance*, ed. Roger Chartier (Cambridge, Mass., 1989), 252–7, and Lawrence Stone, *The Family, Sex and Marriage in England, 1500–1800* (New York, 1977), 102–5 and chs 7–8.
12. Levin, *Sex and Society*, 96.
13. Ibid., 61. On Western teachings about marriage, see Georges Duby, 'What Do We Know about Love in Twelfth-Century France?', 'Marriage in Early Medieval Society', and 'The Matron and the Mismarried Woman', *Love and Marriage in the Middle Ages*, trans. Jane Dunnett (Chicago, 1994), 3–55.
14. *Domostroi*, 181.
15. Ibid., 158, 124, 143.
16. For a description of the icon, see V. I. Antonova and N. E. Mneva, *Katalog drevnerusskoi zhivopisi; Opyt istoriko-khudozhestvennoi klassifikatsii*, 2 vols (Moscow, 1963), 2: 411–12. Other examples of secular figures in icons are rare: a fifteenth-century Novgorod icon includes the donor's family (men, women and children), and in the late seventeenth century the family of the donor is included in the frescos of the Nikitniki Church in Moscow, a church with which Semen Ushakov was associated.
17. See Avvakum's pious devotion to his wife in *Pamiatniki literatury drevnei Rusi (PLDR). XVII vek*, 3 bks (Moscow 1988–94), 2 (1989): 351–453; English version in Serge A. Zenkovsky (ed.), *Medieval Russia's Epics, Chronicles and Tales*, rev. and enlarged edn (New York, 1974), 399–448. Other sources depict-

ing spouses' relations include the death scenes and wives' lament to Dmitrii Donskoi (1389) and Vasilii III (1533) cited in note 5.

18. *PLDR. XVII vek*, 1 (1988): 101. English version in Zenkovsky (ed.), *Medieval Russia's Epics*, 391–9. Dmitrii Donskoi is also praised for chastity in marriage: PSRL, 11: 109.
19. *PLDR. Konets XV – pervaia polovina XVI veka* (Moscow, 1984), 642–7 (my translation). English version in Zenkovsky, *Medieval Russia's Epics*, 290–300.
20. On seclusion, see my 'The Seclusion of Elite Muscovite Women', *Russian History*, 10, pt. 2 (1983): 170–87, and Natalia Pushkareva, *Women in Russian History: From the Tenth to the Twentieth Centuries*, trans. Eve Levin (Armonk, NY, 1997), 88–101. For primary sources, see Adam Olearius, *The Travels of Olearius in Seventeenth-Century Russia*, trans. and ed. Samuel H. Baron (Stanford, Calif., 1967), 158; Grigorii Kotoshikhin, *O Rossii vo tsarstvovanie Alekseiia Mikhailovicha*, 4th edn (St. Petersburg, 1906), chs 1 and 13.
21. *Dukhovnye i dogovornye gramoty velikikh i udel'nykh kniazei XIV–XVI vv* (*DDG*) (Moscow-Leningrad, 1950), no. 17, 45 (ca. 1401–2). For similar citations, see *DDG*, no. 1, 8 (ca. 1339), no. 12, 33, 36 (1389), no. 61, 194, 197 (ca. 1461–2).
22. See my *By Honor Bound*, ch. 2.
23. *Moskovskaia delovaia i bytovaia pis'mennost' XVII veka* (Moscow, 1968), sect 1, no. 17, 38–40.
24. *Gramotki*, no. 290, 155 (1695) and no. 398, 236 (this undated letter is grouped with other letters of the year 1700).
25. Ivan IV, 'the Terrible', is said to have passionately loved his first wife, Anastasiia Romanovna, and to have grieved deeply at her death. The Muscovite-era sources on their relationship, however, reveal little of this and this topos owes most to N. M. Karamzin's romantic rendering of Ivan and Anastasiia in the early nineteenth century. For Karamzin's version, see *Istoriia gosudarstva rossiiskogo* (Moscow, 1989; 1842–4 edn), vol. 8, ch. 3, cols 58–9 and ch. 4, cols 187–8. The Muscovite sources are Ivan IV's First Letter to Kurbskii (J. L. I. Fennell, ed. and trans., *The Correspondence between Prince A. M. Kurbsky and Tsar Ivan IV of Russia, 1564–1579* [Cambridge, 1963], 94–9, 136–7, 148–9, 190–1 and 210–11) and Kurbskii's 'History' (J. L. I. Fennell, ed. and trans., *Kurbsky's History of Ivan IV* [Cambridge, 1965], 152–3). The authenticity of all these sources has been seriously challenged and in my view the controversy is not resolved. See Edward L. Keenan, *The Kurbskii-Groznyi Apocrypha* (Cambridge, Mass., 1971) and his 'Putting Kurbskii in His Place: or, Observations and Suggestions Concerning the Place of the "History of the Grand Prince of Muscovy" in the History of Muscovite Literary Culture', *Forschungen zur osteuropäischen Geschichte*, 24 (1978): 131–62.
26. *PRG . . . 1526–1658*, 1: 3–5 (Vasilii III) and passim (Mikhail Fedorovich, Aleksei Mikhailovich). *PRG*, 5 (1896), passim (Aleksei Mikhailovich).
27. Isolde Thyrêt, *Between God and the Tsar: Religious Symbolism and the Royal Women of Muscovite Russia* (DeKalb, Ill., 2001), ch. 4.
28. *PRG*, 5: 28, 5 May 1654. See Philip Longworth's wishful but unlikely conclusion: 'Presumably he wrote even more often and intimately to Maria [his wife], though these letters have not survived.' *Alexis, Tsar of All the Russias* (London, 1984), 106.

29. N. Ustrialov, *Istoriia tsarstvovaniia Petra Velikogo*, vol. 1 (St Petersburg, 1858), 382–4; English translation in Lindsey Hughes, *Sophia, Regent of Russia, 1657–1704* (New Haven, 1990), 227–8.
30. *PLDR. XVII vek* 1: 55–64; English version in Zenkovsky, *Medieval Russia's Epics*, 474–86.
31. *Iunosti chestnoe zertsalo. Reprintnoe izdanie* (Moscow, 1990).
32. *Polnoe sobranie zakonov (PSZ) Rossiiskoi imperii*, vol. 1 in 40 vols with 5 additional vols of indices (St Petersburg, 1830), 5, no. 3246 (1718).
33. Richard Wortman, *Scenarios of Power. Myth and Ceremony in Russian Monarchy*, vol. 1 (Princeton, NJ, 1995), 56–60.
34. For a concise survey of Peter's relationship with Catherine, see Lindsey Hughes, *Russia in the Age of Peter the Great* (New Haven, 1998), 393–8.
35. *PRG*, 1 (1861): no. 31, 22 (8 August 1712). With regard to Peter's attitude towards love and marriage, the fact that Peter often carried with him a copy of the 'Tale of Peter and Fevroniia' when he traveled is intriguing: L. R. Lewitter, 'Peter the Great and the Modern World', *Russia and Europe*, ed. Paul Dukes (London, 1991), 104.
36. N. V. Kaliazina and G. N. Komelova, *Russkoe isskustvo petrovskoi epokhi* (Leningrad, 1990), nos 4, 98, 114–16, 129, 135, 136. For the 1715 engraving, see M. Alekseeva, *Graviura petrovskogo vremeni* (Leningrad, 1990), 139–41.
37. Wortman, *Scenarios* 1, 55–9; illustration of the wedding banquet on 59. Firework/engraving: V. N. Vasil'ev, *Starinnye feierverki v Rossii* (Leningrad, 1960), 51, plate 29.
38. 1702 law on betrothal: *PSZ*, 4, no. 1907, 191–2. On divorce, see Brenda Meehan-Waters, *Autocracy and Aristocracy: the Russian Service Elite of 1730* (New Brunswick, NJ, 1982), 122–6.
39. On portraiture in this period, see James Cracraft, *The Petrine Revolution in Russian Imagery* (Chicago, 1997), 190–220, and Kaliazina and Komelova, *Russkoe isskustvo petrovskoi epokhi*, 14–53. Martial portraits of Peter are widely reproduced in the above two works. For portraits with symbols of European culture, professional or personal attributes, see ibid., nos 90–3, 96, 101, 108, 112, 119, 121–2, 125–7. For family portraits, see ibid., nos. 104, 135, 136.
40. Smilianskaia, 'Sledstvennye dela'.

3
From Boys to Men: Manhood in the Nicholaevan University

Rebecca Friedman

During a break from classes in the 1840s, a number of Moscow University students headed off to the *dacha* (cottage) of one of their classmates for a weekend of hunting and merry-making. In order to gain permission for the use of the family place, student Blagov made a promise to his mother – one that he would do his best to keep – that no one would consume alcohol during their visit. However, he failed to inform the other young men of this promise. Upon reaching the cottage, the student-guests took out several bottles of wine and were ready to begin their evening of drinking and roistering. When Blagov came into the dining room and saw his comrades toasting, he became sullen, quickly finished his meal and retired to his bedroom. After some time, several of the students peeked inside Blagov's room and found a different world: the quiet, pious interior sharply contrasted with the raucous activity in the dining area. Boris Chicherin records this moment in his student memoir; he highlights the outsider status that Blagov had achieved. 'The contrast,' Chicherin remarks, 'was staggering.' Ignoring his friends' drunken antics, Blagov, 'wearing a nightcap with pink ribbons', knelt in front of an icon reciting his evening prayers.[1] The pious, submissive and effeminate picture of Blagov that Chicherin paints starkly contrasts with the image of the other students gathered around a table drinking and laughing in preparation for the next day's hunting expedition.

For the remainder of their trip, Chicherin explains that the students attempted to teach Blagov their ways of 'debauchery' and to guide him on how to stand up to his mother. The obstacles to re-masculating Blagov turned out to be too great: he not only refused to drink, but also was overpowered by feminine influences – or so his friends believed. 'Besides a strict mother, there was still a virtuous grandmother, and against their combined strength, Blagov felt himself completely feeble.' This feebleness followed him throughout his life: Chicherin implies that as an adult Blagov was unable to satisfy his wife, causing her eventually to run away from him. Ultimately, Chicherin tells his reader, Blagov went mad and became a monk. Blagov's refusal to participate in his friends' drunken and debauched sociability foreshadowed his inability to fulfill his obligations as a man.[2]

Historians have theorized about the connections between drinking rituals and the assertion of masculinity in various historical and social contexts. They explain that the willingness to drink often is linked to a young man's status among his peer group. Writing on students in antebellum colleges in the American south, for example, historian L. Ray Drinkwater explains that despite official prohibitions, for many young men drinking 'was an accepted (and even required) mode of masculine self-expression'. Students who refused to participate would, this historian argues, 'jeopardize their self-worth and position among their peers'.[3] Peer pressure continues today to be a significant inducement to drink among male and now female college students. Over a century and a half ago, Russian students' drinking rituals were, in part, informal testing grounds for one another; those such as Blagov who did not wish to drink risked being perceived as outsiders, less virile and, by extension, less masculine.

The culture of rowdy, drunken behavior exemplified by the student-hunters, however, was not the only path to Russian manhood in the second quarter of the nineteenth century. This ideal stood in stark contrast to the autocracy's official ideology of masculinity, which required a combination of gentility and obedience. To instill the official model of Nicholaevan manhood and transform generations of unruly boys into proper men and self-controlled servitors, the state turned to its educational institutions, and especially to its all-male universities. While at the university over the course of three or four years, fifteen- and sixteen-year-olds were taught how to manage this tenuous balance of official and unofficial prescriptions for masculine behavior. They were required to drink with their comrades, to bow in polite company and, most importantly, to learn how to negotiate these contradictory impulses as they grew into men.

The administrative ideal

In the 1835 *Instructions to the Student Inspector of the Imperial Kazan' University*, the Russian university administration, under the guidance of

Tsar Nicholas I himself, defined its educational priorities. On the one hand, students were required to master the rules of gentlemanly conduct. At the same time, in order to acquire 'a good moral sense' students had to be 'true sons of the Church, faithful servants of the Throne, and useful citizens of the Fatherland'.[4] Coming of age in Nicholas' Russia, according to official university regulations, required students to be men of probity and character who displayed loyalty and obedience before church and state. In essence, these young men were being schooled in the habits of their future professional class; they were expected to learn these values at the university and then bring them into the realm of state service after graduation, whether as teachers, doctors or civil administrators. These prescriptions for gentility and subservience suggest that Nicholas I and his officials were attempting to project an image of Russia as a civilized, European power, while at the same time upholding autocratic principles, wherein deference to rank and obedience to authority were paramount.[5]

At the start of the nineteenth century there was but a single university in the Russian Empire, the University of Moscow, which had opened in 1755. As part of Alexander I's reform-minded programs, the tsar issued an All School-Statute of 1804 that created six educational districts; each district – Kazan', Kharkov, Vilno, Dorpat and, in 1819, St Petersburg – had a university at its administrative and curricular helm. However, it was not until Nicholas' reign that the number of university students grew in earnest. Although enrollment figures differ slightly depending on the source, the total number of students throughout the empire was approximately 1500 in 1836, 2500 in 1844 and 3400 in 1848.[6] After graduation, this relatively small group of young men was to represent Russia at home and abroad as public servants of the tsar.

An understanding of the shifting relationship between the university and state is essential to an exploration of the creation of the administrative ideal of masculinity. During the reign of Nicholas I, the university lost much of the autonomy in such matters as the hiring and firing of professors and the shaping of curriculum that had been granted by Nicholas' brother Alexander I. The central authorities incrementally usurped the universities' decision-making powers as well as the governing of day-to-day operations. After the issuing of the 1835 University statute, for instance, the rector, previously appointed by the faculty, had to win the approval of the tsar himself. Likewise, the student inspector went from being a professor chosen by his peers to a civil servant in the state bureaucracy selected by the Minister of Education.[7] It is interesting to note here that the large degree of state control over the affairs of faculty and students distinguishes the Russian university administrative structure from its western European counterparts. German university students, like Russian, had to endure a large degree of discipline, but their lives were not directly monitored by representatives of the state. By the early nineteenth century, in fact, German universities were claiming considerable autonomy. When the University of Berlin opened in 1810, Wilhelm von Humboldt published a memorandum on restructuring the universities to that effect. He wrote that the 'state should not look to them [the universities] at all for anything that directly concerns its own interests'.[8] Russian students, in contrast to their German peer group, were watched and molded by strict curricular and disciplinary systems overseen by the state in order to satisfy its own needs.

With its channels of direct control over the universities in place, the Nicholaevan autocracy not only provided academic training, but also attempted to mold moral, well-mannered men to fill posts in its provincial and central bureaucracies. The curriculum was geared somewhat towards technical skills in an attempt to satisfy growing administrative needs. Students, who were primarily sons of the lesser nobility, merchants and priests – the middling elites – were socialized to feel comfortable in their new professional and social roles after graduation.[9] The university employed a team of inspectors and sub-inspectors to oversee this process of socialization.[10] From early in the morning until late at night, within the university, in the taverns and on the streets, inspectors were charged with the monitoring of students' academic and personal lives; they exposed students' private behavior to public scrutiny.

The transformation of Russian boys into proper state servitors required students to cleanse themselves of their passionate impulses and to replace willfulness with self-control. The language of the university's disciplinary codes reflects an assumption that the fifteen- and sixteen-year olds who came to the university to study were infested with 'depraved/vicious inclinations and harmful habits'.[11] It was the job of the university inspectors and rectors alike to tame the 'imagination, passions, and . . . the very physical strength' of the youngsters.[12] They were expected to leave the university cleansed of vices, including 'violent gushes of passion', 'stubborn vice', 'depravity', and 'impatience'.[13]

One of the ways in which the administration hoped to create self-controlled servitors was the promotion of sexual discipline. The student disciplinary codes mandated that students resist 'the temptations of . . . debauchery' and rid themselves of all erotic impulses, such as 'licentiousness' and 'shamelessness'.[14] The seduction of a girl and the 'injuring the female sex', for instance, were considered 'serious offenses of order and decency' and guaranteed severe punishment, from long stays in the prison room to military service.[15] In October 1836 in St Petersburg, the head of the Third Section, General A. Benkendorf, went on a general campaign to rid the area around the university of 'public women', that is, prostitutes. Benkendorf voiced his fear that the 'public women' would 'infect' and 'harm . . . the young men studying at the university'.[16] The punishment for sexual involvement of any kind was serious. For instance, in 1850 the city authorities caught Moscow University law student Aleksei Shumilik returning home from what the authorities claimed was a brothel, carrying women's clothing and eighteen rubles. As punishment for his alleged crimes of visiting a brothel and stealing clothes from a prostitute, Shumilik was dismissed from the university and banned from living in Moscow altogether.[17]

As part of the project to create young men who were singularly loyal, university inspectors were charged with discouraging students from forming excessively devoted attachments to one another; state officials were fearful of such possibly sexual intimacies. The following incident highlights this anxiety. While on his usual rounds of the student dormitories, Kazan' University inspector Frants Bronner found students Bazilev and Ardashev in bed together. Bronner threatened that if this intimacy continued he would see to it that Ardashev, the supposed instigator, 'be sent away to the most remote school'. Although this incident occurred in 1816, it suggests the administration's attitude toward students' relationships with one another more broadly. After the tightening of controls under Nicholas it is likely that punishment would have only increased.[18]

Students not only were discouraged from acting on sexual impulses, but also were expected to be, and remain, bachelors. Married men were not admitted to the university, and getting married while a student constituted grounds for expulsion. Although legally a student needed no permission from the university authorities to marry, once he was wed, the university administration released him.[19] In 1850, for instance, a Moscow University student married secretly. When the authorities discovered his new status, they insisted that he was 'obligated to abandon his studies'. The reason, the authorities agreed, was that 'spousal obligations and civil obligations can not be satisfied simultaneously'.[20] Students, at least in theory, were supposed to be asexual, single men.

This Russian administrative ideal – echoing models of gentlemanliness found in western European prescriptive literature[21] – equally emphasized the cultivation of morals and the perfecting of manners.

The Russian word *nravy* encompasses both the English words 'manners' and 'morals'. In other words, external qualities such as a neatly mended uniform, a freshly shaven face or a cleanly scrubbed body were supposed to reflect internal goodness. Students were praised not only for the 'neatness and cleanliness of the body', but also for the 'cleanliness of morals'.[22] Likewise, uncleanliness of mind, exemplified by lying, 'evil words' and rudeness, were forbidden.[23]

When Nicholas visited the universities, he seemed to notice 'little else except dress and social behavior'.[24] Reflecting the Tsar's preoccupations, the university statutes emphasized the perfecting of comportment, including 'gait and gesture', hairstyle, and clothing.[25] There were formal requirements to guarantee that students learned to behave in the desired manner: the university required classes such as fencing and dance that were designed to perfect students' self-presentation in polite society. Fencing developed balance and grace, university officials believed; it was considered a mark of gentlemanly status throughout Europe. Dance taught a student how to 'enter a room, bow, and to hold oneself among well-bred people'.[26]

In this atmosphere, a student's hairstyle and uniform were not simply matters of superficial concern, but were 'the key to maintaining honor and modesty' and expressing devotion to the autocracy.[27] The state's direct concern with civilizing the elite by requiring trimmed beards and smooth faces began under the direction of Peter the Great, as Nancy Kollmann demonstrated in the previous chapter. These external markers of civilization were considered signs of modernity and were thought to assist Russia to assume its place among the respectable European nations. Failing to wear one's hair cropped short, 'according to military length', was therefore considered a serious offense. If a student insisted upon maintaining long hair or any facial hair at all he was assured substantial punishment.[28] In his memoir recalling his student days at Moscow University, P. F. Vistengof describes an argument that he witnessed between an inspector and a student over the length of the student's hair:

> Inspector: What is this! Cut it even shorter! Crop it closer! Are you listening? And you too [he says, looking at another student].
>
> The inspector continues: If you dare again to let your beard, mustache, or long hair grow, I will order to you to get it cut and shaved. . . . I will send you to the prison room (*kartser*) and then to become a soldier. You are not a sexton! (*d'iachki*).[29]

A student's dressing habits also fell within the administration's jurisdiction. Currently enrolled students 'were obligated to show the proper respect for their place... and observe the honor of wearing their student uniforms in public places'.[30] Nicholaevan society at large was one where uniforms were commonplace and official garb not only solicited respect, but also signaled one's status in state service, whether as priest, officer or student. Wearing the student uniform – including the three-corned hat with silver tassels, a student frock coat, and a black silk tie knotted in the back – was considered an important 'external sign of good breeding'.[31] The failure to do so was reason enough to be punished. The privileges of wearing a uniform were the exclusive property of students; former students were forbidden from sporting their old uniforms. In August of 1843, for example, the student inspector of Moscow University charged ex-student Ivan Subbotnik with the offense of publicly wearing his student clothes. The authorities punished Subbotnik by revoking his *zhitel'stvo bilet,* the document allowing him to live in Moscow, and consequently forcing him to relocate.[32]

Emulation of the university's administrative ideal of masculinity required that each student's sense of propriety be combined with *pokornost'* or submissiveness/obedience before God and the autocracy. According to the Kazan' *Instructions to the Inspector, pokornost'* was to be 'the soul of education and the first virtue of a citizen'.[33] Humbling oneself before the authority of God was considered the 'most important virtue of youth'. Through disciplined religious worship, a student could achieve the 'submission (*pokornost'*) of passion [and] restrain the stubbornness of self-love'.[34] Orthodox Christian students were required to regularly attend Church services and say their prayers daily.[35] The achievement of *pokornost'* would guarantee a student the acquisition of 'a *softness* [*miakost'*]' that would last his whole life.[36] Achieving a 'softness' of manner implied not a lack of will, but rather a sense of humility and respect for one's place within status hierarchies.

Respecting the system of order (*poriadok*), which was formalized in the student behavior codes, meant showing deference in the presence of one's superiors.[37] Upon meeting a general, for instance, a student was required, under the threat of punishment, to tip his student cap and respectfully salute his superior.[38] Similar rules and rituals applied to students meeting the tsar himself, whether on the street or in a university auditorium; in the event that a student happened upon Nicholas or a member of the Imperial family, he was immediately to remove his hat with his left hand while bowing.[39]

Whether by neatly darning one's socks or bowing in the presence of a superior, students were required to prove their loyalty and decency through the everyday adherence to the administration's rules. Coming of age in autocratic culture required a young man to be moral, humble, self-controlled, respectable and internally and externally clean; the failure to cultivate these qualities could earn him harsh punishment, such as several weeks in the student prison room with only bread and water. Masculinity, however, was also molded outside of the classrooms and the university hallways, and in the company of one's peers. Students as well as their mentors had their own informal ideas of what constituted acceptable behavior. One of the most popular venues for student social life was the tavern, often located near to the university. In taverns young men found an informal, semi-public/semi-private venue for socializing outside of the university walls and also an alternative school of unofficial masculine deportment.

Tavern sociability

Remembering his journey into manhood during his student years at Moscow University, Ia. I. Kostenetskii writes, 'the university should turn a youth not just into a simple *chinovnik* [bureaucrat], but into a man and a citizen.... For that he needs ... not only lectures and books ... but also comradely society.'[40] Kostenetskii's juxtaposition of the figure of a 'simple *chinovnik*' with a 'man and citizen' highlights the degree to which manhood, for many young students, required more than becoming a respectable servitor in the state's bureaucracy. In the pubs and on the streets students learned how to become men in society and not just, as Kostenetskii chides, *chinovniki* in the system. The alcohol-centered masculine world of tavern sociability included representatives of state culture. In their professional capacity as inspectors, university officials kept up the facade of respectability by formally instilling in their protégés the state's values of orderly conduct. At the same time, they taught their students the secrets of how to function properly within this drunken world and how to move between the cultures of respectability and debauchery without being ostracized.

The particular places where students drank and socialized varied widely; they included local bars, private apartments, and the streets. Students in Kazan', Moscow, and St Petersburg spent many of their non-classroom hours in cavernous pubs near the university.[41] There they drank spirits, beer, and wine and smoked 'to their hearts' content'.[42] In their memoirs, students highlight the central role that the tavern played in their social lives. The pub, one student records, was 'filled with a cloud of smoke and always had a crowd of students'. The daily routines of pub life depended upon the flow of students to and from their classes.[43] There was never any need to wear a watch while sitting in the tavern because students came and went on the hour, with the schedule of classes.[44] The two most popular Moscow student pubs, *Zheleznyi* and *Britaniia*, were located in close proximity to the university itself. As one memoirist remarks, *Britaniia* was 'a simple tavern, standing directly across [the street] from the university'.[45] Although open to a wider clientele than students alone, taverns near the universities gave the student population a chance to create semi-public/semi-private niches of exclusive sociability within the broader public arena; they had separate 'student dormitories' where they drank, sang student songs, and 'felt absolutely at home'.[46] In these exclusive spaces, students educated one another in the arts of manly behavior. As part of that process they could affirm their separate group status, both literally and figuratively – as respectable and socially superior – in front of the other tavern denizens.

Excessive alcohol consumption was a central component of students' social interactions in the corners of their favorite pubs. One evening in *Britaniia*, student Dmitriev and his comrades feasted, drank, and toasted one another throughout the night. At seven in the evening, the owners closed the doors to all but the students. For the students that night, 'the fun was just beginning'. They drank to each other – 'to their brothers' – and to 'beautiful women! beautiful women!' and drunkenly sang of the 'green pockets' of their beloved billiards.[47] At the tavern *Eliseeva* in St Petersburg, student drunkenness was so common that the tavern keeper concocted a strict policy, which institutionalized students' rowdiness. After several episodes of raucous behavior, he made a deal with the young men; both sides agreed that students would be permitted to frequent the pub only under the condition that when they had the urge to throw bottles out of the window (which evidently they often did), they would only throw them out the courtyard side. Fearing the wrath of the police, the tavern owner forbade his student-patrons from breaking bottles on the streets.[48]

The pub, with its rituals of drunken celebrations, often served as a launching point of students' more public rowdiness. They moved from the semi-public venue of their cozy tavern rooms out onto the exposed, public world of the streets. Once there, students often turned to mischief directed at the codes and institutions of polite society. Their disregard for the social expectations of official polite society involved aggressive and destructive behavior, from bar brawls to harassment of lowly government officials.

In his memoirs, Moscow University student F. I. Buslaev shows how he and his comrades spent their evenings together drinking at the tavern and then wandering the streets, breaking the law and disturbing the peace. For example, Buslaev describes one winter evening when, after many hours in a bar, he and several of his friends harassed a carriage driver who was roaming the streets near to the university looking for business. Even though the carriage was intended only for a single pair of passengers at a time, the students stopped the driver and drunkenly demanded that they all be permitted to get in. They succeeded in convincing – even intimidating – the beleaguered driver to give over control and sit below while a student sat on top of the horse and guided the *drozhki* around the garden and back to the university. The humiliation of the driver was part of the students' adventure; by humiliating him they could assert their superiority. 'And so we rode,' Buslaev writes, 'under the light of the moon, through the Alexandrovsky Gardens, laughing all the way.'[49]

Students also targeted the church in their escapades. According to police records as well as memoir sources, during the final week of the Easter fast in 1839, a group of Kazan' University students gathered to celebrate the birthday of fellow student Peter Aristov.[50] Having just received the birthday gift of a large package of food and wine from his father, the young Aristov invited all of his friends to his apartment to eat, drink, and join in his celebration. As the sun began to set in the late afternoon, several students got up to leave and sleep off their headaches. Aristov insisted that they stay, continue drinking and join in the general rowdiness. Under this peer pressure, the young men remained and soon found themselves involved in an increasing amount of mischief. Stumbling around the city, they were passing a church near the university when one of the students yelled: 'Let's break the glass!' Another answered him: 'You are drunk!' and then proceeded to throw a stone through a window. Other students followed suit, one injuring his fist as he punched a window with his hand. After breaking as many as eight windows (the reports vary), the students' activities were curtailed by a priest who had been inside in the church during the incident. The priest shouted for help, causing many of the students to run away.[51]

Outside of the confined environment of their dorm rooms or family parlors, students such as Aristov and his comrades caused trouble in broad daylight in the spaces of pubic life. The spontaneous fights that filled the leisure hours of these young men crossed lines of age and social status. In 1832, for example, a pair of drunken Moscow students was spotted stumbling into a restaurant looking for a fight. Noticing their intoxicated state, the police report states, the restaurant proprietor asked them to leave. This suggestion offended the students and inspired their anger. In retaliation for the humiliation they claimed to have suffered, one of the students caused a commotion by hitting a patron with his walking stick. Meanwhile, the other student put his fist through several restaurant windows, blood splattering everywhere.[52]

Such displays of student aggressiveness were quite common and could grow increasingly violent if a young man's social status was in jeopardy. At a public masquerade ball in January 1845, for example, an officer and a student engaged in a fight over the attentions of a woman. As the ball wound down in the early hours of the morning, student Peter Kupdosov found himself gleefully dancing with an attractive woman. An officer approached the couple on the dance floor and began to flirt with the woman. Rudely staring at the student, the officer suggested to the woman that 'she is not in the proper company' and ought to abandon her partner and dance with him. Upon hearing those words, Kupdosov defended his own sense of manliness by punching his rival in the face.[53]

Far from the state's idea of molding young boys into humble, controlled and proper men, this world of rowdy sociability encouraged students to behave violently and solve their disputes with punches and broken glass. Such uncontrollable, disrespectful behavior was what state and university officials were hired to prevent.

The university and the bottle

Despite the official rhetoric of respectable manhood, there were those in officialdom who not only encouraged students in their escapades, but also served as their mentors. Student inspectors in some instances straddled the lines of official and unofficial culture; they enforced the strict disciplinary regime by following students into taverns and monitoring their social lives, while schooling the same young men in the rites and rituals of drunken, virile manhood.[54] Mentors also taught their protégés how to move fluidly between these worlds, guiding them on what to drink, how to salute, and when to pray.

The career of Platon Stepanovich Nakhimov, Chief Inspector of Moscow University in the 1830s and 1840s, provides one of the most poignant and well-documented examples of a university administrator functioning as both a disciplinarian and an actor in student drinking culture. It is difficult to know with certainty how representative

Nakhimov was of inspectors. There is certainly evidence of inspectors who handed out severe punishments to students for the slightest misstep, whether wearing the wrong hat or hanging around with a suspicious crowd. However, anecdotal evidence of interactions between students and their superiors, including professors who socialized and drank with their students, suggests that Nakhimov was not entirely alone.[55] During his tenure as inspector, Nakhimov enforced the facade of sobriety while he himself indulged in and mentored his protégés in how to properly consume alcohol. He became like a father figure to the young men by protecting them from harsh reprimand and serving as their advocate in dealings with professors, priests and even police. In their reminiscences, students use familial language to describe their feelings towards their beloved inspector. 'Nakhimov,' student Afanasev recalls, 'was loved from the soul and he loved the students, like his own children.'[56] Another student writes that Nakhimov treated his protégés as if they 'were his native family . . . ; he honestly and ardently loved the students'.[57] Students' deep emotional attachment to their inspector stemmed, in part, from the fact that Nakhimov taught them how to negotiate the complexities of becoming men in nineteenth-century Russian elite culture.

Moscow University students learned the rules of drinking from the very man who enforced the administrative ideal of masculinity. One Moscow evening Nakhimov spotted a group of his students in the tavern *Britaniia* hurriedly gulping glasses of dark liquid; he approached them and inquired as to exactly what they were drinking. The students nervously responded to the inspector's question by shouting the word 'tea!' Disappointed, Nakhimov tasted the liquid in each of the glasses. He then proceeded to leave the tavern without punishing the students for their blatant lie and general disrespect for the rules. The following morning, the inspector took action, summoning one of the student 'tea' drinkers into his office and questioning him about the incident. Nakhimov began to reprimand the young man, but then his scolding took an unexpected turn. He sternly looked at the student and asked, 'What kind of rubbish were you drinking?' The student admitted that it was spiked punch. Nakhimov replied:

> I know it was punch. You all had punch. But *you*, what exactly did *you* have? The devil knows. You must have poured two spoons of rum in a glass with tea and then you had some kind of dishwater. Is that what you call punch? Go to the prison room! . . . They drank punch and you drank dishwater![58]

The inspector's reprimands were not because of the fact of alcohol consumption, but rather due to the young man's lack of refined taste; the 'tea' drinker had failed to mix his drink as would a proper, well-mannered man.

The inspector's jovial relationship with a notorious student drunk named Novak demonstrates Nakhimov's role in protecting his protégés. Novak and Nakhimov acted out a charade each time the young man was caught drunk: Nakhimov pretended to be the outraged official and Novak the innocent young man. When Nakhimov caught his student stumbling around campus, he would ask Novak to breathe on him to confirm the intake of alcohol. In response, Novak would complain that his jaw was stuck and therefore he was unable to open his mouth very widely. This so-called medical problem prevented Nakhimov from smelling the alcohol on Novak's breath and therefore from proving that his student had indulged in drink. The two conspired together, went through the official motions, but ultimately circumvented the rules.[59]

By schooling students in the art of drinking, Nakhimov acted as an intermediary between the authorities and the students; he served as a role model, 'a defender, and a friend' for the young men.[60] Nakhimov guarded the students' well-being and protected them from outside discipline, whether from other university authorities or the city police. (No doubt his interventions also saved his own reputation on occasion.) For their part, students turned to Nakhimov in moments of personal or academic crisis; they had an unspoken understanding with their beloved inspector.[61] Upon receiving a low grade in a lecture course, for example, an outraged student approached his mentor and bitterly complained. 'Look at my mark!' he shouted. Nakhimov realized immediately that the student was begging him to intervene on his behalf, but his response was gruff. 'I know you are mocking me,' the inspector told the young man. 'Now get out of here!' Nakhimov then went off to persuade the professor in question to rethink his grading. Several hours later he found his protégé again. 'You have a four,' he declared triumphantly. Grateful and a bit surprised, the young man replied in a quiet affectionate voice: 'Thank you P. S.'[62]

Nakhimov occasionally directly mediated the relationship between his students and the city and church authorities. To protect his charges from outside authorities, Nakhimov habitually snatched drunken ones off the streets. On holidays in particular Nakhimov roamed the most popular student spots in order to ensure that 'students would not loaf about drunken without their uniforms and three-cornered hats and swords'.[63] During a holiday celebration, Nakhimov spotted a medical student absolutely drunk and sitting on the street hunched over with neither uniform nor sword. The student begged to be left alone. Afraid of the consequences if either city officials or other university authorities found the young man, Nakhimov refused to let him remain there and dragged him back to the university prison room. Even though drinking was against the rules, Nakhimov's anger at the student was not due to his drinking. Rather, it was his stupidity for appearing in a public place in such an intoxicated state; next time, Nakhimov warned, he just ought not to go out, 'especially on a holiday'.[64]

Nakhimov's in-between position as representative of formal state authority and participant in informal student culture won him the status of most popular and trusted inspector among the students. As one later remembered, 'each student stored in his heart grateful memories' of him after graduation.[65] Commentaries on Nakhimov's positive qualities abound in students' diaries and memoirs. N. D. Dmitriev remembers how 'his personality was loving and extremely original. He was soft, warm, sympathetic.'[66] During his tenure as inspector, Nakhimov 'comfortably lived among the student youth' and they were so fond of him that 'to be reprimanded by him and in general to look into his eyes after an embarrassing scandal . . . was difficult'.[67] His authority, therefore, stemmed in part from his personal relationships with the young men. In turn, these feelings of personal attachment between inspector and students helped to foster attachments across generations. Nakhimov taught his protégés how to function as men in Russian society, both inside and outside of the university. Students, for their part, would take this precarious balance of respectability, obedience, and rowdiness with them to their posts across the empire.

Conclusion

Far from a distant and ominous figure who wielded punishments for the slightest impropriety, Chief Inspector Stepan Platonovich Nakhimov welcomed students into the tavern and taught them how to enjoy their vodka. His dual role as overseer of the administrative ideal and mentor in the rules of tavern sociability suggests the tensions inherent in nineteenth-century prescriptions for manhood. Coming of age in the Nicholaevan university required a balancing act. A student had to behave respectably one moment and hurl a stone at church windows the next. He had to show humility before his superiors and God, while asserting his authority over those lower down on the social scale, whether in professional status (city officials) or in gender status (mother/grandmother). How could he know when to act the obedient servitor, the civilized gentleman, or the drunken comrade? He had only to look to his mentors, who would guide him through this maze. The lack of appropriate mentoring – as in the case of the poor Blagov who turned to his mother and grandmother for guidance – could lead to ostracism by one's peers, or even worse, to emasculation.

Notes

Funding for research and writing of this article was provided by the International Research and Exchanges Board (IREX), the Social Science Research Council (SSRC), and the University of Michigan Department of History. I would like to thank my co-editors, Barbara Evans Clements and Dan Healey, for their insightful comments.

1. Boris Chicherin, *Vospominaniia B. N. Chicherina*, vol. 1 (New York, 1973), 70–1.
2. Ibid.
3. L. Ray Drinkwater, 'Honor and Student Misconduct in Southern Antebellum Colleges', *Southern Humanities Review*, 27, no. 4 (Fall 1993), 328–31.
4. *Instruktsiia inspektoru studentov imperatorskago Kazan'skago universiteta* (Kazan', 1835), 6.
5. On the question of Nicholas I's attempt to project an image of European civility and respectability, see Richard Wortman, *Scenarios of Power: Myth and Ceremony in Russian Monarchy*, vol. 1 (Princeton, 1995), 255–378.
6. James T. Flynn, 'Tuition and Social Class in Russian Universities: S. S. Uvarov and the "Reaction" in the Russia of Nicholas I', *Slavic Review* 35, no. 2 (June 1976), 236. Although these numbers are small, the universities in the early years of the nineteenth century had even fewer students. The oft troubled Kazan' University in 1815 had a mere 42 students and just 169 four years later. There is a discussion of the problems at Kazan' University in the article by James T. Flynn, 'Magnitskii's Purge of Kazan' University: a Case Study in the Uses of Reaction in Nineteenth-Century Russia', *Journal of Modern History*, 43, no. 4 (December 1971), 598–614.
7. Cynthia H. Whittaker, *The Origins of Modern Russian Education: an Intellectual Biography of Count Sergei Uvarov, 1786–1855* (DeKalb, 1984), 175–6.
8. Friedrich Paulsen, *German Education: Past and Present* (London, 1908), 187.
9. Russian university students were sons primarily of the middling elites, including nobility, junior officials and priests. This group made up approximately 70 percent of the overall student population. The remaining 30 percent were a combination of *raznochintsy* (25 percent), foreigners, and peasants. Nicholas and his officials were engaged in a constant struggle to attract more members of the aristocracy to the universities. In the late 1830s, there was a small degree of success. See Whittaker, *Origins*, 178–9.
10. The university became more closely tied with the central state bureaucracy after the issuing of the General University Statute of 1835. After 1835, inspectors were no longer chosen from among the faculty, but from among a broader pool of civil servants. On this see ibid., ch. 7.

11. *Instruktsiia inspektoru studentov*, 9–10 and 'Instruktsiia direktoru Kazan'skago universiteta', *Kazan'skii vestnik* (February 1821), 93.
12. *Sbornik rasporiazhenii po ministerstva narodnogo prosveshcheniia*, vol. 2 (St Petersburg, 1866), 43.
13. *Instruktsiia inspectoru studentov*, 14.
14. Arkhiv gosudarstvennogo istoricheskogo muzeia g. Moskvy, fond 404, op. 1, d. 24, l. 21ob. From now on GIM. Materials on Kazan' students are found in Kazan's main historical archive, Natsional'nyi arkhiv respubliki Tatarstan fond 977, op. ins, d. 12. From now on NART. In her study about sex and liberalism in fin-de-siècle Russia, historian Laura Engelstein describes how turn-of-the-century Russians preoccupied themselves with male sexuality and declared, in their medical and pedagogical literature, that young boys needed to exercise self-restraint to control their own libidos. Late nineteenth- and early twentieth-century professionals' anxieties about male sexuality had antecedents in earlier decades. On this subject see especially Engelstein, *The Keys to Happiness: Sex and the Search for Modernity in Fin-de-Siècle Russia* (Ithaca, N.Y., 1992), 215–53.
15. *Zhurnal ministerstva narodnogo prosveshcheniia* 7, no. 19 (July 1839), xxv, xxvii. From now on *ZhMNP*. Tsentralnyi istoricheskii arkhiv Moskvy, fond 418, op. 251, d. 1. From now on TsIAM.
16. Rossiiskii gosudarstvennyi istoricheskii arkhiv, fond 735, op. 10, d. 114. From now on RGIA.
17. TsIAM, fond 16, op. 40, d. 236. Since I have no other account of a student caught either in a robbery or at a brothel, it is difficult to discern whether the administration severely punished Shumilik because of one or the other crime. Yet the administration's general intolerance toward students' sexuality suggests that the severity of this punishment was related, at least in part, to his alleged brothel visit. In addition, it is difficult to judge whether Shumilik had indeed visited a brothel, or if the authorities fabricated the charges as an excuse to punish a disruptive student.
18. D. Naguevskii, *Professor Frant Ksvarii Bronner (ego dnevnik I perepiski)* (Kazan', 1902), 128.
19. The punishment of 'release' corresponds to *uvol'nenie*, while expulsion corresponds with *iskliuchenie*. The latter was a much more severe punishment.
20. TsIAM, fond 459, op. 2, d. 1356.
21. Catriona Kelly traces the genealogy of the influence of western European notions of behavior on Russian culture in her manuscript 'Reforming Russia: Advice, Literature, Gender, and Polite Culture from 1760', forthcoming from Oxford University Press.
22. *Sbornik rasporiazhenii*, 2: 56; *Kazan'skii vestnik* (February 1821), 94–6.
23. *Kazan'skii vestnik* (February 1821), 94–6.
24. Whittaker, *Origins*, 174. Historian Richard Wortman notes that during Nicholas' rule the display of proper dress and comportment among members of the Tsar's court, military, and civilian bureaucracies 'were the essential signs of loyalty, showing an officer's [or student's] identification with Nicholas' rule'. *Scenarios of Power*, 1: 311.
25. *Sbornik rasporiazhenii*, 2: 46.
26. Ibid.
27. TsIAM, fond 418, op. 251, d. 1 and RGIA, fond 733, op. 44, d. 26.

28. TsIAM, fond 418, op. 266, d. 84. Whittaker, *Origins*, also mentions the attention paid to students' hair length, 174–5.
29. P. F. Vistengof, 'Iz moikh vospominanii', *Istoricheskii vestnik*, 16, no. 5 (1884), 336. Italics in original. Regulations for students' hair length echoed both Nicholas' preoccupations and paralleled requirements in other branches of the bureaucracy. In 1837, for instance, the Minister of War decreed that hair was supposed to be cut on the forehead and the side no longer than 'one-and-three-quarters inches, from left to right' (Wortman, *Scenarios of Power*, 312).
30. *ZhMNP* 5 (May 1837), clxxx.
31. Ibid., clxxviii–clxxx. Rules for student dress are in *ZhMNP*, 5 (May 1857), clxxx.
32. TsIAM, fond 418, op. 260, d. 48.
33. *Kazan'skii vestnik* (February 1821), 20.
34. Ibid., 90.
35. *Sbornik rasporiazhenii po ministerstva narodnogo prosveshcheniia*, vol. 2 (St Petersburg, 1866), 41–2.
36. *Kazan'skii vestnik* (February 1821), 20.
37. NART, fond 977, op. insp, d. 17, l. 14–15 and *Sbornik rasporiazhenii*, 2: 122–3.
38. TsIAM, fond 418, op. 266, d. 84.
39. RGIA, fond 735, op. 10, d. 175 and TsIAM, fond 418, op. 252, d. 20.
40. Ia. Kostenetskii, 'Vospominaniia iz moei studencheskoi zhizni: III', *Russkii arkhiv* (1887), 335.
41. To describe the places where they drank in the nineteenth century, student-memoirists often use the term *traktir*, which – at least in eighteenth-century usage – was 'primarily a drinking establishment where eating was of secondary importance'. On this see George Munro, 'Food in Catherinian Russia,' *Food in Russian History and Culture*, ed. Musya Glants and Joyce Toomre (Bloomington, 1997), 42.
42. F. I. Buslaev, *Moi vospominaniia akademika F. I. Buslaeva* (Moscow, 1897), 12.
43. A. Georgievskii, 'Moi vospominaniia i razmyshleniia', *Russkaia starina*, 165, no. 6 (June 1915), 428.
44. Nikolai Dmitrievich Dmitriev, 'Studencheskie vospominaniia o Moskovskom universitete', *Otechestvenniia zapiski* 122, no. 1 (January 1859), 3.
45. Ibid.
46. Buslaev, *Moi vospominaniia*, 11–12.
47. Ibid., 5.
48. P. P. Semenov Tian-Shanskii, 'Sank Peterburgskii universitet (1845–1848)', *Leningradskii universitet* (Leningrad, 1956), 44.
49. Buslaev, *Moi vospominaniia*, 14.
50. A description of this incident appears in RGIA, fond 733, op. 42, d. 182.
51. Ibid.
52. Ibid., op. 30, d. 61.
53. NART, fond 18, op. insp., d. 977.
54. The rules appear, for instance, in GIM, fond 404, op. 1, d. 24, l. 10ob.
55. On the informal relationship between students and their professors, see 'Romantic Friendship and Male Intimacy', chapter 4 of my dissertation 'In the Company of Men: Student Life and Russian Masculinity, 1825–1855' (University of Michigan, 2000), especially 180–5.

56. A. N. Afanasev, 'Moskovskii universitet, 1843–1849', *Russkaia starina*, 51, no. 8 (August 1886), 359.
57. N. A. Popov, 'Iz vospominanii starogo studenta', *Russkie universitety v ikh ustavakh i vospominaniiakh* (St Petersburg, 1914), 686.
58. A. N. Afanasev, 'Moskovskii universitet v 1840-kh godakh', *Russkaia starina*, 55 (September 1887), 651. Italics in the original
59. Buslaev, *Moi vospominaniia*, 31. Nakhimov also helped students hide their smoking habits. This is described in Afanasev, 'Moskovskii universitet', 651. There are other student accounts of Nakhimov's drinking, for instance N. A. Popov, in 'Iz vospominanii starogo studenta', *Russkie universitety v ikh ustavakh i vospominaniiakh* (St Petersburg, 1914), 136–7. One student memoirist alludes to drunkenness among the faculty in general. On this see P. F. Vistengof, 'Iz moikh vospominaniiakh', *Istoricheskii vestnik* 16, no. 5 (May 1884), 340–1.
60. Popov, 'Iz vospominanii', 686–7.
61. N. D. Dmitriev, 'Studencheskie vospominaniia o moskovskom universitete', *Otechestvennoe zapiski*, 119, no. 8 (1858), 86.
62. Popov, 'Iz vospominanii', 687. Grades were typically awarded on a scale of 1 to 5, with 5 being the highest.
63. Ibid.
64. Ibid., 686–8.
65. Nikolai Dmitrievich Dmitriev, 'Materialy dlia kharakteristiki', *Russkoe obozrenie*, 19, no. 1 (January 1893), 726–7. A. A. Fet remarked in his memoir that Nakhimov often played a prominent role in the student poetry that he and his peers wrote. He mentions, in particular, a poem that Polonskii wrote to Nakhimov. See his *Rannye gody moei zhizni* (Moscow, 1893), 210–11.
66. Dmitriev, 'Materialy dlia kharakteristiki', 726.
67. Popov, 'Iz vospominaniia', 687.

4
Russian Dandyism: Constructing a Man of Fashion

Olga Vainshtein

In his book *Remarkable Eccentrics and Originals*, M. I. Pyliaev describes the famous Prince Kurakin, a fop of Catherine the Great's era:

> Kurakin was a great pedant about clothes. Every morning when he awoke his servant handed him a book, like an album, where there were samples of the materials from which his amazing suits were sewn and pictures of outfits. For every outfit there was a particular sword, buckles, ring, snuff-box, etc. Once, playing cards with the Empress, the Prince suddenly sensed something amiss; opening his snuff-box, he saw that the ring that was on his finger did not go at all with the box, and the box did not match the rest of his outfit. His displeasure was so great that even though he had a very strong hand he still lost the game, but fortunately nobody except he himself had noticed the dreadful carelessness of his servant.[1]

All of Kurakin's actions were highly typical of the eighteenth-century man of fashion. For him the harmony of the details of his costume were the basis of his spiritual tranquillity and his basic method of self-presentation. He behaved like a classic aristocrat, using fashion as a stable semiotic code, a sign of his high status, wealth, and ability to manage his personal property to the greatest effect. Thus an involuntary neglect of trifles equalled for him a loss of status that left him feeling exposed.

In this story there is also something else curious – the tone of the narrator. For M. I. Pyliaev, writing about this event in 1898, classified it as an eccentricity that betrays peculiarities of character. Such anecdotes were quite commonplace in European biographies of the dandy. By the end of the nineteenth century in Russia, aristocratic dandy culture was already fairly incomprehensible, since even at court a standard of dark frock coats and black tails reigned.[2]

Pyliaev's intonation here contains inevitable irony, but note that there is a nuance of respectful admiration. When he says with obvious sympathy 'Prince Kurakin never in his entire life insulted anyone,' he explains everything.[3] This ethical criterion is decisive, even though it is mentioned in passing. We will return to this important factor later.

The luxurious costume of Kurakin would have been impossible outside the context of an existing vestimentary tradition. Peter I (the Great) established the beginnings of a culture of foppishness (*shchegol'skaia kul'tura*) in Russia by issuing in 1700 his famous decrees ordering 'all ranks of persons' to shave their beards, wear German and Hungarian dress on workdays and French costume on holidays. These decrees were aimed at all social classes except the clergy, coachmen, and peasants engaged in agriculture. The appropriate examples of costume were displayed on mannequins and fines were set for failure to observe the new norms. This dress reform made possible the appearance in Russia of a new European style of daily and formal apparel.

What kind of dress was brought in by the Petrine reforms? According to J. Laver, in Europe the fashionable outfit 'took shape under Louis XIV and consisted of a coat, vest, and knee-length pants'.[4] It had rather complex trimmings – round frills on the shirt front (called *jabots*) and sleeves decorated with buttons (of which there could be over a hundred) and sewn with gold or silver thread and braid. In the first half of the eighteenth century women's and men's costumes were made from the same materials – brocade, velvet, patterned silk – while for men's coats, sequins, gold and silver thread, colored mirror glass, and foil insets were used too. Bright colors – pinks, yellows, greens – were also thought appropriate for men's clothing. They were considered normal for a masculine style and no one accused the aristocratic dandy of the eighteenth century of exaggerated devotion to decoration and color, later considered the attributes of feminine dress, since these were the universal language of fashion at that time.

The importation of this aristocratic fashion with a European accent resulted in the adoption of foppish behavior by some members of the Russian gentry as a specific cultural form of expression. This was an example of successful modernization not only in dress, but in lifestyle, an indicator that Russia was participating in European historical development. During the eighteenth century Russian fashion changed several times,[5] culminating in the male wardrobe of the 1780s becoming simpler under the mediating influence of English clothing. Yet these changes all took place within the European framework laid down by Peter the Great at the start of the century.

In eighteenth-century Russia, fashionable men were chiefly found among the aristocracy nearest to the court, but in Catherine the Great's time (1762–96) there appeared a kind of fop from the middling sort, imitating (sometimes in quite caricatured form) noble fashion. These men of fashion were called in the French manner *petits maîtres* (*petimetry*), that is, fops. The patriarchal structure of Russian society dictated a reserved attitude to finery among most members of the middle class: excessive attention to one's toilet was judged to be evidence of conceit and vanity, and there was widespread moralistic condemnation of fashionable men. Despite this disapproval, some people from the middle ranks of society did aspire to dress according to the latest fashion.

Literary luminaries such as N. Novikov, A. A. Maikov, N. I Strakhov, and I. A. Krylov frequently satirized the *petit maître*. Krylov, the well known author of fables, actively mocked the inclination to French fashion of young fops in the journal *Pochta dukhov* and in his short stories entitled *Nochi* (Nights). One *petit maître* in his satires was called Pripryzhkin (from the verb 'to hop, skip'), another Vertushkin ('to whirl, spin'). In the pamphlet 'Thoughts of a Philosopher on Fashion', Krylov gave ironic advice to the *petit maître* just starting out on 'how to look sensible with having a jot of sense'. One should speak about everything a little bit, prattle using the words of others, joke about important things, forget about modesty, get used to being a 'lucky stiff' who is not obliged to work, and so on. The society man of fashion in this ironic light became a very useless and odious creation. But it was notable that Krylov's attacks on *petits maîtres* were based primarily on gendered arguments, comparing dandies to women and children, unmasking their claims to masculinity.[6]

It is somewhat unexpected that Krylov did not mock the dress of the *petit maître*. He concentrated his analysis on discourse and manners. According to Krylov, fops spoke with voices resembling women's. 'There is another way to speak amusingly without sense, only make your tongue as flexible and agile as a chatterbox's; but this is a difficult art, that can only be learned from women. Strive to imitate them, strain so that your words have no connection nor sense, so that your conversation switches topics five times in a minute, so that abuse, praise, laughter, pity and simple tales, all of it just mixed together, fly past the ears of those who listen to you.'[7] In the paradoxical logic of Krylov, the fop appealed to women the more he spoke as they did. Symbolically denying the man of fashion masculinity in speech, Krylov nevertheless linked him with women, offering disparaging caricatures of their likeness to one another.

An analogous attitude was used in comparing the fop with children, although the pamphleteer's tone was outwardly less aggressive: he rather 'forgives' his unsuccessful hero, as though he were an innocent child. 'You just play quietly with your toys; you are kept quiet with your catkins, carriages, dogs, caftans, women; you often get into scraps, but then children fight over their trifles. Your quarrels are no more important than theirs, and so like theirs are just as innocent.'[8]

The two lines of comparison, with childishness and femininity, hinted at a likening of the *petit maître* to a girl. Krylov wrote that the fop 'in his deliberations about important things was so funny and simple, like a little girl with her dolls'.[9] Thus the fop in his scheme was denied those substantial signs of 'real' men, the ability to reason properly about politics and science. Similar motifs of infantilism and femininity can be heard in the satirical invective against fops from Novikov and Strakhov.

The attraction to European fashion in Russian mentalities was automatically tied to western ideologies, so that those who prized foreign fashion were assumed to prize foreign ideas as well. When relations with the West soured, therefore, men of fashion were forced to endure various indignities. Plainly, in Russia much more than in other countries, attempts to regulate fashion had come from above for purely political reasons, so it was more likely that the fashionable man could become a 'fashion victim' in not only a figurative but literal sense.

Paul I in the first days of his reign in 1796 published special decrees against European dress, which for him symbolized the liberal ideas of the French Revolution. As F. F. Vigel' noted, 'Paul took up arms against round hats, tails, waistcoats, pantaloons, boots and shoes with cuffs. He strictly prohibited wearing them and ordered they be replaced with single-breasted jackets with standing collars, tri-cornered hats, shirts, short undergarments and Hessian boots.'[10] Attempting to influence fashion with purely police methods, Paul sent special detachments of soldiers into city streets to tear offending garments off their wearers, forcing unhappy fashion-plates to find their way home half-dressed.[11]

Attempts to contradict the course of history (in this case, the internal logic of the evolution of men's costume) were always doomed to failure, so it is unsurprising that after the death of Paul in 1801 his clothing reform was spontaneously annulled. 'The first use to which young people put their newly obtained freedom was the alteration of their clothing; not two days after the news of Paul's death top hats appeared in the streets, and after about four days tails, trousers and waistcoats, although previously forbidden as an ensemble, began to appear worn together. Everything changed in St Petersburg in a few days. By the end of April, only the poorest people were still to be found wearing the old single-breasted jackets and shirts.'[12]

These descriptions are interesting not only for the details of the rapid return of the previous style of dress, but for the social geography of these fashions. First, the vestimentary revolution proceeded faster in Moscow, for it was farther from the enforcers of power in the capital, St Petersburg, and men of fashion there had less to fear from them. Second, the most affluent were the first to express themselves in this way, as poorer people simply could not permit themselves to change their wardrobes rapidly, given the significant costs involved.

After the repeal of Paul's decrees, men's fashion began to develop more naturally, within European lines but with Russia's usual time delays. In the decades following the costume changes of the French revolutionary epoch, the minimalist style of the British dandy gradually appeared. It entailed a simplicity of contours and economy of expressive forms, yet with a significant emphasis on the eroticism of the male body. Neoclassic "nude fashion" was primarily achieved through very tight pants. 'Trousers were closefitting; such that *avoir la jambe bien faite* (to have nicely shaped legs) was considered among the prime external qualities of the *petit maître*. This quality was far less marked in other trouser forms then becoming fashionable, such as long and wide "sailor" or "Jacobin" pants.'[13]

This small example of French terminology describes a style and also demonstrates the use of foreign fashion jargon among dandies. In nineteenth-century Russia this was extremely prevalent, and many dandies subscribed to French fashion journals. Meanwhile in Paris, London, St Petersburg and elsewhere in Europe, most tailors and bootmakers were German. Tailors frequently suggested the appropriate types of materials and fashions. Not for nothing did Pushkin complain: 'But pantaloons, suit coats, vest / In Russian such words don't exist.'[14]

The lively debates in the nineteenth century over foreign influences often linked the borrowing of fashion ideas and of West European words. As O. A. Proskurin convincingly demonstrated, partisans of French fashion were perceived to be promoters of a 'freethinking cosmopolitanism', of destructive liberal ideas and of the defiling of the native language. In a polemic against the followers of historian N. M. Karamzin, traditionalist A. S. Shishkov created the image of the literary dandy, the bearer of a 'fashionable-urbane consciousness', for whom the call to revive primordial Russian speech was as absurd as the attempts to bring back old-fashioned homespun coats and caftans.[15]

Shishkov need not have feared the demise of Russian uniqueness. While the Russian dandy externally resembled his European brothers, he nevertheless displayed distinctions that highlighted his national difference. First, Russian dandies trying to prove their affluence through their dress often misused expensive accessories. 'Certain Croesuses contrived to display their wealth by setting large diamonds in the center of each silk button.'[16] English dandies invariably condemned such examples of 'conspicuous consumption'; the very famous English dandy George Brummell, at the very outset of his career, instructed the Prince of Wales to avoid what he considered to be the vulgar passion for diamonds. Russian dandies did not share Brummell's scorn, and they favored expensive pins to fasten crimped cambric shirt frills, rings, and not one, but a pair of watches, preferably by the French firm Breguet. This 'pairing' was a distinctive departure from European fashion; Russian dandies always sought to wear two timepieces while Europeans were normally satisfied with just one.

Russian fashionable men (and women) were criticized for trying too hard, and their efforts were obvious to all. Since they viewed their clothing, in fact their entire outfit, as enormously important, they desperately saw to every detail, especially colors, and what was worse, having acquired the proper outfit, they frequently felt fettered by it, fearing that the tiniest unnecessary movement might spoil their toilet. In their desire to 'out-French' the French, they drew attention to their desperation to 'catch up'. The trend-setting dandies of western Europe permitted themselves, as a rule, departures from the strict requirements of fashion in favor of personal taste or comfort. They affected tranquillity and relaxation, free poses and gestures.

An illustration of the Russian anxiety about dressing correctly is an ingenious little 'machine', popular for decades, that was used to tie a necktie. To achieve the desired effect, clever mechanical devices such as a special wire frame for the knot were used, however strange they seem today.[17] Such mechanical devices were not typical of the toilet of European dandies, who preferred to invent complicated knots for their neckwear. The young Honoré de Balzac even wrote a modest tract about 39 ways to knot one's tie. After Brummell introduced the fashion for starched cloth, it became possible to set the creases of a kerchief, and the Russian *petits maîtres'* 'little device' became nothing more than an extra bit of insurance for those unconfident ones who could not achieve a beautiful knot themselves. More confident western Europeans thought that a dandyish necktie should exhibit some degree of carelessness, or at least the illusion of carelessness.

Another difference in the style of Russian dandies was linked with the necessities occasioned by wintry weather. Whatever the desire to imitate the French, they had to factor in the specifics of Russia's cold climate. For winter wear frock coats were made from heavy wool fabric, and over these were worn full, sleeveless cloaks or fur coats. Indeed the general penchant for furs in winter always caught the notice of travelers and became an 'exotic' national feature. Théophile Gautier, visiting Russia in 1858–9, described street types very precisely:

> The young people who are neither military nor civil-service personnel are dressed in fur coats, the cost of which would surprise a foreigner, and our fashionable types would refuse to pay such prices. Not only are they made from fine cloth and marten or nutria furs, but they sew beaver collars on them that cost between 200 and 300 rubles, depending on how coarse or soft the fur is, how dark its color, and the number of white bristles still protruding from it. A coat with a price of a thousand is not regarded as exceptional, and many coats cost much more. This is a Russian luxury unknown to us. In St Petersburg you could say, 'Tell me what kind of fur you're wearing, and I'll tell you what you cost.' Fur coats mark one's status.[18]

The deliberate conspicuous consumption that made an impression on Gautier was connected to the demands of a harsh climate; no fabric then available could keep one as warm as fur.[19]

An experienced dandy, Gautier understood the importance of an entire outfit and made note of the variations in combinations of headgear and fur coats. 'If, having renounced the useless elegance of a hat, you wear a cap of quilted cotton or mink, then you will not be bothered by a high fur-lined collar [pushing up against the hat brim]. Mature dandies, strict adherents to London or Paris fashion, cannot tolerate quilted, peaked caps and have made for themselves caps without flaps at the back but just a simple peak at the front. But do not even think of opening your collar then; the wind will blow on your bare neck and you will suffer an icy blade as perishing as the touch of steel to the neck of a condemned man.'[20] Forced to avoid the wide-brimmed hats that prevented them from raising their collars, Russian dandies refused to wear ugly cotton caps. This was their form of aesthetic compromise. Théophile Gautier himself, it should be noted, bought a beaver hat while in Russia!

The ideological debates between Slavophiles and westernizers left a special mark on Russian men's fashion in the nineteenth century. They continued in a new historical framework the dispute over old and new language and masculine national dress. For a time one's choice of costume depended on one's position in this old quarrel. European style was favored by liberal westernizers, and there were a number of devotees of dandyism among them. The renowned liberal P. Ia. Chaadaev was known for the 'unusual refinement' of his garments, according to M. I. Zhikharev. 'I do not know,' he wrote, 'how Mister Brummell and his analogues dressed, and so will refrain from any comparison with these world leaders of dandyism, but I conclude that Chaadaev raised the art of costume almost to historical significance.'[21]

Chaadaev's coldness toward women evoked a great deal of curiosity from his contemporaries. Some critics, not troubling to seek specific evidence, consider that Chaadaev was gay,[22] but it is noteworthy that this coldness, in combination with an aesthetic minimalism in dress, was typical of English dandies of the first generation. The clearest example was George Brummell, who never took a female lover and who promoted a strict masculinity. In his case purism reigned both in clothing and erotic preference: economy on all levels became a fundamental principle of his aesthetic system.

European dandyism, which contemporaries sensed in Chaadaev (revered, among others, by Pushkin), contrasted starkly with the Slavophile attempts to return to a Russian national costume. Although there were fashion-plates among the zealots of national tradition, their attempts at fashion *à la russe* looked too contrived and artificial, inevitably arousing the irony of observers. The leading Slavophile Konstantin Aksakov, as recalled by I. I. Panaev, 'made a great fuss in Moscow appearing in blacked boots, a red *rubakha*, and a *murmolka*'.[23] His propaganda had more of a comic effect. 'It is time to become closer to our people, and in order to do that we must first throw off these stupid, short German outfits that divide us from the people (meanwhile Aksakov bowed toward the ground, took off his frock coat and contemptuously threw it away). Peter, tearing us away from our nationhood, forced us to shave off our beards; we should return to our nation and grow them back.'[24] It is funny that while propounding the value of Russian costume Aksakov was normally wearing a frock coat. Of course he did then make a spectacle of himself by taking it off.

Slavophiles did not express their ideological enmity toward dandyism frivolously. They were offended not just by differing attitudes toward national traditions, but the underlying structural principle embodied in dandyism. A genuine dandy was an adept of self-discipline, constantly self-regarding from a distance, checking the refinement of his bearing. Such rational behavior fundamentally contradicted the 'slackness, formlessness, and chaos of the Russian way of life' that Chaadaev and Turgenev among other national authors noted.[25]

In sum European dandyism became a widespread fashion for young Russians during the 1820s. Most were affluent noble youth from very old families, and the aristocratic rank of the Russian dandy not only gave him a clear social character, but suggested reasons for the appearance of dandyish masculinity. Leonid Grossman, the author of 'Pushkin and Dandyism', an article in the spirit of sociological critiques that were so popular in the 1920s in Soviet Russia, noted, 'The exhaustion of an ancient pedigree, the eclipse of a family crest is often expressed in a feminine fragility among its last members. The refinement of the physical organization, the aggravation of the nervous system, the intensification of sensitivity, these are the typical signs of the last bearers of an ancient lineage.'[26] Grossman was writing about the eponymous hero of Pushkin's poem *Evgenii Onegin*, whom Pushkin characterized as 'an exemplary pupil of fashion', comparing him with 'Coquettish Venus'. F. F. Vigel' observed in his 'Zapiski':

> The affectedness that one encountered then in literature was also found in the manners and attitudes of many young people. Effeminacy was not counted as a complete disgrace, and grimaces that would have been revolting to see in women were regarded as the refinements of a society education. Those who traded in such things displayed a kind of delicacy that is indecent in our sex, not concealing any fear, and hardly being amusing, which was even more surprising.[27]

In order to understand this observation it should be remembered that Filipp Filippovich Vigel' was himself notoriously 'gay' and as a result experienced many difficulties in his professional life.[28] He was of course unable to discuss a 'gay' aesthetic openly in his text and as a result there are many passages filled with cautious phrases: 'a kind of delicacy', 'not counted as a complete disgrace', 'hardly being amusing'. Sensing the contradictions, Vigel' added a supplementary conclusion to the end of this discussion: 'The present age, destroying these forms among our young people, forms so abusive especially for Russians, takes them to the other extreme, and their masculinity frequently inspires loutishness (*muzhikovatost'*).'[29] Trying to arrive at a compromise, Vigel' unconsciously hinted at his spectrum of 'masculinity', from 'effeminacy' to 'loutishness', the latter regarded for reasons easy to understand as highly negative.

Such assessments of the gender value of masculine costume are typical of the responses of many members of the nineteenth-century Russian elite. Dandyism was received as a stable virtue if it emphasized masculinity, but with suspicion, if not negativity, if it invoked any shade of effeminacy. In these circumstances practically the only way for the Russian dandy to promote himself without offending public opinion was, however paradoxically, to appear in full dress uniform.

Many young noblemen served in privileged military guards units, such as the elite Semenov and Preobrazhenskii regiments. The military uniform had long been considered prestigious and fashionable, and there were not a few devotees of fashion in this milieu. 'Officers went about strapped into corsets; to look more imposing, staff officers fashioned artificial shoulder pads, with thick epaulets firmly bristling on them.'[30] Corsets stayed in fashion for military men even after they had disappeared from civilian men's wardrobes.

Of all the kinds of uniforms, the most dandyish was considered to be the full military dress uniform. As L. E. Shepelev wrote, 'The attitude towards full dress uniform in Russia has always been enthusiastic, even loving. Dress uniform served to conjure up memories of battle valor, honor and the exalted feeling of comradeship. The military uniform was thought to be the most elegant and attractive of masculine garments. All of this pertained especially to the ceremonial uniform, worn on grand occasions and intended particularly for them.'[31] Russian emperors always appeared in public in ceremonial dress uniform and personally regulated the changes to military dress. As elsewhere in Europe, there was in Russia a practice of using dress uniforms as rewards; government officials were made honorary commanders of military units or were given high military ranks in recognition of long service.

The elegant dress uniform worn only on special occasions was an object of pride and concern for the military dandy. 'In 1886 Adjutant General Count A. P. Shuvalov, former head of the Third Section and leader of the corps of gendarmes, later ambassador to England, was awarded a dandyish "white dress uniform" – the uniform of the Life Guards Regiment of the Cavalry – because that is where he began his service. In November of that year Shuvalov "in full ceremonial cavalry uniform" attended the dedication festivities of the Semenov Regiment.'[32] Among the upper military ranks it was typical to have several dress uniforms and to wear various ones to receptions at court or on holidays, a practice known as 'gracing society with uniforms' (*liubeznichat' mundirami*).

Retired military men had a special motive for 'gracing society'; the various uniforms they were entitled to wear displayed the achievements of their careers. The 1886 social calendar of Prince A. I. Bariatinskii, governor-general of the Caucasus from 1856 to 1862, is a case in point:

> He told funny stories, joked and graced society with his various dress uniforms. The other day he lunched with their Imperial Highnesses in the uniform of a cuirassier in honor of the Empress; yesterday he apparently lunched wearing a hussar's garments in honor of His Majesty; today he wears an adjutant-general's dress since it is the birthday of Grand Prince Aleksei Aleksandrovich; on the sixth of the month he will wear the *kabarda* to mark the regimental holiday.'[33]

There were critics of too much freedom and effeminacy even in military dress. M. I. Pyliaev has written:

> The fashion for earrings flourished especially among military men in cavalry regiments, and though it is hard to believe, hussars of bygone days, 'wicked friends round a bottle', all followed this feminine fashion, and not only officers, but the men too wore earrings. The first to object to this fashion was General Kul'nev, the commander of the Pavlograd Hussar regiment; he published an order that all rings should be removed from soldiers' and officers' ears and turned in to him. They say that the famous saying, 'for a good friend, even the ring from my ear' was thought up by soldiers at that time. Fifty years ago it was not thought strange to whiten and powder the face, and some dandies so adorned their faces with powder that it was shameful to look at them.[34]

For military dandies, wearing dress uniform sometimes demanded certain sacrifices, since the outfits often 'hampered movement; it was hard or even impossible to sit down, for they were easily soiled. Trousers proved particularly inconvenient. In cavalry regiments, for example, white riding breeches made of elk skin had to be put on while damp, so that ideally they would cling to the figure. Nicholas I, who took a dandy's interest in his dress, was forced to spend many days not appearing in public as a result of soreness produced by his military uniforms.'[35] Corsets caused similar suffering.

The dandy's enjoyment of the military uniform was a typical Russian phenomenon. For European dandies, on the other hand, wearing a uniform more often signified the suppression of their individuality in dress. George Brummell sought in vain to resign his commission in the Tenth Dragoons when his regiment was forced to transfer to Manchester, because he wanted to continue his high society life in London. The French writer and dandy Barbey d'Aurevilly in his penetrating fashion noted, 'It was said not without scorn that Brummell could not stand his uniform. His essence as a dandy cannot be explained by the tastes of the young officer. The dandy who places the stamp of refined originality on everything (in the words of Lord Byron) could not help but feel hatred towards a uniform.'[36]

The Guards officer Konstantin Aleksandrovich Bulgakov (1812–65) was a famous dandy among military men at the beginning of the 1840s. He expressed his attitude toward the dress uniform in comic public performances. A. Ia. Panaeva recalled, 'Once in March Bulgakov appeared on Nevskii Prospekt [a main street in St Petersburg] without an overcoat and caught the attention of passersby with his bright green, very long frock coat. The reason was that an order had been issued to change the black cloth in military coats to a greenish one and to lengthen the coats somewhat. Bulgakov was the first to have a new uniform made, but he deliberately overdid it.'[37] Bulgakov made his ironic protest in a purely dandyish way, using the language of clothing, applying hyperbole to the new outfit he disliked.

In the terminology of modern art, Bulgakov's behavior can be called a street performance, and it would not be an exaggeration to say that at this time the theatricalization of everyday life was a frequent occurrence. Iu. M. Lotman has emphasized the great significance of the code of behavioral theatricality that prevailed in the culture of the early nineteenth century.[38] It is possible to extend this idea to later decades. M. I. Pyliaev wrote:

> At the end of the 1840s the model for dandified dress was thought to be the actor playing the part of young, first-time lover. I think that today hardly anyone would slavishly follow the fashions of the young lovers of the Aleksandrinskii Theater and curl their hair tightly into ringlets, but then middle-class dandies, having few good examples to follow, copied actors in everything. In this era young lovers wore olive-colored dolman capes with red scarves at the neck

> in public and to public entertainments. It was considered chic to change the scarf frequently, retaining the rest of the outfit. Young theater-goers, imitating actors, also appeared in the streets in this apparel.[39]

Overall the opportunities for self-expression through masculine dress were actually rather limited, principally because the sphere of regulation of clothing in Russia was much wider than in European countries. Military personnel, civil servants, and nobility were not permitted to appear in public as they wished, but were obliged to dress in accordance with the Table of Ranks introduced by Peter I in 1722.[40] If a man entered the civil service or acquired noble rank, dressing as he wished was no longer possible. Any innovations evoked suspicion and suggested disloyalty. When he was presented at court, Pushkin, regardless of his dandyism, had to wear the uniform of a gentleman of the bed-chamber with lace trimmings, which he openly despised and criticized in his letters.

I. I. Panaev, another fashion-plate, also fell into an ambiguous position because of his dislike of his Treasury Department uniform.

> Once I came to the department in dress uniform with colorful plaid trousers, which had only just appeared in St Petersburg at that time. I was one of the first to wear them and wanted to show them off at the office. The effect created by my trousers exceeded my expectations. When I passed a row of offices in my department, the clerks, both permanent and temporary, threw their work aside, smiled and nudged each other, pointing at me. That was the least of it. Many head clerks and even heads of departments came to my section to look at me; some of them approached me and said, 'May I ask what kind of trousers you are wearing?' and then they touched them. One of the head clerks, a humorist, observed, 'Yes, it seems that they are made of the same material that cooks have their aprons sewn from.' My trousers caused such a noise and stir in the department that V. M. Kniazhevich turned to my desk, looked at me askance, and then, passing in front of me, advised me that I was dressed indecently.[41]

The word 'indecently' in this context did not mean 'obscenely', but rather 'inappropriately for the workplace'. The dandy Panaev caused a sensation because instead of ordinary uniform trousers he wore pants made of Scottish plaid; that was not acceptable in the department. The cloth, a novelty in Russia in the 1830s–1850s, became popular because of the influence of Sir Walter Scott's historical novels. Panaev's vestimentary experiments were not merely a youthful fling, but the mark of a serious passion. Later he began to run the fashion section of the journal *Nash sovremennik* and wrote a series of fashion articles with A. I. Panaeva.

The interest in and passion for fashion may well have been intensified by the government's regimentation of masculine dress. Perhaps as a consequence, menswear expressed a semiotic code of intensely rich meanings throughout the nineteenth century. It was not coincidental that practically all Russian authors devoted much attention to the costumes of their characters. How a man dressed not only suggested his financial position, but indicated what social type he was.

The well-known writer I. A. Goncharov, in a series of sketches entitled 'Letters of a Friend from the Capital to a Provincial Bridegroom' (1840), laid out an interesting classification of fashionable types in Russian high society. Goncharov himself had a reputation as a dandy: he wore a morning coat, grey trousers striped on the outer seams, plum-colored boots with patent-leather spats, and a short watch chain decked with intricate fobs. He addressed his letters to his older brother, whom Goncharov sought to teach *savoir-vivre*, or how to live.

Savoir-vivre for the author was a subtle science, comprehending the arts of personal appearance, of social interaction, and of a certain moral tone. The first fashionable type in his system was the 'Fop' (*frant*), who only acquired the very simplest aspect of *savoir vivre*, how to dress impeccably. 'In order to afford to wear trousers sewn only the day before yesterday, of the right color with side-stripes, or to exchange one watch chain for another, he agrees to eat meagerly for two months. He is prepared to stand on his feet for an entire evening rather than crease his white waistcoat by sitting down; to turn his head neither to left nor right so that he does not spoil his cravat.'[42] For the fop a good outfit was an absolute value, the basic technique of his self-identification, for which he was prepared to sacrifice all comforts and bodily needs. The straitened circumstances of the fop were visible in this neglect of his own body.

The Lion, in contrast to the Fop, distinguished his *savoir-vivre* with a different set of externals. His outfit was not the most significant aspect: 'He never looks over his clothing, does not adorn it, never adjusts his tie or hair; an impeccable toilet is not a quality, not a virtue in him, it is a necessary condition. He is brimming with confidence that he is dressed perfectly, consistent not just with current but with the very latest fashion.'[43] The Lion paid similar attention to all aspects of fashion in his life. He ate well, smoked the best cigars, had the most fashionable furniture in his home. He was a leader of fashion and was constantly imitated, because he had a feel for what was coming next. It was the Lion in Goncharov's classification that most closely resembled the contemporary western dandy embodied by Brummell and Count d'Orsay.

The next type in Goncharov's system was the 'man of *bon ton*',[44] who could permit himself various departures from fashion. The main feature of the man of *bon ton* was his inborn tact, the art of relating to people. He commanded, in Goncharov's view, not only the external but the internal aspects of *savoir-vivre*. '*Bon ton* means knowing how to carry oneself in society and with people *as one must, as one ought to*.'[45] It might be possible to catch the Lion unawares in circumstances in which he would throw off the mask of politeness, but the man of *bon ton* would always know how to divest himself of unpleasant persons in a light and deft manner, outwardly observing the rules of propriety.

The characteristics of the man of *bon ton* in Goncharov's sketch coincide with the general European ethos of the dandy in one significant aspect of masculinity – the imperative of reserve, the prohibition against the display of the individual's emotions. Thus the complaint that such men were heartless was frequently heard, 'You will say that this is just a doll, an automaton, who has discarded from his straitened soul all sensation, all passion.'[46] But Goncharov defended this hero. 'No, he has not discarded these; he merely does not make spectacles of them, so as to keep from disturbing others, to keep from embarrassing and worrying others with endless, constant demands. He expects and desires that kind of behavior in himself and others.'[47] Here the stoic coldness of the dandy is transformed, in Goncharov's interpretation, into the cardinal virtue of intelligentsia behavior.

These rules of *bon ton*, and, to some extent, the imperative of masculine reserve, were the behavioral code of the westernizing Russian nobility during the entire nineteenth century. Consider the words of O. S. Murav'eva: 'The ability to conceal from others "petty disappointments and resentments" was considered an indispensable trait of the educated man/person.' K. Golovin, recalling Prince Ivan Mikhailovich Golitsyn, whom he considered 'one of the finest adornments of Petersburg salons', wrote, 'His indefatigable courtesy never became banal and never gave way to irritation.' And this despite the fact that everyone knew that the prince 'had plenty to be irritated about, his life being far from smooth and carefree'.[48]

It was precisely on this point that the Russian nobility followed literally the commandments of *bon ton* developed by European etiquette. They were all avid readers of Lord Chesterfield's *Letters* to his son, a widely published collection of detailed instructions on manners. Chesterfield, an eighteenth-century English statesman, diplomat and philosopher, stressed the importance of emotional control in gentlemanly behavior. 'This knowledge of the world teaches us more particularly two things, both of which are of infinite consequence, and to neither of which nature inclines us; I mean, the command of our temper, and of our countenance. A man who has no *du monde* is inflamed with anger, or annihilated with shame, at every disagreeable incident; the one makes him act and talk like a madman, the other makes him look like a fool. But a man who has *du monde*, seems not to understand what he cannot or ought not to resent.'[49]

Yet despite the European gloss, Goncharov's man of *bon ton* was not impeccable in a moral sense. He was 'a hero of respectability', but not 'a hero of the moral rules' and could, while calmly observing the external forms, enter into a deception, refuse to pay a debt, or dupe someone in a card game, violating the very same code of gentlemanly honor.

As foil to the man of *bon ton*, Goncharov set up the next type in his classification – the 'honest man' (*poriadochnyi chelovek*). He possessed in full measure 'a close, harmonious combination of external and internal moral *savoir-vivre*',[50] in which the latter dominated. Like the man of *bon ton* he never violated external decencies, but his refined manners flowed from a genuine spiritual delicacy and an inborn sense of justice. He would not take up deception or otherwise violate the principles of a moral way of life. Goncharov admitted that the 'honest man' was practically an ideal type, but he was nevertheless convinced that to live among civilized people it was necessary to be an honest man:

> because select, refined society is the same everywhere in the world, whether in Vienna, Paris, London or Madrid. Like the Jesuit Order it is eternal, inextinguishable, indestructible, whatever the storms and shocks; just like that Order it has its learning, its own rules not accessible to everyone, and it possesses the same spirit, despite tiny differences in form, with one object always and everywhere: to spread across the face of the earth the great science of *savoir-vivre*.[51]

This utopian picture ceaselessly repeats itself in Russian culture as the idea of the spiritual brotherhood of noble people. During Goncharov's day this ideology was based on estate and was linked to aristocratic origin, but in a later era with the strengthening of a middle class in Russia, it became the property not only of a cultured nobility, but of all educated people. And after the Revolution, when it was dangerous even to refer to aristocratic ideology, propriety, and civilized manners, Goncharov's 'moral *savoir-vivre*' became the credo of the intelligentsia, transmitted in intellectual families from generation to generation as a philosophy of life that helped many to retain their dignity and withstand the most difficult moments.

In Goncharov's system there is an ascending hierarchy of types. To the untutored eye it is obvious that he respected the 'honest man' the most and the fop the least. Yet there is another curious gradation present, in the authenticity of character and the degree of *savoir-vivre*. The Fop constantly seemed to pretend, he imitated the Lion, but did not really become one. The Lion, in his turn, possessed more *savoir-vivre*, but even he could be caught unawares in dismaying moments while trying to imitate the behavior of the man of *bon ton*. The latter aspired to become like the 'honest man', who was the sole type to achieve both external and internal *savoir-vivre* and who was distinguished by the genuinely ethical basis of his character.

At the end of the nineteenth and the beginning of the twentieth century the culture of the dandy spread further and as a result, became differentiated into mass and elite types. Specialized fashion periodicals enabled a mass character to emerge; one such journal was *Dendi* ('The Dandy'), published from 1910 in Moscow under the editorship of R. N. Brenner. *Dendi* appeared twice a month and bore the subtitle 'The Journal of Art and Fashion'. *Dendi* carried all the advertisements characteristic of the era – for eau-de-Cologne, for miraculous 'pneumatic trusses', for hypnosis, for the latest medical corsets, and so on. Nevertheless, the journal did justify its title; in articles on men's fashion an observer under the English pseudonym 'Jim' told men, in a dandyish spirit, how to dress.

Yet the fullest expression of the dandy's ideology was not to be found in Jim's articles on menswear, but in a translation of the program-manifesto of European dandyism of the 1840s. Beginning with its first edition, the journal serialized a Russian translation of Barbey d'Aurevilly's 'On Dandyism and George Brummell', the foundation text of European dandyism. Two years later Barbey's essay, with minor amendments, was published as a separate booklet by Al'tsiona publishers.[52]

The writer Mikhail Kuzmin, famous for his 'gay' preferences, was asked to contribute a foreword to Barbey's essay for the separate edition. He agreed to write about Barbey and Brummell because he was personally involved in the theme of dandyism. As memoirists have testified,

Kuzmin loved to experiment with his appearance and outfits. After a period in 1906 when he dressed in a special Russian costume – a cherry-colored *poddevka* (a man's light, tight-fitting coat) and a gold brocade *rubakha* – Kuzmin changed his style and from 1907 was hailed in St Petersburg as a European dandy, admired for his brightly colored waistcoats and even winning the label 'the Russian Oscar Wilde.'

Kuzmin was frequently compared to Brummell in stories that circulated widely. 'Kuzmin is the king of the aesthetes, the lawgiver of fashions and tone. He is the Russian Brummell. He owns 365 waistcoats. In the morning at his place, lycée students, law students, and young guardsmen gather to greet him at his "*petit lever*",' wrote the poet Irina Odoevtseva.[53] When she actually met him, she found that the real Kuzmin fell far short of the reports about him. 'Under the striped trousers are bright green socks and worn-out patent slippers. . . . It is he, Kuzmin, prince of aesthetes and lawgiver of fashions. The Russian Brummell. In a rumpled, stained morning coat, in some kind of velvet Gogolesque waistcoat. Undoubtedly the other 364 vests were pretty much the same.'[54] Irina Odoevtseva's disappointment was understandable; the myth of Kuzmin-as-dandy was very popular at the time, so the memoirist repeated, with obvious irony, her previous characterization: such a Kuzmin clearly did not bear comparison with Brummell. But we must bear in mind that the second description refers to 1920, when the civil war had impoverished everyone in Petrograd, including the perpetual spendthrift Kuzmin.

The dandy's style was particularly valued by the famous circle of avant-garde artists that called itself *Mir iskusstva* (World of Art). Theirs was, of course, not the military style of dandyism of the mid-nineteenth century, but one rather more in the aesthetic, decadent vein. Stylistically derivative, it was oriented toward the fin-de-siècle western literature of Oscar Wilde, Charles Baudelaire, and Joris-Karl Huysmans. The fundamental originality here was not to be found in everyday clothing or the behavior of the *miriskusniki* (The World of Art-ites), but in their artistic innovations in painting and later in the design of scenery and costumes for the Ballets Russes, which had a real influence on European culture. Nevertheless it is worth examining the fashions of the World of Art.[55]

The musicologists Al'fred Nurok and Dmitrii Filosofov had reputations as notorious dandies in the circle. The publisher of its journal and famous ballet impresario S. P. Diagilev was also a dandy. 'His top hat, his impeccable morning coat and jacket were noted by Petersburgers not without mocking envy. He carried himself with foppish looseness, he loved to flaunt his dandyism, he carried in his sleeve a scented silk handkerchief that he would remove coquettishly to place against his trimmed moustache. He could be deliberately impertinent, like Oscar Wilde, refusing to take account of the "prejudices" of good behavior and not hiding his unusual tastes in order to spite virtuous hypocrites,' recalled S. Makovskii.[56] These were clearly the games of European dandyism, by now an established technique of self-presentation. The same can be said of painter and scenery designer Lev Bakst, who also attracted attention with his dandyism. According to I. E. Grabar', 'he was a dandy, spic-and-span in patent leather shoes, a marvelous necktie and a bright lilac hanky stuffed coquettishly in his shirtsleeve. He was a flirt (*On byl koket*): his movements were soft, his gestures elegant, his speech calm; everything in his manner was an imitation of society dandies with their lack of constraint and their artificially "English" dissipation.'[57]

Even among the fashion-plates of the World of Art, Val'ter Fedorovich Nuvel' (nicknamed 'Corsair' and 'Petronius') stood out with his elegance. He was one of the founders of the group and brought Diagilev, Konstantin Somov, and Alexander Benois into its ranks. His character recalled that of Brummell, sarcastic but without Brummell's coldness. 'Valechka Nuvel' was judged a '*magister elegantiarum*', a master of elegance. But he would sooner have been regarded a 'shaker of foundations' since he had a poisonous and shattering skepticism. Yet it was all expressed in such amusing and brilliant, and sometimes merry and cynical, ways, and was so subtle and witty, that it was disarming and had something attractive in it.'[58]

The brilliance of the personal style of these men is undeniable, yet it seems that the fundamental result of Russia's culture of the dandy is not to be found in these examples of elite dandyism, but rather in the far more widespread phenomenon of the dandy of the middle class. These dandies, like the one in Fig. 4 from 1916, were typical in Russian society of the first decades of the twentieth century.

This snapshot from my family archive is of my paternal grandfather, Konstantin Borisovich Vainshtein. He had this picture taken in a photography studio against a decorated background and for the occasion he wore a handsome Prince of Wales check three-piece suit and a walking stick, not forgetting his watch chain and his signet ring. He casually holds a cigar in the tips of his fingers, there is a carefully folded handkerchief in his pocket, and his shoes are polished until they shine. And while the suit does not quite hang perfectly on his frame, his whole appearance and the easy pose testify to his serious dandyish determination. It is clear that for Vainshtein the dandy's style was a sign of self-

Figure 4 Konstantin Borisovitch Vainshtein, a middle-class dandy of the 1910s

confidence and self-control, a deliberate program of self-fashioning, designed to create the image of a man with taste and well-honed masculine manners, a lady-killer.

In his efforts to create an image my grandfather was not alone. Thousands of middle-class young people in pre-revolutionary Russia used the code of the culture of the dandy when they wanted to create the best impression. For them, this code was already a convenient, well-polished stereotype of masculine elegance. In this popularized version of the dandy's code the 'dangerous' connotations – of vanity, frivolousness, and femininity – had been muffled; instead, the semantics of bourgeois masculinity – propriety, responsibility, reliability, and respectability – were accented.

After the Revolution, predictably, the concept of 'dandyism' in all its rich nuances lost any currency. The arduous material circumstances of everyday life made the dandy's life impossible even for the many dandies remaining in Russia. The word itself remained in the lexicon of the intelligentsia, although now with a predominantly ironic shade. The new, fashionable Soviet man sought other means and other labels to construct his identity.[59]

Notes

Translated by Dan Healey. The author wishes to thank R. M. Kirsanova for valuable suggestions made during the preparation of this chapter.

1. M. I. Pyliaev, *Zamechatel'nye chudaki i originaly* (Moscow, 1990), 90–1. Historically there were different words in Russian denoting 'the man of fashion.' In the eighteenth century words in use included *'shchegol'* (fop), *'petimetr'* (petit maître), *'fert'* (coxcomb). In England the word 'dandy' was already in use around 1810, and it was adopted in France between 1815 and 1820. In Russia, 'dandy' appeared in 1820–23, first used by Pushkin in *Eugene Onegin*: 'kak dandy londonskiy odet' (dressed like a London dandy). Characteristically, Pushkin spelled it in English, as it was still a new word, and explained its meaning in a special note. The Russian spelling of the word 'dandy' varied throughout the nineteenth century and there existed other words in this semantic field (*frant, shematon, lev*) but gradually 'dandy' became the most generally accepted term.
2. John Harvey, *Men in Black* (Chicago, 1996).
3. Pyliaev, *Zamechatel'nye chudaki*, 91.
4. James Laver, *Costume and Fashion* (New York, 1986), 103–27.
5. T. T. Korshunova, *Kostium v Rossii XVIII – nachala XX veka iz sobraniia gosudarstvennogo Ermitazha* (Leningrad, 1970), 7.
6. On masculinity in the nineteenth century, see Vern L. Bullough and Bonnie Bullough, *Cross-Dressing, Sex and Gender* (Philadelphia, 1993), 174–84. On the gender aspects of the dandy, Jessica R. Feldman, *Gender on the Divide* (Ithaca, 1993); P. McNeil, 'Macaroni Masculinities,' *Fashion Theory* 4, no. 4 (2000): 375–405.
7. I. A. Krylov, 'Mysli filosofa po mode', *Russkaia proza XVIII veka*, vol. 2 (Moscow-Leningrad, 1950), 757.
8. Ibid., 754. Compare suspicious and disapproving attitudes towards English macaronies, discussed in Peter McNeil, 'That Doubtful Gender: Macaroni Dress and Male Sexualities,' *Fashion Theory* 3, no. 4 (1999): 411–47.
9. Krylov, 'Mysli filosofa,' 754.
10. F. F. Vigel', *Zapiski* (Moscow, 2000), 51.
11. Ironically, the offending fashion was English in origin, having appeared in

France before the Revolution. The top hat was worn instead of the popular tri-cornered hat by British country gentlemen, as were shoes instead of slippers, and so too with the tail-coat, originally a riding-coat, and the short jacket instead of the long nobleman's coat. They eschewed lace on sleeves and jabots and luxurious embroideries, since these attributes of aristocratic finery were ill-suited to the active life in the open air and to British traditional pursuits like fox-hunting. See Laver, *Costume and Fashion*, 149–52.

12. Vigel', *Zapiski*, 78–9.
13. Iu. K. Arnol'd, *Vospominaniia* (n.p., 1892), vyp. 1, 9. See also on this context Anne Hollander, *Sex and Suits* (New York, 1995), 63–116.
14. A. S. Pushkin, *Sochineniia* (Moscow, 1949), 315. On Pushkin's dandyism, see Sam N. Driver, *Pushkin: Literature and Social Ideas* (New York, 1989); M. Greenleaf, *Pushkin and Romantic Fashion: Fragment, Elegy, Orient, Irony* (Stanford, 1994); L. Grossman, 'Pushkin i dendizm,' L. Grossman, *Sobranie sochineii v 4 tomakh* (Moscow, 1928), 4: 14–45; Iu. M. Lotman, 'Russkii dendizm,' in *Besedy o russkoi kul'ture* (St Petersburg, 1994), 123–35.
15. O. A. Proskurin, *Poeziia Pushkina ili podvizhnyi palimpsest* (Moscow, 1999), 328–47.
16. Arnol'd, *Vospominaniia*, 10.
17. 'The entire figure of the *petit maître* presented a particular aplomb and significance, united in the collars, ties and hairstyle. The knot of a necktie was formed by a subtle "little machine" (for there is no other expression I can think of to describe it), consisting of an array of numerous thin spirals of fine brass wire, covered in calico with fine kid or rabbit skin stuck on it. This little device of three inches' width accurately but smoothly was wrapped in a lightly starched and carefully ironed tie that adorned the neck of a *petit maître*. This somewhat massive bandage was fixed on the middle of a neck covered with a wide, high-standing, heavily starched cambric collar that reached up to the ears, and having wound round the whole neck rather smoothly, was tied up at the front in a wide bow that was sometimes decorated with extremely delicate embroidery. This way the head willy-nilly acquired a rather unshakably important pose, and the face looked full and the picture of health.' Arnol'd, *Vospominaniia*, 11.
18. Teofil' Got'e (Théophile Gautier), *Puteshestvie v Rossiiu* (Moscow, 1990), 43–4.
19. Ibid., 68. Gautier was no casual observer of such trivial details. Famous for having worn a red (or in some sources, pink) waistcoat to the première of *Ernani*, he was a dandy all his life and followed fashion strictly. In his novels he described his characters' costumes with detail and feeling. He also wrote an article, 'On Fashion' (1858), in which he wrote intriguingly about the relationship between clothing and the body. Thus Russian fur coats would have excited his imagination and he would have sympathized with the problems of winter outfitting encountered by Russian dandies.
20. The techniques of wearing fur coats stimulated Gautier to write on Russian gestures. Gautier was fascinated by the way in which Russian dandies donned their coats while maintaining their poise. 'They throw on a fur coat, putting an arm in a sleeve and wrapping it deeply inside, placing a hand in a little pocket on the front. To know how to wear a fur coat is an art in itself, not learned overnight. With unnoticeable movement the coat slips across

the back, a hand goes into a sleeve, the coat wraps itself around the body, like swaddling for a baby.' Ibid.

21. M. I. Zhikharev, 'Dokladnaia zapiska potomstvu o Petre Iakovleviche Chaadaeve', *Russkoe obshchestvo 30-kh godov XIX veka. Liudi i idei. Memuary sovremennikov* (Moscow, 1989), 57. Iu. M. Lotman, commenting on Chaadaev's particular style, noted, 'P. Ia. Chaadaev can be an example of exquisite fashion. His dandyism did not consist in the desire to follow fashion, but in the deep conviction that he set it. The strict absence of elegance was the very framework of the elegance of his costume.' Iu. M. Lotman, *Kul'tura i vzryv* (Moscow, 1992), 127.
22. Konstantin K. Rotikov, *Drugoi Peterburg* (St Petersburg, 2000), 252–9.
23. I. I. Panaev, *Literaturnye vospominaniia* (Moscow, 1988), 197. A *rubakha* was a traditional, long shirt worn outside the pants and belted at the waist. A *murmolka* was a hat with a high crown narrowing upwards (BEC).
24. A passionate agitator, Aksakov even pleaded with high society women to array themselves in sarafans, but they reacted with incomprehension. 'Get rid of this German outfit,' he said to one such woman, 'Why are you so keen to wear it? Be an example for all our ladies, wear a sarafan [a traditional dress]. You will look so good in one.' While he was speaking so heatedly to this woman, the then military governor of Moscow, Prince Shcherbatov, approached. She explained to him that Aksakov was trying to convince her to wear a sarafan. Prince Shcherbatov smiled, 'Then we men will have to wear caftans?' he said to him not without irony. 'Yes!', Aksakov said in a triumphant voice, his eyes sparkling and his fists clenched. 'Soon we will all be wearing caftans!' Prince Shcherbatov quickly hastened to remove himself from the enthusiast. 'What has just happened there between Shcherbatov and Aksakov?' someone asked of Chaadaev, who had witnessed this scene. 'It's true that I hardly know,' he replied, smiling slightly. 'It seems Konstantin Sergeich [Aksakov] was trying to convince the military governor to put on a sarafan, or something of the sort.' If we take Chaadaev's dandyish manners into account, his slight smile and deliberate substitution of the men's 'caftan' for the woman's 'sarafan' becomes more than comprehensible. Ibid., 196–7.
25. L. I. Grossman, *Sobranie sochinenii* (Moscow, 1928), 4: 43–4.
26. Ibid., 29–30.
27. F. F. Vigel', *Zapiski*, 66. On various forms of the 'feminine' in fashion, see Marjorie B. Garber, *Vested Interests* (London, 1993).
28. S. Ia. Shtraikh, 'Istoriko-literaturnyi ocherk o Vigele', in Vigel', *Zapiski*, 554–80.
29. Vigel', *Zapiski*, 66.
30. Piliaev, *Zamechatel'nye*, 164.
31. L. E. Shepelev, *Tituly, mundiry, ordena* (Leningrad, 1991), 93.
32. Ibid., 94.
33. Diary of P. A. Valuev, 1876, cited in ibid., 94–5.
34. Pyliaev, *Zamechatel'nye*, 163–4.
35. Shepelev, *Tituly, mundiry, ordena*, 95.
36. Barbe d'Orevil'i [Barbey d'Aurevilly], *O dendizme i Dzhordzhe Brammelle* (Moscow, 2000), 110.
37. A. Ia. Panaeva (Golovacheva), *Vospominaniia* (Moscow, 1986), 94.

38. Iu. M. Lotman, 'Teatr i teatral'nost' v stroe kul'tury nachala XIX veka', Iu. M. Lotman, *Izbrannye stat'i v trekh tomakh*, vol. 1 (Tallinn, 1992), 269–87.
39. Pyliaev, *Zamechatel'nye*, 164.
40. The Table of Ranks established the basic estates of Russian society, their titles, ranks and designations, and the corresponding uniforms. The general legislation was followed by decrees which gave the law substance. For example, in 1782 uniform outfits for Russia's provinces were introduced, with each province assigned its own colors. The motive behind the decree was to 'discourage ruinous luxury' and to 'save resources'; in other words it was a Russian version of Europe's 'sumptuary dress laws' of the Middle Ages. In 1794 an album of provincial uniform designs was published. By the beginning of the nineteenth century, the hierarchy became quite complex: only nobility and civilian estates were counted, each with 14 ranks, but in addition to that there were military noble designations, to say nothing of special army units. A uniform could say much about its wearer – the kind of service, the department (or kind of armed forces), and rank (in the case of military service). There were also women's uniforms in the provinces and at court. Owners of uniforms had to have them made at their own expense, a sometimes heavy financial burden.
41. Panaev, *Literaturnye vospominaniia*, 61.
42. I. A. Goncharov, 'Pis'ma stolichnogo druga k provintsial'nomu zhenikhu', *Velikaia taina odevat'sia k litsu* (St Petersburg, 1992), 20–1.
43. Ibid., 21–2.
44. *Bon ton* is a French phrase that circulated widely in Europe in the eighteenth and nineteenth centuries. It had many connotations: it could indicate high social status, fashion sense, good manners, a general stylishness, or all of the above. In the sense Goncharov is employing it, the best translation is probably 'good manners' (BEC).
45. Ibid., 26. Italics in the original.
46. Ibid.
47. Ibid.
48. O. S. Murav'eva, *Kak vospityvali russkogo dvorianina* (St Petersburg, 1998), 78–9.
49. Lord Chesterfield, *Letters to His Son and Others* (London, 1929), 258.
50. Goncharov, 'Pis'ma stolichnogo druga', 29. In Goncharov's criteria there was an additional important factor – a man's attitude toward his material resources. '[The] Fop and the Lion without money are in trouble. The two, relieved of the means to be fops or lions, return to their primitive, natural state and having disappeared from the horizons of polite society, lose all their significance.' By contrast, the 'man of *bon ton*' and the 'honest man' do not require money to remain who they are. In poverty or in obscurity, they keep their refined manners, their ability to relate to people, and (in the case of the 'honest man'), they observe the moral rules. 'Like precious diamonds, they can get lost in the dust, but do not lose their value' (ibid.).
51. Ibid., 30.
52. There was serious and more than intermittent interest during the Russian Silver Age in Barbey's D'Aurevilly's work. He was eagerly translated (see his *Liki d'iavola* [St Petersburg: 1908]; *D'iavol'skie maski* [Moscow: 1909, 1913], renderings of his *Les Diaboliques*) and quoted. Maksimilian Voloshin devoted

three articles to him for the Petersburg edition, which is highly indicative. D'Aurevilly's heroes became the sources and models for a number of characters in Russian prose fiction. Voloshin saw in him an 'underground classic' of French literature; 'of all the solitary minds he remained, perhaps, the most undervalued.' (M. Voloshin, *Liki tvorchestva* [Leningrad, 1988], 41).

53. I. Odoevtseva, *Na beregakh Nevy* (Moscow, 1989), 96–7. A lycée was an elite, college-preparatory secondary school. 'Petit lever' (literally, little rising) is here a sarcastic reference to the custom of heads of state receiving guests; originally it meant the morning reception during the French king's dressing ritual (BEC).
54. Ibid., 101.
55. Here I disagree with Julia Demidenko who thinks the dandyism of the World of Art was genuinely innovative; see J. Demidenko, 'Russkie Dendi,' *Rodina* no. 8 (2000): 111–14.
56. S. K. Makovskii, 'Diagilev', *Sergei Diagilev i russkoe iskusstvo*, vol. 2 (Moscow, 1982), 309.
57. E. Grabar', 'O Bakste', ibid., 2, 290.
58. M. Dobuzhinskii, *Vospominaniia* (Moscow, 1987), 203.
59. On variations of Soviet dandyism see M. A. Svede, 'Twiggy or Trotsky, Or what the Soviet dandy will be wearing this next Five-Year Plan,' in *Dandies: Fashion and Finesse in Art and Culture*, ed. S. Filliu-Yeh (New York, 2001), 243–70.

5
Masculinity in Late-Imperial Russian Peasant Society

Christine D. Worobec

Two seemingly contradictory images of the Russian peasantry stand out in the representations of the late eighteenth through early twentieth centuries. One image is that of the peasant as child. Like a child, he is at times docile and other times willful, but he is always ready to cower fearfully before authority. The other representation is of the fierce, out-of-control peasant who can no longer contain his personality under the mask of the child but instead becomes violent as a raging beast, destroying everything that stands in his way. In both cases the peasant by definition is male. The peasant-as-child image surfaced at the height of the oppressive serf system in the late eighteenth century, when a paternalistic state and nobility viewed bondaged peasants as requiring their continual guidance and superior knowledge. The specter of the dangerous raging-beast-of-a-peasant originated with the 1773–4 Pugachev Rebellion, when peasants led by Emelian Pugachev in protest against the extension of serfdom into the southeast threatened the security of Moscow. So powerful was the image of the violent peasant that Tsar Alexander II was able in 1856 to invoke it before the Russian nobility as a justification for emancipation. By noting that the peasants would free themselves if the government did not liberate them, he implied that the peasants would murder their owners. Not surprisingly, the figure of the irrational and violent peasant re-emerged in the revolutionary upheavals of 1905 and 1917.

The representations of the peasant as child and raging animal stemmed from a need on the part of the autocratic state and its noble supporters to control peasants who, either in bondage or freedom, undergirded the political and economic systems of a vast empire. As a subaltern group, peasants, in their superiors' eyes, were devoid of masculine characteristics. According to landowners and government officials, peasants displayed feminine qualities by being inferior, weak, irrational, and potentially disruptive. Distinguishing itself as masculine and superior, strong, rational, and orderly, the state was able to preserve hierarchical power relationships and avoid fundamental reforms in the agrarian sector until after the first bursts of revolutionary fervor in 1905–6, when it appeared that if the state did not tame the savage peasant, it would be destroyed.

Official images of emasculated peasants may have undergirded power relationships between the government and countryside, but they obscured village reality. This essay proposes to look beneath the surface of official discourse to uncover those aspects of peasants' lives that structured their masculinity. While the state tried to deprive male peasants of their masculinity for its own purposes and the peasants were only too willing to take advantage of the state's penchant to view them as weak and childlike, village life was organized in such a way as to endow men with authority, responsibility, and respect.

Russian peasant society after all replicated the structure of the hierarchical patriarchal state. Women and children found themselves subordinated to husbands and fathers just as peasants as a whole were subordinated to the tsar, the supreme father. Young men also had to pay deference to elderly men in a society in which equality and competition among men was intra-generational rather than inter-generational. Peasant men's authority and identity stemmed from their roles as procreators of large families, managers of their household economies, and protectors of their families' as well as their individual honor. So too did the tsar's power and reputation derive from the multitudes of his subjects and his ability to manage and defend the country.

An examination of the internal dynamics of peasant life and of the ways in which men competed and socialized with each other, upheld their own and their families' reputations, and acculturated youngsters reveals the cultural constructions of masculinity and manhood within Russian peasant culture. We shall find there a good deal of violent behavior. However, as in other honor-bound peasant societies, violence was 'rooted in an ethic of honor' that had its own rituals and guidelines.[1] Those same rituals and guidelines also structured peasant violence against social superiors and government officials.

The Russian lineage system rested on a patriarchal structure with the household head or *bol'shak* at its apex. In the pre- and post-emancipation periods the *bol'shak* enjoyed absolute authority over all the members of his extended household, including married sons and their wives. The *bol'shak* managed the household economy as well as collective familial property and determined the labor shares of every productive family member. Under serfdom he decided which family members farmed the household's own allotted lands and which members were to work the serfowners' demesne to fulfill the household's labor requirements on those estates in the rich agricultural south where *barshchina* or *corvée* prevailed. On serfowner estates in central and northern Russia that collected quitrents in lieu of labor, the household head still had to delegate labor responsibilities, this time with a view to ensuring that agricultural work was completed to satisfy the household's subsistence needs and that work involving the production of artisanal goods or off-farm labor generated income sufficient to cover the household's quitrent and the state poll-tax. When emancipation of the serfs occurred in 1861, household heads continued to delegate labor responsibilities along the lines developed under serfdom, as peasants continued to work on large estates (now as day-laborers working for a wage), and as the opportunities in the center and north for off-farm labor expanded considerably.

The power structure of individual households was mirrored and supported in the peasant commune, the governing body of village communities both under serfdom and after emancipation. All households were represented by their male heads in the communal assembly. Run by village elders who were elected on the basis of their experience or the backing of particular factions within the community, the assembly made decisions regarding land use and payment of taxes, punished community members for delinquent behavior, and took extra-legal measures against strangers who through theft or arson threatened the community.

The meeting of all senior males in the communal assembly (younger men and women were excluded) also served as an arena in which household heads competed with each other. Rivalries among men, notes Miguel Vale de Almeida, are commonplace 'in the competition for the symbolic capital of masculinity'.[2] In Russian peasant society, where material resources were so limited and reputation became the most important delineator of status, such rivalries took on a particular intensity. In the communal assembly the reputations of individual households were prominently displayed and challenged. A household whose standing in the community had previously been unjustly sullied or questioned by a public shaming that cast aspersions, for example, on an unmarried daughter's virginity could have its status raised in a communal meeting if the pranksters came before it to apologize for their actions and to treat the whole gathering to vodka in a symbolic gesture of reconciliation. Woe to the household head, however, whose household's reputation had been justifiably questioned according to community values and norms. He was responsible for the actions of an adulterous wife or daughter-in-law and for any family member who had committed petty theft. His voice would not carry the same weight in the communal assembly until he and his family were able to repair the damage.

A household head's reputation and authority rested primarily on his advanced years, experience, diligence as a laborer when he was of laboring age, and competence as a manager of his household economy. According to the autobiographical writings of the peasant V. A. Plotnikov (1906–94), a true man was a laboring man.[3] But labor in itself was insufficient to make or break a household head's reputation. As the peasant proverb pointed out, 'A young man [is good for] work, an elderly man for advice.'[4] The experience that came with age, family responsibilities, and the obligations of managing a household economy, together with a solid work record, conferred respect upon a man within the community.

In a system in which all peasants shared responsibility for taxes, a household head was a liability if he was a drunkard, squandered the patrimonial property, or prevented his family from fulfilling its communal obligations. The village administration might protect the common interest by assigning a guardian to a troubled household in an attempt to restrain the head's behavior. It might also transfer his authority to another family member, normally the next-eldest male in the household. If, however, all males in the home were underage, authority temporarily devolved to the household head's wife, the *bol'shukha*.

All community actions against a delinquent household head were humiliating for the recipient, but none so much as the devolution of authority to a wife. A man's subordination to a woman temporarily turned the patriarchal system on its head. For a man to be respectable, he had to be in charge and have a public presence, as a peasant proverb stated emphatically: 'The peasant as well as the dog are always in the yard, whereas the *baba* ['woman' with a pejorative connotation] and the cat are always in the hut.'[5] The moral of a Russian peasant folktale that a man who does women's work will lose his penis would not have been lost on a man who forfeited his leadership role to his wife.[6] Peasants would have ridiculed the offending former household head on the street, perhaps even subjected him to a charivari that paraded his symbolic emasculation before the entire community. Such public shaming naturally resulted in a severe loss of face for the victim.

To ensure the proper working of a patriarchal system in which reputation was so highly valued, household heads were obliged to teach boys and adolescents how to become men. A household head's reputation stemmed in part from his virility and ability to procreate many children, preferably sons, but peasants also considered parenting skills important. Fathers schooled their male offspring in the demanding world of work and also in the various tests that developed masculinity. According to a Russian proverb, '[As] unripe grapes are not tasty, a young man has not been tested.'[7] By encouraging fraternization and competition among adolescent boys, patriarchs saw to it that young men gained the attributes of manhood and learned the value of reputation. Using course language, learning to drink, smoke, and behave with women, engaging in fistfights with other lads, leading shaming rituals, playing pranks on neighbors, and testing neighbors' hospitality in the New Year were all part of sons' education. At the same time, household heads had ways to stem the generational tensions that naturally arose in a system that encouraged youths to cultivate their own reputations.

Training began with small boys whose parents encouraged them to use colorful language. As in other peasant societies, vulgarities allowed sons 'to sever their emotional dependence' on their mothers.[8] The late nineteenth-century ethnographer Semenova Tian-Shanskaia was appalled to report that Ivan, her archetypal peasant, 'learned swear words from his older brothers and sisters, even before he could put together a complete sentence'. Rather than punish a son for calling her a 'bitch', his mother encouraged him by praising him as a 'sly little rascal' or blaming herself for not heeding her little man. She might even call him an 'ataman', a chieftan, to demonstrate to others his self-assertiveness and leadership role in engaging other children in brawls or other mischief. Semenova Tian-Shanskaia also reported that children frequently used such words as 'cur, bitch, bastard, whore'; indeed, they knew 'almost the entire repertoire of abusive peasant words'.[9] These were the same words that appeared later in criminal cases involving insult to honor. Boy children, however, could use them in a carefree manner without consequence as they distanced themselves from their mothers.

Separation from the domestic sphere also occurred when fathers took their young sons out to the fields or to market and introduced them to the responsibilities of work. In his memoirs V. A. Plotnikov bragged about his young sons' holding their own during the backbreaking toil of haymaking. 'It was [a] happy [time]: the boys were young, but they worked with [great] strength. Mikhail did not break one pitchfork; he turned the hay over vigorously, a fine fellow.'[10] According to migrant laborer Semen Kanatchikov's memoirs, peasants slept only five or six hours during the harvest season. They got up 'as early as two o'clock' and mowed for five hours. While the hay was drying they did other harvesting work, returning to the hay in the evening to move it to a shed.[11] It is little wonder that Plotnikov was proud of his sons. Clearly, his own initial exposure to the men's world of work had made a strong impression upon him, for he fondly recalled his father taking him out for the sowing of crops when he was six years old and then letting him go along to the train station when it was time to buy additional seed.[12]

A boy's detachment from his mother was complete when a father assumed responsibility for punishing his son for disobedience or laziness. Peasants believed that only the rod would ensure that a son would not default on his responsibility to provide for his elderly parents. According to proverbs, not only did 'An unpunished son ha[ve] no respect for his father', but 'If you did not teach your son when you fed him, you will not teach him when it is time for him to feed you.'[13] So strict a disciplinarian was his father that Kanatchikov described him as a 'despot' who 'kept the entire family in mortal fright. We all feared him and did everything we could to please him.'[14]

As boys grew into young men ready for courtship and the military draft, labor remained an important feature of their schooling in manhood, but now drink was introduced. Summer was a time when youths helped in the fields belonging to their fathers as well as their neighbors. On Sundays and holidays, particularly during the harvest season when early frosts threatened, a villager requiring help would summon a group of youths to work for him in exchange for vodka and food. Twenty to thirty young men would come, knowing that when they became household heads they too might need extra laboring hands.[15] After work they would drink together. Ostensibly the lads were just relaxing at the end of a hard day, but such group conviviality had a similar function in Russian peasant society to that it still holds today among the young. Through binge-drinking, young men were initiated into the adult world of responsibility and sociability. Drink held symbolic importance among Russians in sealing work and marriage contracts. It also advanced sociability and hospitality among peasants in family and religious celebrations and among men in taverns. An adolescent had to learn to hold his drink and even to outdo his peers as he developed his self-assertiveness and reputation. Drinking with friends probably also built bonds between young men of the same age.

In the fall, young men and women participated in elaborate courtship rituals as they maneuvered within a social arena that by the end of the nineteenth century increasingly permitted them to select their own marriage partners. Despite the move toward individual choice, however, courtship was conducted in a public setting to instill in youths collective responsibility for maintaining community values and morals. Young men and women formed groups along gender lines. The male youth groups charged themselves with providing vodka and musical entertainment for working bees, that is, evening gatherings organized around girls' need to spin flax and wool as well as embroider linens and clothing for their trousseaus. Once the girls had finished their handiwork for the evening, the bees turned into social occasions. According to Kanatchikov, 'the village lads . . . moved in crowds from village to village; they played their accordions, sang outlandish songs in their strained voices, shouted, danced their village dances, drank vodka, acted rowdy, and fought over girls with the boys of other villages.'[16]

Non-villagers who attended these evening socials had to follow certain rules or fistfights were guaranteed. According to David Gilmore, masculinity continuously involves 'confrontations with dangerous foes' that must occur in public.[17] Following the rule of reciprocity that dictated village relations in general, the host village invited outsiders to its parties fully expecting their guests to return the favor. Ugly incidents, however, occurred when the reciprocity was not forthcoming, when guests and hosts exchanged insults, and when uninvited young men appeared at the festivities. If an uninvited guest did not assuage his hosts' anger by treating them to vodka, they beat him up. Subsequently, the injured party might seek revenge by rounding up friends from his own village, plying them with vodka to solidify their camaraderie, and then leading them into battle with the young men of the opposing village. If the host villagers won, they were permitted to participate in the social events of the outsiders' village free of charge; if they lost the fight they had to provide the victors with vodka at future dances.[18] Vodka thus served as a social leveler, a symbol of restitution, and a token of generosity.

Because of their important functions, fistfights among contending suitors and youth groups were common in Russian peasant society well into the twentieth century. They served as opportunities for asserting community and peer loyalty as well as building individual reputations for bravery and physical prowess. In the following *chastushka* (a modern song with rhyming couplets), youths boasted, 'We made merry in Tutilovo,/And we will go to Petrovskoe;/Our fists are bigger,/We will not lose anywhere [we go]!'[19] Male posturing in the physical confrontations they sought with other youths was also closely tied to courtship rituals which encouraged frank sexual commentary and tested men's virility. Although obscene games and gestures at evening gatherings asserted men's sexual domination of women, eligible maidens enjoyed some leverage in the mating game by commenting on their suitors' sexual attributes. A woman's praise or condemnation of the size of man's sexual organ and remarks on his sexual practices could enhance or destroy his reputation.[20] At fistfights female spectators undoubtedly continued to act as arbiters of male virility, separating the men from the boys. For a young man to have suffered a split head in one of these altercations was a mark of courage.

Oblivious to the social functions of these rituals of male sociability, local officials and outside observers viewed the fistfights and rowdy gatherings as signs of the peasants' immorality and savagery. Like nineteenth-century social reformers elsewhere in Europe, upper-class Russians were disconcerted by the peasant youths' abandonment from the 1880s onward of folk dances in favor of urban dances such as the waltz and polka, in which couples embraced one another. The new dances, their critics charged, 'transformed village festivities into "savage, disorderly affairs"', reminiscent of '"a sectarian orgy"'.[21] Observers were even more appalled by the fistfights, especially since migrant peasant laborers brought their rituals of sociability with them to the city. One commentator went so far as to equate the youths' weapons with those used in the Stone Age! What had earlier been understood as typical mischief-making among boys became hooliganism by the turn of the twentieth century.[22] Like their European counterparts, Russian local officials tried banning working bees, but they succeeded only when local peasant elders supported them, having decided that rowdiness at these events had indeed gotten out of hand. Many elders persisted in believing that the gatherings still served important labor and social functions, however. What frightened the official and educated elite most was the fact that peasant youths did not confine their ruffian ways to their own peer groups but periodically attacked other community members and officials.

The same groups of male youths who showed off during the evening socials also took it upon themselves to police fellow villagers' behavior by punishing moral and social failings. Adulterers, suspected thieves, impotent men as well as women with sullied reputations became the objects of their pranks. Singing a song that blamed a young girl for inflicting an out-of-wedlock pregnancy upon herself, they smeared tar or dung on the gates of her home.[23] They might also blockade the entrance to her house with logs, harrows, and carts, while they stood outside singing obscene, mocking songs and indulging in riotous laughter. Similar activities occurred during New Year celebrations when youths went from house to house dressed up as animals, women, and individuals of a higher social standing. They sang *koliadki*, wishing household heads prosperity if they treated the youths to food and drink or alternatively disaster in the coming year if a household head refused to entertain the boys in proper fashion.[24] Believing that wealthier peasants and local authorities were obliged to share their prosperity with the poor in a moral economy that emphasized social equality as an ideal, youths retaliated against those villagers who denied them hospitality by smashing and burning their gates or fences, smearing their gates with dung, breaking windows, stuffing hay down their chimneys, or letting animals loose. Youths similarly attacked peasants who tried to take advantage of the Stolypin reforms from 1907 onward by separating from the village commune.[25]

Having been encouraged to join male youth groups to develop and test their masculinity, the same youths also periodically questioned their elders' authority. Indeed, Russian peasants perennially complained of sons' disrespect for the elders. Although generational tensions were commonplace in other peasant societies, they were particularly acute among Russian peasants because married sons were expected to remain in the patrimonial household and had to await their fathers' deaths to be freed from their authority. Insubordination, however, could not be tolerated in a patriarchal system that discouraged intergenerational socializing and so the communal assembly members invariably supported patriarchal relationships.[26]

With community support, a *bol'shak* had several means at his disposal to contain the disobedience of adult sons who no longer feared his strength. Village assemblies and peasant cantonal court judges might sentence disobedient sons to the lash. This humiliating punishment involved whipping the prostrate delinquent on his naked buttocks with willow switches before witnesses. Solicitous of a father's authority, cantonal judges also allowed fathers to set the terms of their sons' punishment. For example, the judges of Prigorod cantonal court, Borisoglebsk district, Tambov province, on 8 May 1871, ruled that three disrespectful sons, ranging in ages from 20 to 26, should be disciplined with the number of lashes their father indicated, as long as he did not exceed the legal limit of twenty lashes per offender. In an extreme 1863 case of a son beating his mother, the Shalov cantonal court judges of Borogordsk district, Moscow province, were willing to waive the limit in view of the heinousness of the offense. Judges granted the father's demand that his son be administered forty lashes. They further warned the young man that if he did not mend his ways he would be sent to a criminal court.[27] Such actions were meant to deter sons from challenging patriarchal authority.

A father had still other means of dealing with disobedient adult sons. He could threaten a son with partitioning him off from the household with little or no property and then disinheriting him in his will. Since threats of disinheritance lost some of their force in a growing cash economy, a father might instead choose to deny a son permission to obtain a work passport and have it renewed. Without such a passport, the younger man could not legally take a job away from the village. Or a father could force his son out to work for wages if he neglected his share of the agricultural labor. In the event that a migrant son did not send a portion of his earnings back to his father to help pay the household's taxes and lend support to the family he had left behind, a father could demand that the communal assembly order the return of the delinquent to the village under police escort. According to medical doctor D. N. Zhbankov, 'Coming home as a prisoner in transit is considered a disgrace in the village. . . . The community indiscriminately looks upon every returnee as a person of drunken behavior, not zealous toward his household, and as such he is usually sentenced by the cantonal court to punishment or arrest of "the birch". . . .'[28] As deterrents 'to inspire obedience and fear among village members', such extreme measures against delinquent sons could not 'be used often'.[29]

In spite of the controls that a father had over a son, peasants and observers alike complained about the waning of patriarchal authority after emancipation. In 1888 an observer of peasant life noted that parental authority had previously been buttressed by the steward and serfowner. 'The master had only to say a word and everything would be done as he wished. But now our authorities keep changing, and they are peasants like ourselves. Besides, the young have begun to read newspapers and even to look at books. They know their rights . . . ; before you would do what you were ordered out of fear.'[30] In the same year, a peasant correspondent in Podol'sk District, Moscow Province, pointed to the indecent and drunken behavior of peasant migrants who had returned to their village for holiday celebrations. Unlike upper-class Russians who accused the savage village of inundating the civilized city, this peasant observer blamed the city for corrupting youths. There had once been peasants, he wrote, whose 'amusements' were 'innocent and decent, that is, uncorrupted by vulgar urban habits'.[31] For this educated peasant then, the village of memory was an idyllic pastoral oasis.

To be sure, there were changes in the late nineteenth-century countryside as the number of young men who went off to the cities increased dramatically, especially in the industrial provinces. Historians who have studied the phenomenon of out-migration have pointed to the migrants' growing self-assertiveness and their acculturation in urban ways.[32] Disposable income also made a difference in these men's lives. Once they returned to the village for good, some could afford to set up their own households independent of consanguineal family members who had remained in the countryside. At the same time, most of these migrants left behind wives and elderly parents who continued to live together as they farmed the household's allotments, ever dependent upon the migrant husband/son to send them part of their earnings. When men returned to the village to retire at the age of 40 or so, the likelihood of their fathers being still alive was reduced and defiance of parental authority for many had become somewhat of a moot issue.

The lessons that young men had learned in their peer groups and the solidarity they had developed among men their own age were not forgotten when they married and assumed family responsibilities. Socializing now moved from youth groups and working bees to the tavern and other public locations where men continued to compete with one another. The saloon (*shinka*) served increasingly from the 1870s onward as a public space for male sociability and the testing of male respectability.

While the peasant hut remained the preserve of women, the locus of much of women's labor and hospitality, the tavern became 'the men's home', a place where men who were finished with their labors could freely 'drink, smoke, share, talk, compete and play' freely.[33] In this male space language became coarser than in mixed company and subjects of conversation varied widely. During winter evenings, observed a peasant cantonal court clerk from Kaluga province, men 'gather here not just to be here, but in order to get together with other villagers and to exchange a few words. Wealthy [peasants] drink vodka, while poor [peasants] look on. There are all sorts of conversations – scabrous, narrative, or agricultural – and sometimes in the saloon a resolution of the next meeting of the communal assembly is prepared.'[34] Although he notes the social distance between prosperous and poverty-stricken peasants, the clerk's remarks focus more on the sociability of communication wherein men of all classes exchanged information, regardless of whether they were drinking. They also swapped stories but over a level playing field of generosity and reciprocity as they bought each other drinks. According to the rules of the moral economy in which the better-off peasants were supposed to help less fortunate neighbors, the richer men should have been buying drinks for the poorer neighbors.

Men came to the tavern to be seen and heard as well as to exchange information. It was not unusual for a rural community's prominent citizens – village elders, the church elder, and cantonal elder – to frequent a saloon. Information about the price of grain, the whereabouts of horse thieves, the details of a murder in a nearby village, as well as national and world affairs were shared among men who sat on benches in front of tables rather than at a bar. So important was news about the world outside the village to the peasant A. A. Zamaraev of Vologda province that he interspersed his sparse diary entries about agricultural labor and the weather with notes on international and national events. On 20 April 1912, for example, he wrote,

> I went into the forest, I chopped wood. . . . The day was bright, but cold, it is freezing in the mornings. In Siberia at the Lena gold fields 150 men – peaceful workers – were killed; they went on strike. Dreadful. A disgrace.

Earlier that month Zamaraev recorded that the Norwegian Roald Amundsen had discovered the South Pole and that 'a large British ship', the *Titanic*, had sunk.[35] More than likely Zamaraev read newspapers aloud to his friends or one of his friends performed that function in a tavern, village reading room, or store. According to a peasant correspondent from Volokolamsk district, Moscow province, peasants frequented the saloon, 'waiting to listen to the reading of the newspaper'.[36]

Drinking socially in a male space was widespread in the Russian countryside. In the last several decades of the nineteenth century, factories took over the production of vodka, making it 'better, cheaper, and stronger' and more broadly available.[37] In exaggerating the volume of drink the peasants consumed as another sign of rural depravity, however, government officials and urban observers of peasant life ignored the fact that the exchange of cigarettes and drink among men created an environment of comradeship and sharing. That exchange 'replaces the male social incapacity for offering cooked foods, something women can do, or expressing affection through domestic hospitality, an exclusive of the close fmaily'.[38] Among adult Russian peasant males, as among men in other cultures, social drinking was less for the sake of alcoholic intoxication than to express their camaraderie. Not only did a drunkard earn a poor reputation among his peers, but that reputation slid further if his wife had to fetch him from the tavern. According to a popular anecdote, 'A woman came to an inn and asked about her husband: "Was not my drunkard here?" "He was." "Ah, the scoundrel, the knave! How much did he drink?" "Five kopecks' worth." "Well, give me ten kopecks' worth!"'[39] The woman doubly humiliated her husband by inquiring for him in a male space and by out-drinking him. 'The altered state of consciousness' that alcohol produced was supposed to be 'occasional, festive, and shared'.[40]

Within the tavern a man's reputation could be tested, for the equality achieved through drinking rituals contained 'communion and competition, friendship and rivalry'.[41] Similar to urban taverns, rural saloons were spaces where men used rough language to assert their masculinity and in doing so sometimes offended each other by casting aspersions on one another's reputations or those of family members. Fistfights and knife fights could easily break out among men who as youths had honed their fighting skills. The peasant diarist Zamaraev recorded on 1 April 1912, 'Today they gave the shepherd Gavrilo Bulatov 65 kopecks for [looking after] the cows. In the evening we drank vodka with him and then we fought. Carpenters pulled a knife on Alexei'.[42] Unfortunately, Zamaraev does not provide more detail, but it is clear that Bulatov, having just gotten paid for his labors, wanted to celebrate with his friends and may have treated them to drinks. It appears that the return of migrant carpenters had upset the village's equilibrium. The locals undoubtedly resented the superior attitudes of migrants who had firsthand experiences of a larger world. We can only speculate that Alexei, one of the men in Zamaraev's account, insulted the migrants in an attempt to enhance his own social standing and that of the locals. As court cases make clear, insults would have involved the use of off-color words that attacked a man's virility, his morals, or the reputations of his family members. 'Erotic language,' according to Thomas Gallant, 'acts as a non-lethal mechanism for establishing status hierarchies in a community, as a means of maintaining communal standards of behavior and of fostering intragroup social coherence.'[43] Verbal sparring may have gone back and forth between the men, until finally the carpenters decided to defend their reputation with violence. According to Father Mikhail Sokolov of Vladimir province, writing at the turn of the twentieth century, '[Russian] peasants in general are a people who are very self-respecting and proud. Endeavor to offend a peasant . . . with a word, [expressing] some unflattering opinion about him, and he will remember it until he is presented with the chance to avenge [the offense].'[44] Not all verbal insults, however, ended in physical assault.

In an honor-bound society that had a well-established legal tradition dating from Muscovite times of allowing individuals from all social classes to seek restitution for an unfairly damaged reputation, Russian peasant men could turn to the court system in their contests over reputation.[45] In the courtroom the plaintiff and defendant continued their quarrel and contestation of each other's reputation, while witnesses provided testimonies about their respective characters. In an 1871 case heard before a cantonal court in Iaroslavl' province, one peasant charged another with publicly referring to him as a 'cunt-chaser'. The accused readily admitted to having insulted not only the plaintiff but also the plaintiff's daughter in retaliation for the plaintiff's having enjoyed an adulterous relationship with his (the accused's) wife. Ignoring the allegation of adultery, the judges ordered that the defendant pay restitution to the plaintiff as well as his daughter. According to a recent study by Stephen Frank, 40 percent of criminal cases heard before cantonal courts and just over 20 percent of crimes tried in municipal courts and before land captains in 1890 in Kursk province involved similar examples of 'insult to honor'. Similarly, in Riazan province over half the criminal cases before cantonal courts dealt with charges of insult, although assault and violence were involved in a significant portion of them.[46] Even in these latter cases, men's public airing of grievances in a courtroom was simply the last act of a drama that had begun in the tavern or on the street.[47]

The code of honor that guided men's interactions with each other and permitted restitution of honor when a reputation had been challenged also came into play when the village community found itself threatened by thieves or government officials bent on putting down a disturbance. Having enjoyed the solidarity of his youth group in his bachelor days, a peasant knew that he could count on all the other household heads to band together to protect the community from harm and seek justice. Taking extra-legal action against a horse thief extended the parameters of shaming rituals to include violence that ended in the crippling or death of the victim. Dealing with government authorities was obviously more complicated, but peasant men often applied to such situations the values and methods they employed in dealing with each other. In disputes with the police or the military, for example, household heads sometimes sent women and children ahead of them to the initial confrontation, hoping that the authorities would make some move to arrest or hurt the women. Any attack on the women was an insult to the men that would justify their retaliating with physical force.[48] Little did government authorities understand that the peasants they disdained had an entire repertoire of everyday actions that repeatedly asserted their masculinity and honor. The seemingly out-of-control, violent peasant that the government and upper classes feared was often fighting, in fact, to defend his own reputation and the reputations of his household and community.

Like peasants around the world, Russian peasants highly valued their honor. For the proper functioning of the patriarchal society, men had to arbitrate disputes and defend reputations. Competition between males in everyday life was part of the natural order in a materially impoverished society. The workings of the moral economy demanded that peasants learn to share resources with each other and that the more prosperous peasants help out their poorer neighbors, for they themselves might one day need the help of others. That cooperation was nonetheless riddled with tensions as men competed with each other for status and authority. Youths were acculturated in the values of this society as they discovered the merit of work, the importance of friendship, the social roles of drinking, and the authority that came with being able to assert their independence and defend their reputations. While the older generation might complain about youthful insubordination and take measures to stem that insubordination, it valued the male bonding that developed among youths. Older men understood that the lessons learned in their adolescence and early adulthood became critical when younger men took on their own responsibilities as family men and managers of household economies.

Notes

1. Thomas W. Gallant, 'Honor, Masculinity, and Ritual Knife Fighting in Nineteenth-Century Greece', *American Historical Review*, 105 (April 2000), 361.
2. Miguel Vale de Almeida, *The Hegemonic Male: Masculinity in a Portuguese Town* (Providence, R. I., 1996), 89.
3. Introduction in V. A. Plotnikov, *Avtobiograficheskie zapiski sibirskogo kres'tianina V. A. Plotnikova*, ed. B. I. Osipov (Omsk, 1995), 31.
4. V. I. Dal', *Poslovitsy russkogo naroda*, 2 vols (1957 rpt.; Moscow, 1989), 1,309.
5. Vladimir Dal', *Tolkovyi slovar' zhivogo velikoruskogo iazyka*, 4 vols (1880–2 rpt.; Moscow, 1978–80), 2,357.

6. Aleksandr Afanas'ev, comp., *Erotic Tales of Old Russia*, selected and trans. Yury Perkov (Oakland, Calif., 1988).
7. Dal', *Poslovitsy russkogo naroda*, 1,314.
8. Almeida, *Hegemonic Male*, 54.
9. Ol'ga Semenova Tian-Shanskaia, *Village Life in Late Tsarist Russia*, ed. David L. Ransel and trans. David L. Ransel and Michael Levin (Bloomington, 1993), 29–30.
10. Quoted in 'Introduction' to Plotnikov, *Avtobiograficheskie zapiski*, 32.
11. Reginald E. Zelnik, ed. and trans., *A Radical Worker in Tsarist Russia: the Autobiography of Semen Kanatchikov* (Stanford, 1986), 148.
12. Plotnikov, *Avtobiograficheskie zapiski*, 113.
13. I. I. Illiustrov, *Sbornik rossiiskikh poslovits i pogovorok* (Kiev, 1904), 167–9.
14. Zelnik, *A Radical Worker*, 4–5.
15. Patricia Herlihy, 'Joy of the Rus': Rites and Rituals of Russian Drinking', *Russian Review*, 50, no. 2 (April 1991), 139.
16. Zelnik, *A Radical Worker*, 159.
17. David D. Gilmore, *Manhood in the Making: Cultural Concepts of Masculinity* (New Haven, 1990), 12.
18. I. G. Orshanskii, *Izsledovaniia po russkomu pravu obychnomu i brachnomu* (St Petersburg, 1879), 43; S. V. Maksimov, *Nechistaia, nevedomaia i krestnaia sila* (St Petersburg, 1903), 295–6. A. A. Titov observed the same practice in Rostov district, Iaroslavl' province, in his *Iuridicheskoe obychai sela Nikola-Perevoz Sulostskoi volosti, Rostovskago uezda* (Iaroslavl', 1888), 27.
19. V. I. Simakov, *Sbornik derevenskikh chastushek Arkhangel'skoi, Vologodskoi, Viatskoi, Olonetskoi, Permskoi, Kostromskoi, Iaroslavskoi, Tverskoi, Pskovskoi, Novgorodskoi, Peterburgskoi gubernii* (Iaroslavl', 1913), 560, no. 2897.
20. For a brief description of obscene games during social gatherings for courting youths, see Stephen P. Frank, '"Simple Folk, Savage Customs?": Youth, Sociability, and the Dynamics of Culture in Rural Russia, 1856–1914', *Journal of Social History*, 25, no. 4 (1992), 719–20. The popular tale 'A Lover Meets His Lass' centers on a peasant youth's conquering his love with his substantial penis, while the tales 'The Marvelous Ointment' and 'The Shepherd' focus on girls ridiculing youths by accusing them of bestiality. See Alexander N. Afanasyev, comp., *The Bawdy Peasant: a Selection from the Russian Secret Tales Collected by Alexander N. Afanasyev* (London, 1970), 19, 78–80, 84–6.
21. Frank, '"Simple Folk"', 717. For the Western European perspective, see Michael R. Marrus, 'Modernization and Dancing in Rural France: From "La Bourrée" to "Le FoxTrot"', *The Wolf and the Lamb: Popular Culture in France from the Old Regime to the Twentieth Century*, ed. Jacques Beauroy et al. (Saratoga, Calif., 1976), 141–59.
22. Stephen P. Frank, 'Confronting the Domestic Other: Rural Popular Culture and its Enemies in Fin-de-Siècle Russia', *Cultures in Flux: Lower-Class Values, Practices, and Resistance in Late Imperial Russia*, ed. Stephen P. Frank and Mark D. Steinberg (Princeton, 1994), 85, 88.
23. For examples of such songs, see Simakov, *Sbornik derevenskikh chastushek*, 541–2.
24. An example of a *koliadka* that threatened a household head with retaliation went as follows: 'If you don't give us a tart – /We'll take your cow by the

horns,/If you don't give us a sausage – /We'll grab your pig by his head,/If you don't give us a pancake – /We'll give the host a kick.' Roberta Reeder, trans. and ed., *Russian Folk Lyrics* (Bloomington, 1992), 85, no. 1.

25. Frank, '"Simple Folk"', 725.
26. Almeida in his study of men's relationships in a contemporary Portuguese town concludes that son–father deference is incompatible with competition among men. (*Hegemonic Male*, 91.)
27. Christine D. Worobec, *Peasant Russia: Family and Community in the Post-Emancipation Period* (Princeton, 1991), 212.
28. D. N. Zhbankov, *Bab'ia storona: Statistiko-etnograficheskii ocherk* (Kostroma, 1891), 55; quoted and translated in Jeffrey Burds, 'The Social Control of Peasant Labor in Russia: the Response of Village Communities to Labor Migration in the Central Industrial Region, 1861–1905', *Peasant Economy, Culture, and Politics of European Russia, 1800–1921*, ed. Esther Kingston-Mann and Timothy Mixter (Princeton, 1991), 79.
29. Burds, 'Social Control', 80.
30. Titov, *Iuridicheskoe obychai*, 32; quoted and translated in Barbara Alpern Engel, 'Peasant Morality and Pre-Marital Relations in Late Nineteenth Century Russia', *Journal of Social History*, 23, no. 4 (1990), 701.
31. T. S. Stepanov, 'Promysly i vne-zemledel'cheskie zarabotki v zimu 1888–89 gg.', *Statisticheskii ezhegodnik Moskovskoi gubernii za 1889g.* (Moscow, 1889), sec. 3, 21–2; quoted and translated in Jeffrey Burds, *Peasant Dreams and Market Politics: Labor Migration and the Russian Village, 1861–1905* (Pittsburgh, 1998), 31.
32. See Burds, *Peasant Dreams*; and Barbara Alpern Engel, *Between the Fields and the City: Women, Work, and Family in Russia, 1861–1914* (Cambridge, 1994).
33. Almeida, *Hegemonic Male*, 88–9.
34. Quoted in Burds, *Peasant Dreams*, 175.
35. *Dnevnik Totemskogo krest'ianina A. A. Zamaraeva 1906–1922 gody*, ed. V. V. Morozov and N. I. Reshetnikov (Moscow, 1995), 40, 39.
36. Quoted in Burds, *Peasant Dreams*, 177.
37. Herlihy, 'Joy of the Rus'', 131–47.
38. Almeida, *Hegemonic Male*, 88.
39. Aleksandr Afanas'ev, comp. *Russian Fairly Tales*, trans. Norbert Guterman (New York, 1945), 184.
40. Almeida, *Hegemonic Male*, 88.
41. Ibid., 91.
42. *Dnevnik Totemskogo krest'ianina*, 39.
43. Thomas W. Gallant, 'Turning the Horns: Cultural Metaphors, Material Conditions, and the Peasant Language of Resistance in Ionian Islands (Greece) during the Nineteenth Century', *Comparative Studies in Society and History*, 36, no. 4 (October 1994), 707.
44. Quoted in Burds, *Peasant Dreams*, 201.
45. For a path-breaking book on honor in seventeenth-century Muscovy and eighteenth-century Imperial Russia that suggests a new periodization of Russian history, see Nancy Shields Kollmann, *By Honor Bound: State and Society in Early Modern Russia* (Ithaca, N.Y., 1999).
46. Stephen P. Frank, *Crime, Cultural Conflict, and Justice in Rural Russia, 1856–1914* (Berkeley, 1999), 148–50.

47. I borrowed this notion from Thomas Gallant's study of knife dueling among nineteenth-century Greek men. ('Honor, Masculinity, and Ritual Knife Fighting', 380.)
48. For a discussion of the symbolism of peasant resistance, see Barbara Alpern Engel, 'Women, Men, and the Languages of Peasant Resistance, 1870–1907', *Cultures in Flux*, 34–53.

6
Masculinity in Transition: Peasant Migrants to Late-Imperial St Petersburg

S. A. Smith

The Russian peasant family was a patriarchal institution in which men held power over women, elders over youth, adults over children and mothers-in-law over daughters-in-law.[1] The male head of household was responsible for maintaining order within the household and had the right to dispose of the labor power of its members and to take crucial decisions concerning their lives. Within the household the *bol'shak* was expected to assert his authority and to control female sexuality; the anxieties aroused by these responsibilities may explain the prevalence of wife-beating. Outside the household the head's authority extended into village life, since the *mir*, to which only heads of household belonged, ordered the life of the peasant community. Gender identities were thoroughly enmeshed with the age hierarchies of the household, serving to maintain male dominance and to enforce male as well as female conformity to prescriptive norms. The inequality of men and women was perceived to be part of the natural order, it being assumed that men had God-given authority to rule over women by virtue of their superior physical and moral strength. Full masculine status was achieved only with marriage, and it was marriage that entitled a man to a share in communal land. 'Without a wife and family, a peasant is not a peasant.' Single men were not considered 'peasants' (*muzhiki*), since they had no entitlement to a land allotment.[2] The words for 'man' or 'husband' (*muzh*) and for 'peasant' (*muzhik*) shared the same root, the term *muzhik*, or 'little man', suggesting an analogy between the incomplete legal status of the peasant and that of a minor.[3] Over time, this common etymology may have come to suggest that a key basis of masculine authority in peasant society lay in the right and capacity to work the land. Outside the household young men related to one another on the basis of a rough equality, rooted in friendship, play, and dalliance with women, but within the household their dominant experience was one of subordination to older males and, in particular, to their fathers. According to Semen Kanatchikov, 'My father was strict in disposition and despotic in character. He kept the entire family in moral fright. We all feared him and did everything we could to please him.'[4] His father may not have been typical, but he was certainly not unusual.

During the last third of the nineteenth century, growing numbers of young men left the village in search of work. By the 1890s there were over six million migrant workers in European Russia, two million of whom were in the Central Industrial Region, the area from which migration was most intense.[5] Most found work in agriculture or transportation rather than in the city; and the minority that moved to the city came to be employed in services, trade, construction, or artisanal manufacture rather than in factories. Only a minority of migrants ended up living permanently in the cities, and of those only a minority ended up as workers in modern industry.

Nevertheless the cities and the urban industrial labor force grew rapidly as a result of peasant migration. By 1900, 63 percent of the population of St Petersburg were classified by the census takers as belonging to the 'peasant' estate and of these no fewer than 79 percent were 'immigrants' (*prishlie*).[6] The bulk of these were men aged between 16 and 35.[7] Migration almost certainly lessened the contact these men had with women. In 1897 there were 121 men for every 100 women in the city, a disparity that had fallen by 1910 to 110 men for every 100 women.[8] In the peasant estate, however, there were 124 men per 100 women in 1897.[9] Young men coming to St Petersburg in search of work frequently came as members of an *artel'*, or work gang, hiring themselves out for work on construction sites, docks, and in factories, such as the sugar mills, which employed workers on a seasonal basis.[10] By the end of the nineteenth century, an *artel'* also denoted a cooperative living arrangement among migrant workers.[11] The worker, P. Timofeev, describes one such arrangement, where eighteen men lived in one large room infested with cockroaches and bedbugs. Eleven were married, but their wives were in the village; indeed one had not seen his wife for five years. The men elected an elder (*starosta*) to lead the group, and he bought provisions and paid a woman to serve as their cook and landlady. 'Native-place ties linked them into one family and they put up with a lot for its sake.'[12] As this suggests, the experience of migration for most men was one of separation from women and immersion in a largely homosocial world. Men lived, worked, and played together rather than alongside members of the opposite sex as they had done in the village.

The present chapter asks how the social construction of masculinity changed for those who severed their ties with village life and took up a new identity as urban workers. It emphasizes the persistence within the city of a 'traditional' model of masculinity, in which mechanisms of male bonding and status differentiation were determined by physical strength, fighting prowess, a capacity to hold one's drink, womanizing, and certain types of wit and quick-wittedness, but it suggests that these elements were reconfigured, some becoming more prominent, others less so, as the social practices to which they were attached underwent transformation. Secondly, the chapter argues that for a minority of migrants, a more 'modern' style of masculinity emerged, in some respects more open-ended than the 'traditional' model, which was supported by the discourses and practices associated with new forms of work, new forms of family life and, not least, with new forms of commercial culture that were on offer in the city.

R. W. Connell has suggested that the primary dimension of adult masculinity is one of embodiment: to be an adult male is to occupy space, to have a physical presence in the world. Men's presence depends on the promise of power they embody, and although this promise of power may relate to wealth or social prestige, for lower-class males it is crucially about physical embodiment.[13] Physical strength was always a vital element in the 'traditional' model of Russian masculinity, but in the urban-industrial environment it acquired heightened salience since male migrants were deprived of alternative ways of demonstrating masculine status in relation to women. For unskilled laborers, in particular, masculinity became strongly associated with toughness, with a capacity to sustain heavy labor over long periods and with the exertion of sudden force in lifting and shifting. Outside work, masculinity also became more strongly articulated around traditional pastimes associated with the demonstration of bodily force, such as fighting prowess or the capacity to drink. Organized fights had taken place in the village, but in the cities they took on a new importance. On holidays, fights involving up to several hundred men would be organized, wherein the two sides, each representing a different street, would form 'walls' that would struggle for control of a no-man's land. These had a few basic rules – 'don't hit someone when he's down', 'hit with a clean fist' (that is, with no weapon) – and were significant occasions which would be talked about for weeks afterwards. When individuals got into fights – often over a woman or some matter of personal honor – a crowd would gather and provide a running commentary: 'He's smashed him in the ribs. He's wheezing! He's keeling over! . . . How the hell can the puny-chested thing hope to stand up to him?'[14] Again, the exploits of the victors would be celebrated and talked about and much fun would be had at the expense of those with black eyes. Demonstration of fighting prowess thus acquired importance in the homosocial world of the migrant worker in establishing status hierarchies within the all-male group. When young boys took up apprenticeships, for example, they could expect to be set upon by older apprentices and any tale-telling would result only in an even bigger thrashing.[15]

At the same time, in the new commercialized entertainments of the city the preoccupation with physical strength took on more refined, narcissistic forms in sports such as wrestling, boxing and weight-lifting that were often associated with the circus.[16] Wrestlers such as the Estonian Sergei Lurikh became icons of the perfect masculine body, matching muscular perfection to physical skill and grace.[17] Connell argues that the embodiment of masculine identity can take two forms: the first is associated with a desire for force, which he defines as the irresistible occupation of space; the second with a desire for skill, which he defines as the ability to operate upon space or the objects within it (including other bodies).[18] We shall see below that in relation to work, skill became a site for the construction of a new model of masculinity, but in relation to leisure, too, men began to reconfigure ideals of masculinity around new sport which prized facility over brute strength. Soccer, for example, slowly began to take on organized form in the 1890s, although it did not become massively popular among working-class men until the 1920s. By 1914, 23 teams played in the Petrograd Football League, but alongside these official clubs there existed so-called 'wildcat' (*dikie*) teams of working-class footballers, such as the Murzinka club of the Obukhov workers and the Putilov team, which were refused entry to the Russian Football Association.[19]

Heavy drinking constituted another element in the 'traditional' style of masculinity that was gradually reconfigured in the city. Like fighting prowess, it was associated with a form of embodiment that valorized 'force' rather than skill. The city tavern was a lively site of sociability for male migrants. As early as 1865, there were 1840 taverns (*kabaki*), 562 inns, 399 alcoholic-beverage stores and 229 wine cellars in St Petersburg.[20] David Christian has argued that the late nineteenth century saw the evolution of a 'modern' drinking culture in which drinking became regular, recreational, and individualistic, centered on specialized locales, in contrast to the rural drinking culture, which was communal, periodic, associated with festive occasions.[21] By the 1890s, heavy drinking had reached epidemic proportions in St Petersburg. On pay-day one could stand on Malyi Prospekt in Vasilevskii Ostrov district and watch 'the taverns, inns and ale-houses filled to bursting, prostitutes strolling nearby and anxious wives waiting for their husbands to come out before they had spent all their wages'.[22] As this suggests, male sociability based on drinking was secured largely through the exclusion of women. Drink also served as a way to suffuse the culture of the workplace with masculine significance. At the Semiannikov metal works in the 1890s, Buzinov recalls: 'Drunkenness was almost universal. Among the blacksmiths and hammer-men I don't recall a single teetotaler. A good third were drunkards in the full sense of the word.'[23] At the Skorokhod shoe factory '"treats" (*prival'nye*) were almost written into the work regulations. They were considered obligatory, and if a new worker did not treat his fellows to a round of drinks they would not let him have the tools he needed.'[24]

The culture of the workplace was masculinized in other ways apart from the collective consumption of alcohol. Tales of sexual conquest and the use of obscene language (*mat*) in the form of the uproarious *chastushka*, the bawdy pun, the humorous anecdote, the sexual innuendo or verbal banter were all ways in which male bonding and status differentiation were established.[25] Obscene talk served to amuse one's fellows and to stave off the boredom of the job. One compositor recalled:

> Foul language . . . was used for almost everything, in every situation, without the slightest modesty before the young apprentices (there were still no women). . . . And when they swore, they swore strongly with force, usually triply compounded obscenities, facetious sayings and proverbs all in the same breath. It was a kind of game. . . . For the most part, the talk among workers was about boozing and about various adventures with women and sexual encounters. All was spoken openly, shamelessly, down to the last detail.[26]

An essayist in the newspaper of the printers' union in 1907 complained that in print shops: 'After holidays each comrade considers it his "moral" duty to relate to others his "holiday adventures", calling things by their proper names without any embarrassment in the presence of women or apprentices.'[27] A minority of class-conscious workers objected to such casual, unbridled talk about sex, since they were committed to ideals of self-development and self-control. At the Leman letter foundry a group of 'conscious' workers condemned their boss: 'We know quite well why the more conscious and steadfast workers are not to Haupt's liking . . . He can't show his favorite pornographic pictures to his conscious workers since they have no interest in such "artistic" filth. . . . Yet the drunkards in the workshop are proud of the fact that their boss behaves so informally towards them. . . . Now Haupt is saying that he will only hire workers from Moscow, and that no one who is dressed smartly will be taken on.'[28] Although what was at issue for these 'conscious' workers was a political ideal of class consciousness, this ideal did imply a model of masculinity at odds with the prevailing norm. For the majority of 'unconscious' workers, swearing, dirty jokes, and sexual boasting were ways of letting off steam and of demonstrating that you were one of the lads, a way of gaining acceptance from the group. More crucially, they were a way in which men sustained their manliness in the new environment of the capitalist workplace, which conspired to make them feel powerless in a way they had not felt when working the land.

In the capitalist workplace masculine identity still continued to depend on the subordination of women. After 1905 employers began to hire women as cheap labor, which male workers perceived both as a challenge to their economic position and to their masculinity.[29] One consequence was that the masculinized culture of the workplace – with its ubiquitous references to *baby* (a mildly pejorative term for women) – was mobilized against female 'interlopers', in order to remind them that they were on 'male' territory. At the New Aivaz engineering works a group of 'conscious workers' complained about the behavior of the majority of their fellow males. When a new woman asked for advice it would provoke 'immodest innuendos'. 'They say things that directly diminish women's dignity or insult women's honor. Sometimes they go as far as directly criminal actions, making filthy suggestions and attempting to carry them out.'[30] In the No.1 Cable Shop of the Cable Works where five women were employed in 1914, 'The women workers will only go to the toilet when the foreman is not there; otherwise they have to listen to vulgar abuse from him. . . . The male comrades are completely indifferent to this.'[31] As this suggests, for those who had no families or were living apart from their families, the workplace took on a sharpened significance as an arena in which the meanings of masculinity could be reinforced or reworked.

Crucial to the formation of a more 'modern' style of masculinity was the acquisition of work-related skill. For the majority of unskilled migrants, physical strength and stamina were the key ways in which work bolstered their identity as men. For the growing minority of skilled workers, however, masculine status became attached to the exercise of visual, tactile, and auditory sensitivity, to rapidity of reflexes, to the knowledge of materials and machines, and to the ability to take decisions and to control the work process. In Connell's terms, this was still masculinity expressed through physical embodiment, but connected to the ability to operate upon, rather than merely to occupy, social and physical space. Moreover, the acquisition of skill corresponded to the transition into adulthood, since the normal entry into a skilled trade was through an apprenticeship that started at the age of thirteen or fourteen. Apprentices, who were generally known as 'boys' (*mal'chiki*), spent the first years of their working lives doing little more than fetching and carrying for adult males. Constantly reminded of their juvenile status, they were patronized at best, brutalized at worst.[32] Completion of their apprenticeship, however, marked their entry into manhood, as marriage had done in the village. I. V. Babushkin, who began work at the age of fifteen in the torpedo workshop of Kronstadt port, recalled: 'At the age of eighteen, according to the local rules, I was recognized as an adult and transferred from the apprentices into the ranks of the skilled craftsmen.'[33] Skilled craftsmen, such as pattern-makers, instrument-makers, fitters and turners, styled themselves *masterovye*, masters of their craft, a term that resonated with masculine authority. Theirs was an exclusive fraternity that distinguished itself from the world of unskilled workers. The craftsman's sense of honor would not allow him to do the job of an unskilled worker, even if his pay were guaranteed.[34] Indeed up to 1905, many *masterovye* considered it an insult to be called *rabochie*, the term applied to workers in general, possibly because the distant etymology of that term lay in the word for 'slave'.

In their desire to break free from the culture of the 'backward' majority, with its drunkenness, physical aggression, and misogyny, the 'conscious' minority composed primarily of skilled workers strove to forge a new model of masculinity. This stratum, which began to emerge in the 1880s, modeled itself on the intelligentsia, seeking to advance itself – and ultimately the class to which it belonged – by means of education and acquiring *kul'turnost'* (culturedness).[35] Convinced of their innate dignity as human beings, 'conscious' workers aspired to demonstrate their self-respect – and to claim the respect of others – through intellectual self-improvement and the acquisition of certain forms of social respectability, evinced in personal hygiene or dress (an example is the reference to dressing smartly in the aforementioned complaint by the Leman letter-foundry workers). This was a model of masculinity that valorized self-control, the assertion of reason over emotion, autonomy in personal relations, and a more respectful, but not necessarily egalitarian attitude toward women. For some it entailed an ideal of companionate marriage and a nuclear family based on emotional intimacy rather than the hierarchies of age and gender characteristic of the patriarchal family. For a few, whose 'consciousness' led to revolutionary political commitment, it entailed the deliberate rejection of family life as a distraction from the all-embracing demands of the struggle.

A crucial step on the road to achieving 'consciousness' lay in the repudiation of patriarchal authority. This can be seen in the way that many worker memoirists construct their childhood as a narrative of rebellion against their fathers. Kanatchikov tells us, 'I loved my mother intensely and hated my father with an animal hate.'[36] Kirill Orlov, eldest of seven children in a desperately poor family from Iakovlevskaia district, Orlov province, recalled: 'At the age of 11, having overcome many obstacles, I succeeded in entering the village school. For this I was beaten many times by my father, who demanded that I leave school and resume my old duties as a nurse [to his younger siblings]. But I was resolute and won for myself the right to learn.'[37] At the age of twelve, A. I. Svirskii began work as an apprentice ironsmith, but his boss, a drunkard, beat him until he bled, so he ran away. When his father found out, he too gave him a beating. Later, already aged twenty, Svirskii got a job as a day laborer at the Baltic works in St Petersburg, where he begged the principal craftsman, Panteleich, to teach him a trade: 'Be my true father. Teach me to work.'[38] S. K. Volkov, the son of a poor carpenter in a family of nine in an enserfed village in Simbirsk province, tells how as early as 1865 he refused to be cowed by the owner of the iron foundry where he was an apprentice. 'He cursed me with obscenities and I was driven to such rage that I grabbed a stick about two feet long and would have smashed him round the head had not the workers standing behind me snatched the stick from my hands. Even so, the owner did not sack me, since I had labor power which he needed, but after a month I left of my own accord.'[39] The struggle against patriarchal authority spearheaded by these 'conscious' workers came in time to have resonance for a much larger group of workers, influencing the city-slickers examined below, who embraced a more urbane model of masculinity. That it also had political significance for workers who were not otherwise 'conscious' became evident on the eve of the 1905 Revolution, when many rose up against the use of corporal punishment, seen as metonymic of a larger illegitimate system of authority. In 1904 the right of *volost'* courts to sentence male peasants to a beating was abolished, and in the course of the revolution of the following year workers demanded the elimination of corporal punishment from the workplace.[40] The impulses behind this were complex, rooted fundamentally in a growing sense of self-worth (*lichnost'*) felt by female and male workers alike, but for younger males in particular, the refusal to submit to beatings from bosses and foremen was bound up with rejection of subordination to the authority of older men, the linchpin of patriarchy.

To 'traditional' patriarchy 'conscious' workers counterposed a 'fraternal' alternative. Workers' songs are stocked with references to 'brothers' and 'lads' (*rebiata*), by no means only in the discursive context of class.[41] It is perhaps not surprising that migrants, who lived and worked in environments where women were largely absent, should find the idiom of brotherhood appealing. In the village, filiality, not fraternity, had been the dominant idiom of male relationships, but in the urban environment, where fathers were absent, this was no longer the case. For political ends, the 'conscious' workers played upon this idiom of fraternity as a metaphor for class solidarity and human community, apparently unaware of the fact that the fraternal community was built upon the exclusion of women. In a curious twist, however – one that raises a question mark against Carole Pateman's counterposition of a patriarchal model to a fraternal model of political authority – their discourse still invoked an ideal of the family.[42] Indeed it is striking how often 'conscious' workers articulated an identification with the working class in familial terms, usually that of leaving behind their natural family and entering the new family of workers. Buzinov recalls: 'I noticed that as my strength grew, my mother gradually acquired the aspect of a "weak creation". I no longer saw things her way, I desired to follow my independent path. I thus cut myself off from my mother and headed for the family of workers.'[43] I. V. Babushkin similarly writes: 'Although by birth I am a peasant and lived until the age of fourteen in the village, surrounded by forests, far from any town . . . the life of my native village . . . was forgotten and discarded for the rest of my life. I was never fated to return there . . . Mine was to be another life – an urban, metropolitan, industrial, factory life, the life of a skilled craftsman . . . The family of workers was to become my family. I understood it well and had feelings for it.'[44] This was, of course, a strange kind of family, in that it consisted entirely of brothers, yet it qualifies as a version of what Lynn Hunt has called, à propos the French Revolution, the 'family romance'.[45] It suggests that even as they rebelled against the father and sought to separate from their mothers,[46] these men saw in the family, once purged of its relations of hierarchy and subordination, a model of mutual cooperation, solidarity and submersion of self into the collective which the working class could emulate.

So far as real families were concerned, the city offered growing opportunities for a minority of migrants to settle there with their spouses and children. In 1897, 43.7 percent of male workers in St Petersburg were married, yet only 13.3 percent actually lived with their wives and children, the proportion being highest among relatively well-off workers, such as printers (38.2 percent), metalworkers (30.9 percent) and chemical workers (28.5 percent).[47] The Stolypin reforms, which made it easier for peasants to cut their ties with the land, together with improved employment prospects for women, intensified the trend for married workers to bring their families to St Petersburg.[48] By 1918 no fewer than 71 percent of all married workers lived with their families, though this figure needs to be treated with caution, since workers with close ties to the countryside had by that date left the capital because of unemployment and food shortages.[49] Barbara Engel has suggested that in working-class families a new ideal of the man as breadwinner and the woman as homemaker was taking root.[50] A survey of 765 factory and artisanal families showed that in only 48 percent did the wife go out to work. However, only 6.6 percent of wives went out to work in families where the husband earned more than 50 rubles a month, compared with almost 60 percent in families where the man earned less than 20 rubles a month.[51] Among less well-off workers, then, the breadwinner ideal was much less achievable. A survey of 39 textile-worker families, while noting that the 'worker family strives to keep the mother at home', found that in 20 cases the wife worked at the mill, compared with 12 where they were housewives and 7 where they lived in the countryside with the children. However, the surveyor opined that the actual proportion of families where the wife was engaged full-time in the home was probably only about 10 percent.[52] This study suggests that the 'breadwinner' ideal of a man supporting his wife and family through his wages was beyond the reach of all but the best-paid workers.

Contemporaries were wont to claim that in the working-class family relations between husbands and wives were more 'comradely' than in the peasant family.[53] What this meant was indicated by another survey of textile-worker families in 1909:

> While the woman hurries straight home from the factory to the children, the husband goes off to market and to the shops to buy provisions for supper and next day's dinner. . . . And since so many

> of the domestic chores done by the woman (sewing and repair of linen and dresses, the laundry, looking after the lodger) have a relatively high value in terms of the family budget . . . in his spare time the husband must always look after the children. If you go in May around 7 p.m. to any street off Palevskii Prospekt in Nevskaia Zastava you will see on the streets and in the courtyards fathers with the full complement of their children.[54]

This suggests that the man's involvement in childcare was more determined by economic need than emotional intimacy, but even this may be too optimistic, since a writer in the journal of the textile workers' union in 1917 commented far more scathingly on the division of labor in textile-worker families.

> Having finished work at the factory, the woman worker is still not free. While the male worker goes off to a meeting or just takes a walk or plays billiards with his mates, she has to cope with the housework – to cook, to wash and so on . . . ; she is seldom helped by her husband. Unfortunately, one has to admit that male workers are still very prejudiced. They think that it is humiliating for a man to do 'woman's work'. They would sooner their sick worn-out wife did the household labor (*barshchinu*) by herself. They would rather tolerate her remaining completely without leisure, illiterate and ignorant, than condescend to help her do the housework.[55]

In fact, there is little doubt that for most married women the heavy burdens of being housewives and mothers were piled on top of long, gruelling hours of waged work and that men were generally reluctant to do 'women's' work. A time-budget survey carried out among 76 worker families in Petrograd, Moscow, and Ivanovo-Voznesensk in 1922 showed that whereas men did two hours eight minutes unpaid domestic labor per day, women did five hours twelve minutes, even though they were doing roughly the same amount of paid work as their menfolk. And whereas men got eight hours sleep, women only managed six hours and forty-four minutes.[56] Nevertheless, if these figures are to be believed, men still performed as much as 40 percent of the domestic labor done by women which – while hardly a 'comradely' division of labor! – may have accorded with a more urbanized conception of the male role in which the father aspired to be a 'family man', in charge of a respectable home, whilst the wife fulfilled her housewifely duties without becoming a drudge.

Single men comprised a slight majority of male migrants in St Petersburg. In 1910, 58.1 percent of men and 55.6 percent of women were unmarried.[57] There is indirect evidence that a minority may have chosen to remain single in a way that was hardly possible in the village, where the social pressure to reproduce was intense. In 1897 no fewer than 20 percent of workers aged 40 to 59 in St Petersburg remained unmarried.[58] Some may have taken advantage of the increased opportunities in the capital for same-sex relations, as Dan Healey suggests in a later chapter in this book.[59] In the main, however, the high proportion of single people reflected the tendency of urban-dwellers to marry later than in the village.[60] It was these single workers, earning reasonable wages and choosing to postpone marriage, who were most susceptible to the images of sexual attraction and romantic love that circulated in the commercial culture of the city.

Until recently, historians have paid little attention to the role of consumer culture in shaping social identities in late-imperial Russia. Yet gender was a key focus upon which the discourses of modernity, individualism, and consumerism, inherent in mass consumption, mass entertainment and advertising, played. The mass entertainments of the city, for example, explored issues of romantic love, individual choice, and sexual freedom with an exuberance that was historically unprecedented. In the village the idea of marriage for love was already ensconced by the late nineteenth century, although parents still intervened in the choices of their offspring where they felt that practical considerations so advised.[61] However, in the pulp fiction, music halls, pleasure gardens, theaters, and cinemas of the cities, representations of romantic love and of sexuality circulated with a new explicitness. The street ballads known as 'cruel romances', for instance, told of passionate courtship, illicit love, pained rejection, and even suicide, and these melodramas were further popularized through music hall and gramophone records.[62] Similarly, the cheap novels and serialized stories in the 'yellow press', which were produced for the newly literate lower-class reader, exposed migrants to hitherto undreamed-of vistas of individual choice and adventure. The much-recycled, and in many respects rather traditional, story of the 'Terrible Bandit Churkin' (1885) was typical in the frankness with which it depicted sexual attraction:

> Churkin fell in love at first sight and could not take his eyes off her. The girl frequently returned his gaze, because he was a handsome lad – tall, broad-shouldered, his striking face framed by a thin dark beard. Curls hung over his eyes, which shone with audacity and brazen

> resolve. A blue cotton kaftan was draped around his body, and his legs, in shiny boots, were slender and attractive. In general, he had a nice body and the other guys looked at him with envy.[63]

This ideal of masculine beauty was in fact rather conventional; we know, for example, that in the villages of Vladimir province women admired men who were of proud bearing, bold aspect, tall and curly-haired.[64] Yet there is here depicted an emphasis on sexual possibility and a calculated weighing-up of the sexual attractiveness of the potential partner which was altogether new.

Around 2000 silent movies were made in Russia during the second decade of the twentieth century, about half of which were melodramas based on themes of seduction, betrayal, revenge, and destruction. With their penchant for opulent mises-en-scène and sensational plots, these films played on fantasy and the desire for escape and made little attempt to deal with social problems of the day.[65] Yet we should not underestimate the extent to which they allowed lower-class spectators vicariously to explore new social possibilities and to work through moral dilemmas. The film *In Moscow's Maelstrom* (*V omute Moskvy*) tells of Dmitrii who comes to Moscow and finds a job as a waiter in a teahouse, so as to earn enough money to return to the countryside, build a house, and marry his sweetheart. These innocent intentions are soon forgotten amidst the temptations of the city. Dmitrii meets and falls in love with Ulia, a hard-working, modest seamstress, who gives herself completely to him, never doubting his sincerity. Meanwhile, Avdot'ia Dmitrievna Popova, the landlady of the teahouse, a beautiful and powerful widow, has her eye on the handsome youth. Dmitrii becomes besotted by her and spurns Ulia when she appears at the teahouse carrying his baby daughter in her arms. Then begins Dmitrii's steady descent into drinking, extortion, and, ultimately, murder. He is jailed for ten years and emerges from prison a broken, haggard man. The film ends with his walking past the house where Ulia lives with his daughter and her new husband, but they do not recognize him.[66] Like almost all these melodramas, *In Moscow's Maelstrom* has an unhappy ending and may be read as a cautionary tale, which advises its lower-class spectators to stick to the tried-and-tested rules, to feel contentment with their lot and not to seek to rise too far above their station. Yet it also, however badly, portrays the dilemma of the young migrant worker faced by fateful choices that test his character in a situation where conduct is no longer regulated by custom and community censure. In representing city life as a test of character, and in suggesting that moral qualities count for more than physical beauty, *In Moscow's Maelstrom* probes some of the tensions in the more individualistic representations of masculinity purveyed by the cultural products targeted at lower-class consumers, which valorize physical attractiveness, sexual choice, and aspirations for self-betterment.

The signs of a more individualistic style of masculinity, associated with urban sophistication, polished manners, and self-display, were particularly evident in the realm of dress. In the village clothing was a marker of social standing, linked to age and marital status, and peasants in general paid little heed to fashions in clothing, hairstyles, or household furnishings.[67] The move to the town liberated clothing from the hold of local custom and subjected it to the forces of the market. A study of mainly skilled metalworkers in St Petersburg in 1908 showed that they spent 15.6 percent of their income on clothing and footwear, with single men spending a higher proportion than married men.[68] This reflected a new concern with one's public appearance. Style was now as important as utility. As a young apprentice at a samovar factory in Tula, A. Frolov refused to dress in the 'uniform' of a worker – that is, 'simple boots, a smock, wide trousers, a jacket and a peaked cap' – when he went out. Instead he wore a hat and a European suit, ignoring gibes from his workmates.[69] The young Kanatchikov bought himself a holiday outfit, a watch, and, for the summer, a wide belt, grey trousers, a straw hat, and some fancy shoes. 'In a word, I dressed in the manner of those young urban metalworkers who earned an independent living and didn't ruin themselves with vodka.'[70] In 1900 a journalist noted the contrast at a temperance fair between those young men still doing their native round-dances and the 'dandified factory lads with greased-back hair in German outfits and shiny boots' who were doing 'some indecent dance, picked up from some variety-stage actress . . . trying to reproduce the cheeky movements of the cancan'.[71] Dressing well in public was an assertion of self-respect, intended to command the respect of one's peers and superiors. Through clothes, young men shaped their appearance, asserted themselves visually, and sought to improve their social status. Not least, stylish dress helped to attract a sexual partner. In Soligalich and Chukhlomskii uezds in Kostroma province local women preferred men who had lived in St Petersburg. They were 'much more sophisticated than local men; their conversation was often indistinguishable from that of an urban-dweller, though adorned with fanciful expressions; their manner was copied from that of the metropolitan petty-bourgeois; they could dance; they wore dandified suits'.[72]

What we see in the years up to 1917 is increasing differentiation in, and conflict over, the meanings of what it meant to be a man. The tens of thousands of young males who migrated to St Petersburg brought with them an essentially 'traditional' understanding of masculine identity: male status derived from marriage, work on the land, and a form of 'embodiment' that emphasized physical strength and stamina. In the city, this continued to be a dominant idiom, but it was freed from the yoke of patriarchal authority. With the likelihood that they themselves would ever acquire such authority diminishing the longer they lived in the city, young migrants came to reconfigure elements of that 'traditional' idiom. In the village the status of the patriarch within the family was not differentiated from his status in the spheres of work and community. In the urban-industrial environment, by contrast, work, family, and leisure became differentiated sites upon which men constructed their understanding of what it meant to be a man. Elements of the 'traditional' model such as drinking and fistfighting were subtly reconfigured, becoming attached to new, mainly homosocial sites, such as the tavern and the workplace. These new institutions – above all, the workplace – were no longer based on kinship and the meanings of masculinity were no longer securely attached to the procreative role of the father (or indeed the aspiration to that role). In the capitalist workplace men struggled to compensate themselves for their powerlessness by creating a work-based culture suffused with masculinity and based on the exclusion of women. Within the workplace, too, new and old styles of masculinity vied with one another. 'Conscious workers' created a community of brothers that rejected a male status hierarchy based on the display of physical strength or endurance in favor of one based on skill, self-development, autonomy in personal relations, the dominance of reason over emotion, and affective family ties. Among mainly better-off workers a new form of family life emerged, in which men aspired to be breadwinners and wives, still very much subordinate to their husbands, aspired to be homemakers. This was always more ideal than reality, but it testified to the gradual displacement of the patriarchal model of family relations by those of companionate marriage. Of greater social significance, especially for young, single men, was the impact of urban consumer culture and mass entertainment on traditional notions of masculinity. For the great majority of migrants, of course, consumption continued to be dictated largely by the exigencies of survival, by need, rather than desire. Nevertheless the cultural products and consumer goods aimed at a lower-class market, with their messages of sexual choice, romantic love, self-betterment, and self-refinement, put into circulation an urbane, even narcissistic model of masculinity that tied male status to individual refinement, fashionable self-display, and a consciously crafted sexual attractiveness.

The shifting and conflicting meanings of masculinity did not become an issue on the political agenda in 1917. Revolutionaries, particularly the Bolsheviks, believed that consciousness arose from economic forces, not clothing styles or pulp fiction, and therefore paid little attention to how masculinity was defined in the swirl of Imperial Russia's last days. The transformations of social identity that were taking place in the late-imperial period, such as the changing understandings of masculinity and femininity examined here, have continued long after the Revolution to be marginalized in a dominant narrative which writes the history of Russian workers exclusively in terms of a transition from 'peasant' to 'proletarian'. Though always inflected by the formation of class identity, changing gender identities, and the growing sense of self with which they were intimately connected, were potent sources of personal and collective meaning that deserve to be examined in their own right. Indeed, in their subliminal fashion, they contributed profoundly to that destabilization of patriarchal authority which was at the heart of the crisis of the old regime.

Notes

1. Boris N. Mironov, 'Peasant Popular Culture and the Origins of Soviet Authoritarianism', *Cultures in Flux: Lower-Class Values, Practices and Resistance in Late Imperial Russia*, ed. Stephen P. Frank and Mark D. Steinberg (Princeton, N.J., 1994), 57.
2. Christine D. Worobec, *Peasant Russia: Family and Community in the Post-Emancipation Period* (Princeton, N.J., 1991), 119.
3. Maks Fasmer, *Etimologicheskii slovar' russkogo iazyka*, 2 vols (Moscow, 1967), 2, 671.
4. R. E. Zelnik, trans. and ed., *A Radical Worker in Tsarist Russia: the Autobiography of Semen Ivanovich Kanatchikov* (Stanford, 1986), 4–5.
5. Jeffrey Burds, 'The Social Control of Peasant Labor in Russia: the Response of Village Communities to Labor Migration in the Central Industrial Region, 1861–1905', *Peasant Economy, Culture and Politics of European Russia, 1800–1921*, ed. Esther Kingston-Mann and Timothy Mixter (Princeton, N.J., 1992), 55, 57.
6. U. A. Shuster, *Peterburgskie rabochie v 1905–1907gg.* (Leningrad, 1976), 17–18.
7. In 1900 62 percent of the population of St Petersburg was male. Among members of the peasant estate between the ages of 10 and 65, 64 percent were aged 16 to 35. Shuster, *Peterburgskie rabochie*, 23.
8. Joseph Bradley, *Muzhik and Muscovite: Urbanization in Late Imperial Russia* (Berkeley, 1985), 34; *Statisticheskie dannye Petrograda* (Petrograd, 1916), 9.

9. Barbara Alpern Engel, *Between the Fields and the City: Women, Work and Family in Russia, 1861–1914* (Cambridge, 1994), 72.
10. Olga Crisp, 'Labor and Industrialization in Russia', *Cambridge Economic History of Europe*, vol. 7, part 2 (Cambridge, 1978), 377–8.
11. For a detailed account of the different types of *artel'*, see I. Eremeev (ed.), *Gorod S-Peterburg s tochki zreniia meditsinskoi pomoshchi* (St Petersburg, 1897).
12. P. Timofeev, *Chem zhivet zavodskii rabochii* (St Petersburg, 1906), 16.
13. R. W. Connell, *Which Way is Up?: Essays on Sex, Class and Culture* (Sidney, 1983), 18.
14. A. M. Buiko, *Put' rabochego: zapiski starogo bol'shevika* (Moscow, 1934), 15; Zelnik, *Radical Worker*, 60.
15. E. O. Kabo, *Ocherki rabochego byta* (Moscow, 1928), 126.
16. James Riordan, *Sport in Soviet Society* (Cambridge, 1977), 17.
17. Louise McReynolds and Cathy Popkin, 'The Objective Eye and the Common Good', *Constructing Russian Culture in the Age of Revolution, 1881–1940*, ed. Catriona Kelly and David Shepherd (Oxford, 1998), 76–7.
18. Connell, *Which Way*, 18.
19. Riordan, *Sport*, 26–7.
20. R. E. Zelnik, *Labor and Society in Tsarist Russia: the Factory Workers of St Petersburg, 1855–1870* (Stanford, 1971), 247.
21. David Christian, *Living Water: Vodka and Russian Society on the Eve of Emancipation* (Oxford, 1990), ch. 3.
22. Eremeev, *Gorod S-Peterburg*, 632.
23. A. Buzinov, *Za Nevskoi Zastavoi* (Moscow, 1930), 22.
24. *Pravda*, 102, 28 August 1912.
25. S. A. Smith, 'The Social Meanings of Swearing: Workers and Bad Language in Late-Imperial and Early-Soviet Russia', *Past and Present*, 160 (1998), 167–202.
26. Cited in Mark D. Steinberg, *Moral Communities: the Culture of Class Relations in the Russian Printing Industry, 1867–1907* (Berkeley, 1992), 242.
27. Ibid., 78.
28. *Pravda*, 174, 21 November 1912.
29. Rose L. Glickman, *Russian Factory Women: Workplace and Society, 1880–1914* (Berkeley, 1984), 204–8.
30. *Rabochaia Pravda*, 6, 9 July 1913.
31. *Rabotnitsa*, 2, 16 March 1914.
32. Kabo, *Ocherki*, 125; *Vyborgskaia storona: iz istorii bor'by rabochego klassa za pobedu velikoi oktiabr'skoi revoliutsii* (Leningrad, 1957), 5.
33. E. A. Korol'chuk (ed.), *V nachale puti: vospominaniia peterburgskikh rabochikh, 1872–1897gg.* (Leningrad, 1975), 305.
34. Timofeev, *Chem zhivet*, 10.
35. Tim McDaniel, *Autocracy, Capitalism and Revolution in Russia* (Berkeley, 1988), ch. 8; *Rabochie i intelligentsiia Rossii v epokhu reform i revoliutsii,1861-fevral' 1917*, ed. S. I. Potolov et al. (St Petersburg, 1997); S. A. Smith, 'Workers, the Intelligentsia and Marxist Parties, St Petersburg, 1895–1917, and Shanghai, 1921–27', *International Review of Social History*, 41 (1996), 1–56.
36. Zelnik, *Radical Worker*, 5.
37. Kirill Orlov, *Zhizn' rabochego revoliutsionera. Ot 1905g. do 1917g.* (Leningrad, 1925), 3.

38. A. I. Svirskii, *Zapiski rabochego* (Moscow, 1925 [orig.1907]), 12.
39. Korol'chuk, *V nachale puti*, 141.
40. Laura Engelstein, *The Keys to Happiness: Sex and the Search for Modernity in Fin-de-Siècle Russia* (Ithaca, N.Y., 1992), 71; S. Gvozdev, *Zapiski fabrichnogo inspektora* (Moscow, 1911), 119.
41. A. I. Nutrikhin (ed.), *Pesni russkikh rabochikh XVIII–nachalo XX veka* (Leningrad, 1962).
42. Carole Pateman's path-breaking work contrasts classic patriarchalism of the seventeenth century, where masculine political creativity is rooted in the procreative power of the father, with contract theory where men act as brothers in order to transform themselves into a civic fraternity. She argues that in so doing, the 'brothers' split apart the two dimensions of political right that were formerly united in the figure of the father: patriarchal right is extended to all men, but the civil sphere gains its universal meaning only in opposition to a private sphere which subordinates nature and women. C. Pateman, *The Sexual Contract* (Cambridge, 1988), 77–133.
43. Buzinov, *Za Nevskoi Zastavoi*, 18. Buzinov's identification with the family of workers here appears to come about a result not just of the repudiation of the authority of the father, but of the threat of maternal re-engulfment. Such a reading is in line with 'object relations' psychoanalysis, which posits that whilst a boy's sense of self begins in union with the feminine, his sense of masculinity arises against it. See Nancy Chodorow, *The Reproduction of Mothering* (Berkeley, 1978).
44. Korol'chuk, *V nachale puti*, 304.
45. Hunt suggests that during the French Revolution, revolutionaries, having slain the king, sought to replace him with a different kind of family, one in which parents were effaced and children, especially brothers, acted autonomously. She draws the idea from Freud who used the term to denote the neurotic's fantasy of 'getting free from the parents of whom he now has a low opinion and of replacing them with others who, as a rule, are of higher social standing'. L. Hunt, *The Family Romance of the French Revolution* (London, 1992), xiii.
46. The theme of separation from one's mother is less explicit in the memoir literature than that of rebellion against the father, but there is no doubting the power of the cultural archetype of the strong, self-sacrificing, long-suffering mother. See Joanna Hubbs, *Mother Russia: the Feminine Myth in Russian Culture* (Bloomington, 1988). Some writers have gone so far as to suggest that women were the stronger sex in Russian culture, masculinity being 'reluctant to detach itself from the shelter of the feminine principle'. Vera S. Dunham, 'The Strong-Woman Motif', *The Transformation of Russian Society*, ed. Cyril E. Black (Cambridge, 1960), 470.
47. Shuster, *Peterburgski rabochie*, 26; Evel G. Economakis, 'Patterns of Migration and Settlement in Pre-revolutionary St Petersburg: the Case of Peasants from Iaroslavl' and Tver' Provinces', *Russian Review*, 56 (1997), 8–24.
48. L. Haimson, E. Brian, 'Changements démographiques et grèves ouvrières a Saint-Petersbourg, 1905–14', *Annales ESC*, 40, no. 4 (1985), 797.
49. S. G. Strumilin, 'Problemy ekonomiki truda', *Izbrannye proizvedeniia*, 3 vols (Moscow, 1964), 3, 69–71.
50. Engel, *Between the Fields*, 222.

51. N. Vigdorchik, 'Detskaia smertnost' sredi Peterburgskikh rabochikh', *Obshchestvennyi vrach*, 5, no. 2 (1914), 212–53.
52. M. Davidovich, 'Khoziaistvennoe znachenie zhenshchiny v rabochei sem'e', *Poznanie Rossii*, 3 (1909), 119, 121. A survey of thirteen mills in 1900–2, with a total workforce of 11285, showed that families in which both husband and wife worked comprised 90 percent of the total number of families. W. Leont'ev, *Die Lage der Baumwollenarbeitern in St Peterburg* (München, 1906).
53. Timofeev, *Chem zhivet*, 87; L. M. Kleinbort, 'Ocherki rabochei demokratii', *Sovremennyi mir*, 5, part 2 (1913), 154.
54. Davidovich, 'Khoziaistvennoe znachenie', 120–1.
55. *Tkach*, 2 (1917), 7.
56. S. Strumilin, 'Biudzhet vremeni russkogo rabochego', *Voprosy Truda* (1923), 192.
57. *Statisticheskie dannye Petrograda*, 9.
58. In 1897 only 10 percent of all Russian men between 40 and 59 were unwed. Engel, *Between the Fields*, 136.
59. Dan Healey, *Homosexual Desire in Revolutionary Russia: the Regulation of Sexual and Gender Dissent* (Chicago, 2001), ch. 1.
60. Engel, *Between the Fields*, 40.
61. *Byt velikorusskikh krest'ian-zemlepashtsev: opisanie materialov etnograficheskogo biuro kniazia V. N. Tenisheva (na primere Vladimirskoi gubernii)*, ed. B. M. Firsov and I. G. Kiselev (St Petersburg, 1993), 245.
62. James von Geldern and Louise McReynolds (eds), *Entertaining Tsarist Russia* (Bloomington, 1998), xxii; Steve Smith and Catriona Kelly, 'Commercial Culture and Consumerism', *Constructing*, 129.
63. Von Geldern and McReynolds, *Entertaining*, 223.
64. *Byt velikorusskikh krest'ian-zemlepashtsev*, 239–40.
65. Zorkaia, *Na rubezhe*, 184, 186; Richard Stites, *Russian Popular Culture: Entertainment and Society since 1900* (Cambridge, 1992), 32.
66. N. M. Zor'kaia, *Na rubezhe stoletii: u istokov massovogo iskusstva v Rossii 1900–1910* (Moscow, 1976), 195.
67. Mironov, 'Peasant Popular Culture', 19.
68. S. N. Prokopovich, *Biudzhety peterburgskikh rabochikh* (St Petersburg, 1909), 52.
69. A. Frolov, *Probuzhdenie: vospominaniia riadego rabochego* (Kiev, 1923), 17.
70. Zelnik, *Radical Worker*, 71.
71. Cited in E. Anthony Swift, 'Theater for the People: Urban Culture, Society and Politics in Russia, 1861–1917' (Ph.D. diss., University of California, 1992), 275.
72. D. N. Zhbankov, *Bab'ia storona: statistiko-etnograficheskii ocherk* (Kostroma, 1891), 27.

7
Marriage and Masculinity in Late-Imperial Russia: the 'Hard Cases'

Barbara Alpern Engel

This essay, part of a larger study of marriage, its discontents, and the state in late Imperial Russia, represents an exploratory appraisal of the ways that Russian men experienced and exercised the near-absolute authority in the family that they enjoyed by custom and law. Such a study is long overdue. As early as 1975, Natalie Zemon Davis expressed the hope that it would soon become second nature for the historian to consider 'the consequences of gender' as readily as those of class. In order to understand 'the significance of the *sexes* [emphasis hers]', she urged historians to study the history of men as well as women: 'we should not be working only on the subjected sex any more than an historian of class can focus exclusively on peasants', Davis wrote.[1] Yet while the field of Russian women's history is by now well developed, no comparable attention has been paid to the history of Russian men, as *men*. As a result, many of the otherwise pathbreaking studies of the personal and psychological consequences of men's social status stop short of interrogating the consequences for their male subjects of the authority that they exercised as a result of Russia's patriarchal social, economic, and cultural systems. Thus, the history remains to be told of the men to whom Russia's women were subordinated by custom and law, in whose 'field of power' women lived.[2]

This relative invisibility of masculinity both as a social construct and an aspect of human experience seems especially regrettable in the case of Russia, where until well into the twentieth century, production continued to be household-based and social relations among a vast majority of the population remained patriarchal in the old-fashioned, almost Biblical sense of the power of the father over his household. Patriarchal family relations were upheld by law, which defined family relations in terms of authority and duty and required wives to give unconditional obedience to their husbands. Imperial law placed few constraints on men's exercise of matrimonial authority: husbands enjoyed the power to control the activities of their wives and children and to use corporal punishment if they failed to obey. And while in return the law did require a husband to 'love his wife as his own body, live in accord with her, respect, defend and forgive her her weaknesses and ease her infirmities' and to support her according to his station,[3] the law offered almost no relief for the wives of men who failed to fulfill their responsibilities or abused their authority, except in life-threatening cases. The limited grounds for divorce did not include cruel treatment.[4] Even establishing a separate residence was exceedingly difficult for a wife, unless her husband was willing to let her go. Marital law strictly forbade any act that might lead to the separation of spouses;[5] a husband who sought to reclaim a runaway wife could, and in many instances did, summon the help of the police. Inscribed upon her husband's internal passport and lacking a document of her own, a married woman could neither rent an apartment, nor enroll in school, nor take up gainful employment. Thus, in Russia, married men enjoyed an unusually powerful 'ideological support system' to sanctify their authority over their wives.[6] In this chapter, I propose to explore the way some men experienced and exercised that authority in the domestic sphere, and within the constraints of my sources, examine the relationship of that domestic authority to their sense of themselves as men, both within their own households and outside of them.

The source base for this study derives from separation cases preserved in the archive of the Imperial Chancellory for Receipt of Petitions (from 1881–4, the Petitions Chancellory). Offering Russian subjects direct access to the throne, the Chancellory enabled the 'weak' and the 'unfortunate' to appeal to the tsar for mercy. As his agents, Chancellory officials held the authority to circumvent the law forbidding separation of spouses and to issue an abused wife the residency permit (*vid na zhitel'stvo*, henceforward, *vid*) she required to live apart from her husband.[7] Officials did not exercise that authority lightly. Highly reluctant to violate the marital bond, Chancellory officials first made concerted efforts to reconcile the quarreling couple before investigating the substance of disputes. Deliberating behind closed doors and on the basis of written evidence, most of it labeled 'secret', they granted a woman's request for separation only under 'exceptional' circumstances. Between 1890 and 1902, about 20 percent of women's petitions were granted over a husband's objections, and most of these, only until such time as the husband ceased his offensive behavior (*do polnago ero ispravleniia*).[8]

Between 1881 and 1914, when passport law was revised to permit a wife to obtain her own document, tens of thousands of women, the overwhelming majority married to men from the peasantry or lower middle class (*meshchanstvo*), requested separation from the Chancellory. About 2200 such cases have survived in the Chancellory archive, of which I have now examined 200. Although the majority of the petitions derive from the peasantry, I have chosen a more socially diverse sample: approximately 50 of the cases I have read derive from the wives of townsmen, and another 65 from members of the privileged orders, primarily merchants, professionals, and petty civil servants.[9] Because I am interested in comparing the Russian experience with its counterparts elsewhere, in this chapter I focus on groups that were resident in a city and/or belonged to the emergent middle and lower middle classes, groups that have been most thoroughly studied by historians of Europe and the United States.

How 'typical' are the marital relationships reflected in these cases? It is hard to know for certain. According to the findings of William Wagner, by the early 1890s, about 2000 discontented wives submitted separation petitions every year; thereafter, the numbers grew steadily, reaching a high of 3469 in 1896.[10] That figure represented a mere 0.41 percent of the 842 631 marriages that were concluded in the Russian empire during the previous year, 1895.[11] However, about two-thirds of women petitioners (2324) resided either in the city of Moscow or St Petersburg, where the number of marriages in 1895 totalled 12 932,[12] thus giving us a far higher rate of separation – 17.9 percent of marriages. This percentage is certainly too high. It is inflated by the inmigration of an unknown and unknowable number of unhappy couples who married elsewhere, and by the presence of unhappy runaway wives, who selected a big city as their destination. To complicate matters further, cases that came to the Chancellory's attention were not necessarily typical even of 'unhappy' marriages, because a husband retained the right simply to agree to his wife's separate *vid* and so to part with her amicably, without involving the Chancellory or state officials.

Thus, cases that came to the Chancellory's attention tended to be extreme ones, the 'hard' cases, in which husbands stubbornly refused to relinquish the authority vested in them. Even so, the languages Russians employed – men to defend that authority, others to challenge it – can tell us much about the meanings that they attached to manhood in the period under study.

The hard cases

Although their provenance differed, spouses' narratives in separation cases share the 'fictional' quality identified by Natalie Zemon Davis in her exploration of sixteenth-century French pardon tales. That is, their authors 'shape[d] the events' of their marriage into a story, embellishing in the process. As Davis observes, the element of artifice does not necessarily render a particular account 'false'; indeed, it could well introduce verisimilitude or a 'moral truth'.[13] But what about competing moral truths? The cases to be examined offer not one story, but two, each invoking particular gender constructs to give shape and meaning to the narrative and lend gravity to the 'moral truths' embedded therein. What guided husbands as they shaped their stories?

In the cases I have read, a husband's unrestricted right to exercise his domestic authority served as the cornerstone of the narrative. These men appear to have been not only acutely conscious of the 'ideological support system that sanctioned their authority', as were the middle-class husbands studied by James Hammerton, but also supremely confident that the state would take their side. They had good reason. As William Wagner emphasizes, patriarchal family law in Russia served a conservative political function. Because respect for state authority derived from the respect for patriarchal authority fostered by the family, wives who challenged their husbands by subverting family authority threatened public order as well.[14] The connection between the autocrat's authority and their own encouraged husbands to assume that they could treat their wives (and children) as they pleased, that they could exercise, as it were, autocratic authority in their households. Equally important, the ideology of domesticity that had accompanied the rise of the European middle class and, by elevating women's moral status, 'honed the rough edge of patriarchy,' was at best weakly developed in Russia.[15] Consequently, most presented their wives' attempts to set limits to their authority as sheer insubordination.

Take, for example, the case of the townsman (*meshchanin*) Eremeev and his wife, Evdokiia. Mrs Eremeev first petitioned the Chancellory in 1891, after six years of marriage, complaining of cruel treatment by her husband, a metalworker at the San Galli machine works in St Petersburg, who, she claimed, had beaten her 'for trifles' and threatened to murder her.[16] In this case, the Chancellory's routine effort to reconcile a quarreling couple was initially crowned with success, producing a written agreement in which the husband promised henceforward to treat his wife affectionately (*laskovo*), to behave peaceably, and to cease to beat her. For her part, she would refrain from aggravating her husband and entertaining her mother in their apartment, and would no longer spend the night at her mother's place, where she had often sought refuge from her husband's violence.[17] The agreement, which seemed to this reader clearly aimed at preserving an essentially patriarchal relationship by ameliorating its worst excesses, was interpreted in quite a different fashion by the husband: according to his understanding, it signified that the Chancellory had taken his side. This became clear when, in February 1892, he himself petitioned the Chancellory, asking for their help in putting his wife in her place. In his appeal, he claimed that the Chancellory had denied his wife's petition, whereas in fact their reconciliation had simply brought the case to a close. Likewise, he creatively interpreted the language of their agreement to suit himself: 'My wife was ordered to live with me well and not leave the house without telling me and never spend the night elsewhere or at her mother's,' he wrote. Invoking a superior authority to reinforce his own, he claimed that the Chancellory had threatened her with exile from St Petersburg if she disobeyed him. Now, he wanted the authorities to discipline his stubbornly resistant wife, who had hit him on the cheek with a samovar chimney during a recent quarrel and then fled their apartment. He asked for their assistance: 'I can't live without a wife and so I ask Your Majesty to have the goodness to summon my wife before the commission [sic!] and again instill in her the duties of a good wife: to live peacefully with me and not to go off to live with her mother and also, to stop meeting with her sister, who will lure her into something bad.'[18]

As head of his household, Eremeev felt confident of his entitlement to his wife and children's unquestioning obedience as well as his right to enforce obedience with his fists, which he never denied doing. As he became more successful professionally, his sense of entitlement grew. By the turn of the century, Eremeev had become the boss of his own small machine-building shop on the Kriukov canal. This success as a breadwinner, to his mind, should have been sufficient to secure his status in his household. 'I worked almost 30 years at the Sangali [sic!] factory and acquired a shop (*khoziaistvo*) of my own and I thought everything would get better, now that I've created a nest [*ochag*, literally, hearth] for my family.' He also seemed convinced that he need do no more: everyone who knew the couple concurred that he drank incessantly, abused his wife, and spent every kopeck he earned on himself. His behavior prompted his wife to petition the Chancellory again in 1904 and every year thereafter; each time, however, she reconciled with him (for economic reasons, I suspect) until finally, in 1911, she left him for good, taking their five children along. To the bitter end, Eremeev accepted no responsibility for the difficulties in his family life and recognized no need to mend his ways. Setting forth his version of their relationship in a lengthy letter to the Chancellory, Eremeev painted a portrait of wifely defiance of his legitimate efforts to maintain order. Their most recent conflict had erupted when his wife stood up for their seventeen-year-old daughter, whose behavior he had attempted to control. This kind of defiance was typical: 'See what I've had to put up with in 25 years of marriage?' he rhetorically inquired.[19]

Men commonly reacted with outrage when their wives' narrative brought intimate matters to the attention of others. Although Chancellory deliberations occurred behind closed doors and officials sought to maintain 'strict secrecy' in their investigations, a petitioning wife nevertheless threatened her husband with 'dishonor', or so men often claimed. To be sure, domestic disorder could have negative consequences for a husband, as it did in the case of a teacher who lost his state-owned apartment because it was 'inappropriate for a teacher with family problems' to live there.[20] But mainly, dishonor appears to have meant 'losing face' and honor, the right to privacy in family life. Thus, Chancellory officials believed that the approximately 29 percent of husbands who agreed to issue the wife a passport once she petitioned acted primarily to avoid having their intimate life subjected to scrutiny.[21] Honor was all the more at stake because, the emphasis on secrecy notwithstanding, police investigators and witnesses almost inevitably learned the sordid details of a case. In response to his wife's allegations that he denied his family financial support and had carried on with other women under their very roof, for example, the physician Popov maintained that his wife's petition in 1901 showed her desire to 'destroy' him at any cost: 'She shows me no mercy as a man, as a husband, or as father of her children.'[22] 'You call yourself my wife but you've stained my name and my reputation which no one has done before, you shameless thing!' the peasant Shibanov, the owner of a painting workshop in the city of Moscow, wrote in an irate letter to his wife after she petitioned the throne seeking relief from his 'unnatural' sexual demands, among other failings.[23] The investigation that followed her complaints involved depositions not only from family members, but also from neighbors and even workers in his shop. 'I'm upset Mr. Poroshin,' he complained to the investigating officer in 1897, 'at the way you are making me out to be a scoundrel (*podlets*) before my workers. What will they think of me?'[24] Likewise, when the wife of the hereditary honorary citizen Stefanovskii, a former teacher and resident of the city of Viatka, wrote, accusing her husband of excessive drinking, outrageous behavior, and the rape of a domestic servant, her husband responded that his wife's petition to the Chancellory was merely her attempt to 'insult me, humiliate me and nail me to the shaming post [*pozornaia stolba*] in front of Your Majesty, the provincial authorities and the police'.[25]

In their efforts to retain their authority, many husbands crafted extended 'counter-narratives', that is, narratives designed to undermine the effectiveness of the wife's narrative by invoking a different 'truth'. Almost invariably, such counter-narratives cast aspersions on the wife's sexual morality by alleging that she had lost her virginity before marriage or carried on with other men afterwards or both. In his testimony to the police, for example, Shibanov accused his wife of having been pregnant by another man when they married. Stefanovskii, the former teacher from Viatka, claimed that his wife's alleged pregnancy by another man is what led him to take up drink 'if only to forget the shame . . . and the fact that a woman of 32, a mother, conducted her love life so carelessly.'[26] It was a rare husband indeed who refrained from accusing his discontented wife of conducting illicit relations with another man. Boarders, neighbors, relatives, friends, tutors – anyone who enjoyed any access at all to the conjugal nest risked accusation as the alleged lover of the wife.

In most cases, the husband's claims of wifely infidelity proved fallacious, or so Chancellory officials concluded following investigation. These false accusations resemble those leveled by husbands in the divorce cases in late nineteenth-century California that have been studied by Robert Griswold. Griswold explains them with reference to the 'social and legal significance of female chastity' for men and women alike. Thus, men employed sexual epithets in order to shame and disgrace their wives in the eyes of the public.[27] Accusations of wifely immorality served a similar purpose in Russia, where female chastity also carried considerable significance, although chastity never became the very essence of ideal womanhood, as it became in the United States.[28]

But such accusations also gave men moral leverage, invoking as they did a man's longstanding role as custodian of women's morality. His custodial role also lent force to a husband's argument. A wife's infidelity or sexual audacity could in fact humiliate a husband: several files contain anonymous letters criticizing the husband for his failure to preserve his wife's sexual honor, for example.[29] Thus, some husbands argued that if the wife had not yet fallen, she would certainly do so if permitted to live on her own. The Chancellory should not grant his wife a passport, the Moscow merchant Andreev contended in 1891, because if allowed to live as she pleased at the young age of 25, she was likely to 'fall into error', for which he would bear moral responsibility.[30] Likewise, the hereditary honorary citizen Skachkov, a clerk from a bank in Tiumen, Siberia, wrote in 1901 that he considered it his 'moral responsibility' to reject his wife's request for a passport, because she required his guidance to restrain her from 'evil influences'.[31]

These virtually ubiquitous efforts to impugn a wife's morality can also be seen as men's effort to counteract the linguistic advantage that Chancellory procedures offered to women, at least initially. Intended to 'protect the weak and assist the unfortunate', the Chancellory presented women with a ready-made idiom of supplication and victimization, which in the 200 cases I have read thus far, only one woman entirely eschewed.[32] A husband would have known his wife's story of suffering, having learned the contents of her deposition during the investigatory process. Accusing his wife of infidelity or engaging in premarital sexual relations enabled a husband to counter his wife's story of victimization with a victimization tale of his own. Husbands' narratives presented them as victims in other ways as well, for example, as exploited by a wealthy father-in-law, who used his wealth to subborn witnesses and bribe local officials in order to obtain a favorable decision for his daughter.[33]

What exactly *was* expected of a proper husband? Rarely the domestic virtues, judging by the detailed self-defense offered by husbands in these cases. To be sure, many referred to the fact that they 'loved' their wives and some claimed to have treated them affectionately. However, in the language of these errant husbands (or their wives or witnesses, for that matter) there is little evidence of the domestic ideals that governed bourgeois marriage – expectations that a man would respect his wife, treat her thoughtfully and tenderly, spend his free time with her, and the like.[34] Instead of their private behavior, men stressed their public achievements, often framed in terms of service to society and the public good, rather than individual financial success or social mobility (Eremeev being an exception here).[35] 'I was such a successful teacher that I won teaching awards every year,' claimed Stefanovskii in his counter-narrative.[36] The physician Popov digressed at considerable length about his professional record, relating how he traveled long distances to treat peasants from whom he asked no compensation, taking money only from the rich.[37] 'I've worked for the social good,' claimed the Moscow townsman Samodurov, who according to his wife was a despot and a drunkard, and who had squandered all their property. 'I was an elder in the Lazarev cemetery church and a delegate to the Moscow Society of Townsmen, which appointed me guardian of the Alexander Shelter and the almshouse of Moscow townsmen.'[38] To give weight to his appeal to regain custody of his only son, the merchant Morozov invoked the public contributions of his entire clan: 'Merciful monarch! My ancestors are known to almost all of Moscow, as honorable factory owners and equally, as fully moral citizens who have raised more than one generation and have given to the fatherland useful and honorable citizens.'[39]

The privileging of public over private in men's counter-narratives is nowhere clearer than in the cases in which men professed their loyalty to the throne while denouncing the politics of their wives. Defending himself against allegations that he had married his wife for her money, Skachkov, the clerk in a Tiumen bank, insisted that his wife did not deserve to be granted a *vid*. To demonstrate why, he quoted a letter from her in which she 'dared to condemn the actions of the government'.[40] The physician Popov, who had openly conducted liaisons with other women, claimed in his counter-narrative that his wife, who had been arrested while a student, now sympathized with the radical views of their children's tutor and had also become the tutor's lover. According to Popov, the student had once declared that 'only students stand for the truth and will bring Russia happiness and freedom', to which his wife allegedly agreed. Popov, by contrast, had remained steadfast in his loyalty: 'I'm prepared to fall upon my sword for the Sovereign Emperor,' he claimed that he had responded to the wife and the student.[41] It was his wife's brothers who were at fault for their problems, wrote the townsman Semenov, a resident of Moscow and a representative for the Mal'tsev factory owners, in 1906. He, Semenov, considered himself a monarchist, while his wife's brothers held excessively liberal views, 'for example, they justify workers' strikes, and the looting and burning of estates and so forth', and they had won the wife to their side.[42]

In asserting the primacy of their public role, men laid claim to their place in the hierarchy of political authority in which, as in a great chain of being, the tsar stood at the apex and they, as husbands and fathers, provided the final link. Implicit in this hierarchical vision was an assumption of common interest: if one link broke, might it not endanger the rest? Some men referred to the threat explicitly. Accused of excessive drinking, failing to support his family, and beating his wife and children, the townsman Kotliarov warned that if his wife gained a separate *vid* as a result of her allegations, 'then all wives will begin to demand separate *vidy*'.[43] Without addressing any of his wife's allegations that he drank, carried on, and was unable to keep a job, the Moscow merchant Efremov referred to the same slippery slope in 1912, underscoring the convergence of the tsar's interests with his own: 'I am convinced that the all-merciful monarch is not going to destroy family life merely on account of the whims of one of the family members, since the happiness of a person and at the same time, the well-being of Russia consists precisely of family life . . . ; if [the monarch] satisfies my wife's request, then there will be millions of women who also, for the sake of their whims, will begin to trouble His Majesty the Emperor with false denunciations of their husbands and petitions for a separate *vid*.'[44]

In these 'hard' cases, husbands clearly assumed that the way that they treated their wives was no one's business but their own. Emphasizing the public roles from which they drew authority, most were unwilling, unable, or believed it unnecessary to craft a counter-narrative in which they figured, for example, as tender and loving husbands. Instead, they offered tales of their wives' improprieties, most often sexual, which served both to undermine the woman's moral stature and to present themselves as by far the greater victim, betrayed and humiliated in their masculine honor. Having constructed this argument with bits and pieces of evidence, I want to conclude by exploring at some length two cases, which reflect these themes with particular clarity, and also allow us to learn something about the responses of Chancellory officials.

The first case came to the Chancellory's attention in 1899, when the wife submitted a petition complaining about cruel and arbitrary treatment by her husband, the townsman Iartsev, a widower 21 years her senior, who was a trader in fish products and lived in the city of Revel. Iartsev responded to her allegations by portraying himself as a model of piety and his wife as a virtual monster of depravity, who had behaved immodestly even at their wedding.[45] When he consummated his marriage, he learned the reason why: his wife had been seduced at fifteen by a police officer, she allegedly confessed, and had contracted syphilis. Now she was in the advanced stages of disease, as he could tell from her soft, drooping breasts 'like those of an old woman', her teeth which were black from the mercury she took for a cure, her tongue covered with suspicious white spots, her thinning hair and viscous saliva. Thus, he had come to realize that his wife had married him only in order to conduct her 'vicious life' without having to carry the 'ticket of a public woman'.[46] Now that she had petitioned for separation, it was time to tear off the mask 'behind which she shamelessly wallows in mud', blackening his hitherto unstained reputation. However, he refused to grant her a *vid*; rather, as a 'good and true Christian', he was prepared to take his wife back, 'to love and forgive her' once she was cured of syphilis.[47]

In this case, a lengthy investigation convinced the Chancellory of the merits of the wife's complaints. While the husband's witnesses upheld much of his story, those whom his wife named supported her allegations that his difficult character, groundless jealousy, and quest for her dowry had led to their problems. Their testimony provided detailed descriptions of his violent behavior, and relentless efforts to extort money from the wife and her mother.[48] Dismissing the husband's accusations of premarital sex and infection as 'relating to the period before her marriage' and the witnesses who supported him as 'his friends', the Chancellory found the husband solely responsible for the breakdown of the marriage. Concluding that the 'antagonistic relations between the spouses' made it impossible to re-establish cohabitation at present, the Chancellory granted her a one-year *vid*.[49]

Iartsev refused to accept this decision, complaining to the Chancellory about its investigation and threatening to go to court. After three years of fruitless efforts to rescind her *vid*, he lost patience. In an angry letter to the Chancellory, he accused officials of interfering with his moral and legal authority as a husband. Instead of preserving his marriage, as the law required, the Chancellory had helped to destroy it by releasing his wife from her husband's lawful authority and guidance and encouraging her insubordination. If the Chancellory had not granted his wife 'freedom' from the very start, he maintained, then 'she would have made her peace with her lawful husband and would have lived with me in complete happiness'.[50] Summoned to the Chancellory, he repeated his allegations about his wife's morality, refused to sign the protocol of his statement and then left the office, muttering invectives against the Chancellory. In 1904, Mrs Iartsev received the permanent right to live on her own.

The second case, involving the Moscow merchant and hereditary honorary citizen Kuprianov, opened in 1901 when Mrs Kuprianov petitioned the Chancellory, complaining that her husband had been impossible to live with virtually from their wedding day 19 years earlier. Witness after witness upheld her allegations and provided telling detail. Kuprianov routinely abused his marital authority to an extraordinary degree. He was in the habit, for example, of coming home at three or four in the morning, waking his wife and forcing her to read to him until he fell asleep, and if her voice grew too weak, of shouting at her and even striking her. Even when she was in the advanced stages of pregnancy, he did not spare her this ordeal. He demeaned her before the servants and the children and encouraged them to insult her, too. He even betrayed her sexually under their roof, with their servant, to whom he showed greater concern when she became pregnant than he did for his simultaneously pregnant wife.

Kuprianov's own self-representation, however, was completely at odds with the portrait of him drawn by everyone else. In his own eyes, he was a loving husband: his wife had always been 'dear and close to me,' he wrote in a lengthy deposition, 'and I've always loved her and love her now, as a wife and as the mother of my nine children'.[51] And by his own account, he had fulfilled his marital obligations, which he defined in terms of his abilities as provider and protector: 'The family lived in plenty' and the children were educated well. 'I've always protected [my wife] from bad people and given her good counsel.'[52] The entire blame for their problems rested with his wife, a woman who was 'secretive and reserved, incredibly stubborn yet utterly lacking in backbone', and a failure as both wife and mother. If he did raise a hand to her, she was at fault: 'as a person who works a lot, I sometimes failed to control myself when faced with her sickly stubbornness or the disorder in our household'.[53] Likewise, her behavior, not his, threatened the children by offering a bad moral example. He concluded, 'Let my wife return to the home she has abandoned, let her forget the egotism that tore her from the family hearth.' For the sake of the children's morality, Kuprianov asked that the Chancellory restore his wife to his home.[54]

Kuprianov drew the Chancellory's attention to his public accomplishments and his role in Russia's emergent public sphere. He had been elected to various responsible positions in the merchant community, including membership in the Moscow Commercial Court, and had served as an elder of the Moscow Orphan court. Confident in his public role and knowledgeable about the law, he chided the Chancellory for the secrecy in which it maintained the testimony of witnesses. He wanted to confront his wife's witnesses, many of whom, he insisted, could not possibly know the details of their family life. Referring to the appropriate article of the criminal code, he reminded Chancellory officials that 'the evidence of the accusing side cannot and should not be kept secret from the accused; if it is, the investigation will be conducted incorrectly.' This was all the more important because of the seriousness of the matter: false testimony could 'destroy the family'. He demanded, in vain, that his legal rights be restored.[55] In any case, officials had already made up their minds. In a concluding statement that upheld every one of the wife's allegations, the Chancellory recommended that her request for a *vid* be granted. Drawing in part upon the vocabulary of women's rights that had developed during the 1860s and 1870s, in 1902 the Chancellory's report summarized the relationship between the Kuprianovs with the following words: 'As time passed the petitioner increasingly lost her will, and finally, she became a toy in the hands of her despot husband, who crushed in her all that is human and turned her into a silent slave.'[56]

When it decided in favor of abused wives such as Iartseva and Kuprianova, the Chancellory played a role which was in some respects comparable to that played by divorce courts elsewhere – that is, officials resolved marital disputes in order to mitigate some of the worst extremes of a family order that they nevertheless supported.[57] According to historians of marital conflict in Great Britain and the US, judicial decisions in favor of abused wives reflect changing ideals concerning appropriate masculine behavior. Surveying divorce cases that came before rural California courts between 1850 and 1890, historian Robert Griswold notes the broad range of grievances against autocratic male behavior that women articulated. In his opinion, the fact that local judges affirmed the validity of women's complaints and that appellate judges expanded the definition of matrimonial cruelty is evidence that an important change in attitudes was underway. Among judges as well as female plaintiffs and witnesses in court, he finds a growing consensus concerning the need to curtail men's prerogatives in the family, implicit in which was a 'new definition of masculinity, one less domineering and forceful, and more sensitive and cooperative'.[58] By the late nineteenth century, the language employed by female plaintiffs and Chancellory officials suggests that a process of redefinition was taking place in Russia as well, reflecting at least in part the growing number of Chancellory officials who had received either a higher education or training in the law.[59] However, the Chancellory's redefinition of the role of the husband reflected the particularities of the Russian context. While highly critical of wife-beating and infidelity, of failure to support the wife, of 'crude' or 'insulting' or drunken behavior, officials did not set forth a companionate ideal of marriage – that is, they did not expect husbands to spend free time with a wife, to treat her tenderly and be attentive to her, to share decision-making with her. Rather, their decisions emphasized a kind of benevolent paternalism, which preserved family hierarchy but required husbands to exercise their authority neither arbitrarily nor despotically, but with affection and moral constraint, and in a way that did not hinder the personal development of the wife.[60]

The autocratic political context affected Russian proceedings in other ways as well. Most significantly, the Chancellory's role differed fundamentally from that played by divorce proceedings elsewhere. Robert Griswold has argued that legal proceedings in California, which were open to the public and reported at length in the newspapers, offered a 'moral theater' in which a new, and widely accepted definition of manhood might take shape. Testimony in legal proceedings, he asserts, offered community members the opportunity to express opposition to an offense, to bear witness against the offender, to reaffirm the bonds of cultural solidarity and thus, to increase the authority of the violated norm, thereby marking out new cultural boundaries.[61] While other historians of separation and divorce have not examined their data from this perspective, their studies nevertheless suggest that a comparable process was at work.[62] In Russia, by contrast, separation proceedings were kept almost completely from entering the public sphere. Separation hearings were held in private and the evidence was entirely written and held in strictest secrecy. Although elements of the rhetoric that gave elevated and unprecedentedly moral meaning to wifehood and motherhood in, for example, Great Britain and the United States can occasionally be heard in the statements of husbands, wives, and witnesses, Chancellory proceedings prevented them from becoming part of a public discourse. Instead, access to information about violations of community standards remained largely hidden, even, as we have seen in the case of the merchant Kuprianov, to some degree from the accused himself. The only people informed about the Chancellory's decision were the tsar, the plaintiff, the defendant, and the policeman delivering the verdict.[63] As a result, although by the late nineteenth century Chancellory officials had begun consistently to enforce more demanding expectations of men, instead of contributing to a new consensus about appropriate male behavior, their decisions appeared arbitrary and personalized. Moreover, they extended the paternalistic authority of the state and its agents into the families of discontented wives, in some cases demonstrating the powerlessness of husbands in the face of state authority. The effect is comparable to that observed by Natalie Zemon Davis in her study of pardon petitions in early modern France: by displaying the king's capacity for mercy and reminding subjects of his power, she notes, the pardoning process served to enhance the sovereignty of the king.[64]

Yet not unambiguously. By disciplining husbands for their marital misbehavior, the Chancellory revised the terms of the implicit contract that the autocrat had made with men. Recall again the sense of entitlement with which the husbands in these 'hard cases' exercised their marital rights, confident of the link between political absolutism and their own authority in the home. Might not this redefinition of authority's appropriate exercise work both ways? Here, the defiant reaction of both Iartsev and Kuprianov is instructive. If the state could challenge his authority in the one sphere in which Russian law granted men virtually unrestricted rights, might a man become more willing to challenge the authority of the state, and to hold the autocrat, too, to a higher standard? Here it is worth returning, if only briefly, to the insistence of so many of these husbands upon the role they played in public life. In addition to locating them along the chain of political authority, such assertions also suggest a growing perception among Russia's emergent middle class that the power of manhood included, among other things, 'the power to wield civic authority',[65] a perception already widely held by professionals as well as radical critics of autocracy. Unlike the French kings who entertained pleas for pardon, the Imperial Chancellory had to weigh the merits and moral claims of two stories and not one. Charged with protecting the weak and unfortunate, Chancellory officials who responded sympathetically to compelling, sometimes quite harrowing, narratives of men's marital abuses were led to violate the legal rights of men. While such decisions might have enhanced the tsar's authority in the eyes of the wife and perhaps her friends and relatives, they are likely to have made his own political powerlessness far less tolerable to the husband. Thus, in a very small way to be sure, Chancellory officials would have helped to undermine the autocratic political order they were utterly committed to upholding.

Notes

For their comments on an earlier version of this article, I thank Lee Chambers-Schiller, Susan Johnson, and Daniel Kaiser. Research for this article was supported in part by a grant from the International Research and Exchanges Board (IREX), with funds provided by the National Endowment for the Humanities, the US Department of State, and the US Information Agency. None of these organizations is responsible for the views expressed.

1. Natalie Zemon Davis, 'Women's History in Transition: the European Case', *Feminist Studies*, 3, no. 3/4 (Spring–Summer 1976), 90.

2. The phrase is from John Tosh, 'What Should Historians Do with Masculinity? Reflections on Nineteenth-Century Britain', *History Workshop*, 38 (Autumn 1994), 179.
3. *Svod Zakonov Rossiiskoi Imperii* (St Petersburg, 1857) (hereafter *SZ*), x, pt. 1, article 106.
4. The Russian Orthodox Church limited the grounds for divorce to adultery (preferably in front of eyewitnesses), unaccountable absence of the spouse for over five years, exile to Siberia after a conviction for a felony, or long-standing sexual incapacity that had arisen before marriage and could be certified by a medical examination. Gregory Freeze, 'Bringing Order to the Russian Family: Marriage and Divorce in Imperial Russia, 1760–1860', *Journal of Modern History*, 62, no. 4 (December 1990), 709–46.
5. *SZ* (1857), x, pt. 1, art. 103.
6. The phrase belongs to A. James Hammerton, *Cruelty and Companionship: Conflict in Nineteenth Century Married Life* (New York, 1992), 108.
7. S. N. Pisarev, *Uchrezhdenie po priniatiiu i napravleniiu proshenii i zhalob, prinosimykh na Vysochaishee imia 1820–1920gg. Istoricheskii ocherk* (SPb, 1909), 138.
8. Percentage based on figures in Wagner, *Marriage, Property and Law in Late Imperial Russia* (Oxford, 1994), 91.
9. Separation cases were identified by the legal estate to which the petitioner's husband was ascribed.
10. Wagner, *Marriage*, 90. Internal Chancellory documents reckon the number of petitions received in 1902 as about 4000.
11. *Statistika Rossiiskoi Imperii. Dvizhenie naseleniia v Evropeiskoi Rossii za 1895 god* (SPb, 1899), 88.
12. Ibid., 70, 80.
13. Natalie Zemon Davis, *Fiction in the Archives: Pardon Tales and Their Tellers in Sixteenth Century France* (Stanford, Calif., 1987), 3–4.
14. William Wagner, 'The Trojan Mare: Women's Rights and Civil Rights in Late Imperial Russia', *Civil Rights in Imperial Russia*, ed. Olga Crisp and Linda Edmondson (Oxford, 1989), 79–80.
15. Robert Griswold, *Family and Divorce in California, 1850–1900: Victorian Illusions and Everyday Realities* (Albany, N.Y., 1982), 121. For a fuller development of this argument, see Barbara Alpern Engel, *Mothers and Daughters: Women of the Intelligentsia in Nineteenth Century Russia* (Evanston, Ill., 2000), esp. chs 1 and 2.
16. RGIA, fond 1412, op. 217, ed. kh. 13, Eremeeva, 1891, 1–2. I have included this case because of Eremeev's *meshchane* status and because he subsequently became the owner of a small workshop. Although other factory workers are to be found among the cases I have examined, all the others derive from the peasantry and none was so upwardly mobile.
17. Ibid., 8.
18. Ibid., 9.
19. Ibid., 40–4. Eremeev finally agreed to grant his wife and children a separate *vid*.
20. Ibid., op. 235, d. 27, Shniavina, 1892.
21. On the relationship of honor to social standing, see Nancy Shields Kollmann, *By Honor Bound: State and Society in Early Modern Russia* (Ithaca, N.Y., 1999).

For a comparable response in France, see William Reddy, 'Marriage, Honor, and the Public Sphere in Postrevolutionary France: Separations de Corps, 1815–1848', *Journal of Modern History*, 65 (September 1993), 437.
22. RGIA, fond 1412, op. 226, ed. kh. 111, Popova, 1901, 23.
23. Ibid., op. 220, ed. kh. 25, Ilin, 1893, 69.
24. Ibid., 113–14.
25. Ibid., op. 226, ed. kh. 106, Stefanovskaia, 1895, 10.
26. Ibid., 13. It is worth noting that Chancellory investigation found no basis whatever for his allegations.
27. Griswold, *Family and Divorce*, 74.
28. See Julie Brown, 'Female Sexuality and Madness in Russian Culture: Traditional Values and Psychiatric Theory', *Social Research*, 53, no. 2 (Summer 1986), 369–85.
29. See, for example, RGIA, fond 1412, op. 222, d. 12, Lazurkina, 1908, 10.
30. Ibid., op. 212, ed. kh. 148, Andreeva, 1891, 23–4.
31. Ibid., op. 228, ed. kh. 59, Skachkova, 1901, 21, 94.
32. The woman was Anna Boldyreva, a textile worker and socialist and in 1905 a Bolshevik organizer, who had married while in exile for political activity.
33. See, for example, RGIA, fond 1412, op. 225, ed. kh. 55, Sinitsyna, 1909 and op. 227, ed. kh. 6, Razaeva, 1909.
34. Griswold, *Family and Divorce*; John Tosh, *A Man's Place: Masculinity and the Middle Class Home in Victorian England* (New Haven, 1999), esp. chs 1–3.
35. On the genesis of the service ideal for men see Marc Raeff, *Origins of the Intelligentsia: the Eighteenth Century Nobility* (New York, 1966).
36. RGIA, fond 1412, op. 228, ed. kh. 106, Stefanovskaia, 1895, 10.
37. Ibid., op. 226, ed. kh. 111, Popova, 1901, 30.
38. Ibid., op. 228, ed. kh. 14, Samodurova, 1895, 30.
39. Ibid., op. 223, ed. kh. 114, Morozova, 1885, 21.
40. Ibid., op. 228, ed. kh. 59, Skachkova, 1901, 21.
41. Ibid., op. 226, ed. kh. 111, Popova, 1901, 29.
42. Ibid., op. 228, ed. kh. 35, Semenova, 1906, 6. Such political accusations were most likely to derive from educated men, whereas peasants brought charges of religious apostasy. The Chancellory showed little interest in the truth of such allegations.
43. Ibid., op. 221, ed. kh. 132, Kotliarova, 1895, 25.
44. Ibid., op. 217, ed. kh. 24, Efremova, 1912, 12.
45. Ibid., op. 239, delo 11, Iartseva, 1899, 102.
46. Ibid., op. 239, delo 11, Iartseva, 1899, 5–11. He refers to the document registered prostitutes were required to carry, which, among other things, obligated them to undergo regular internal examinations. See Laurie Bernstein, *Sonia's Daughters: Prostitutes and their Regulation in Imperial Russia* (Berkeley, 1995).
47. Ibid., 12.
48. Ibid., see especially 94–9.
49. Ibid., 111.
50. Ibid., 163.
51. Ibid., 23, 27. Evidently in his own way, he did, as witnesses who completely verified his wife's account of his abusiveness also noted that he was devastated each time she left.

52. Ibid., op. 221, ed. kh. 214, Kuprianova, 1901, 20, 27.
53. Ibid., 20, 23.
54. Ibid., 20.
55. Ibid., 4.
56. Ibid., 90.
57. Both Robert Griswold, 'Divorce and the Legal Redefinition of Victorian Manhood', *Meanings for Manhood*, ed. Mark Carnes and Clyde Griffen (Chicago, 1990), 96–111 and Hammerton, *Cruelty and Companionship*, draw attention to this function of the divorce courts.
58. Griswold, 'Divorce and the Legal Redefinition of Victorian Manhood', 98.
59. This point will be explored at length in my book on late Imperial marriage and divorce.
60. See Wagner, *Marriage*, esp. 131.
61. Griswold, 'Divorce and the Legal Redefinition of Victorian Manhood', 99.
62. See Hammerton, *Cruelty and Companionship* and Reddy, 'Marriage, Honor, and the Public Sphere'.
63. A summary report of each case was also prepared for the tsar. These summaries remain in Chancellory files and are listed alphabetically.
64. Davis, *Fiction*, 52–8.
65. Gail Bederman, *Manliness and Civilization: a Cultural History of Gender and Race in the United States, 1880–1917* (Chicago, Ill., 1995), 14.

8

The Education of the Will: Advice Literature, *Zakal*, and Manliness in Early Twentieth-Century Russia

Catriona Kelly

One of the most salient qualities of the Soviet citizen, or, to adopt the term used in Soviet sources, the *kul'turnyi chelovek* (cultured person), was that of *zakalennost'* or *zakal*, 'steeliness'. The term denoted a combination of physical and mental virtues – fitness, endurance, capacity for boundless quantities of hard work, and resolution – that was the result of a process of *zakalivanie*, or 'tempering'. It was meant to be inculcated not only by submission to the military discipline of Party, workplace, and social institutions and by exposure to the rigors of revolution and civil war,[1] but also by the performance of exercise programs (*zariadka*), by other kinds of participation in 'physical culture' (*fizkul'tura*), and by a range of hygiene practices or 'procedures' (*protsedury*), most particularly hydrotherapeutic ones, such as the submission of the body, from early childhood, to douches of cold water and to alternating extremes of temperature. Right up until the end of Soviet power, manuals for nursery-school teachers instructed that children should undergo *zakalivanie* from, at the latest, three years old.[2]

One proclaimed benefit of *zakalivanie* was that the systematic exposure of the body to low temperatures helped prevent the colds and chills that were otherwise believed to be a constant danger from cold draughts (*svozniaki*). But this benefit was marginal to the main one – a regimentation and strengthening of the body and an assurance of regularity in physical habits (eating, drinking, urination, and defecation).[3] Brochures for adults propagandized a more rigorous variant of the exercise and bathing routines, with strenuous packages of exercises and passages expostulating upon the merits of the cold splash, sea and river bathing, and so on.[4]

With physical self-improvement went mental and moral self-improvement. Soviet readers were constantly hectored upon the benefits of 'the hygiene of mental labor' (*gigiena umstvennogo truda*), which required fresh air, frequent breaks, and study that was useful to the collective rather than an end in itself. They were exhorted to maintain punctuality and to streamline work tasks, and sometimes to chart their day minutely in order to ensure that each duty took no more and no less time than it should. The famous 'Gastev system' of work notation was only one of a number of such methods in circulation in the 1920s. *How to be Cultured* (1929), a handily complete guide for the *homo sovieticus* in search of ways to temper himself, set out a model chart aimed at the white-collar worker or low-level Party official: 'Wake up 7; body care 7–7.16; food preparation and breakfast 7.16–8.03; journey to work 8.03–8.48; discussions with colleagues 8.48–9.52; answering letters 8.48–9.52', and so on. Once home, cultured people were supposed to occupy themselves with reading and a quick meal; the only leisure envisaged was attendance at a film (no doubt of suitably edifying content) between 20.27 and 22.01 precisely.[5] A still more important aspect of *zakal* was the cultivation of strong will, 'steeliness' in the moral and mental sense: here again, a host of how-to guides advised on how to inculcate resolve in the self and to suppress shyness and other manifestations of inferior willpower.[6] These qualities were desirable in ordinary citizens and essential in members of the Party, who were supposed to manifest exceptional capacities for self-discipline and 'political and moral steadfastness'. They were most perfectly manifested, though, in the mythic heroes of Soviet power – Stakhanovites in official sculptures, rippling their steely muscles, Arctic explorers, and test pilots. A hero belonging to two of these categories at once, a pilot killed while flying in the Arctic, is commemorated in an epitaph on a tombstone at the Vagankovo Cemetery, Moscow, as 'a man of iron will and large heart', whose 'bright image' was 'stronger than death'.[7]

Zakalivanie was not intended to be exclusively a masculine program, or at any rate not in the early Soviet period. However, there was a sense in which 'self-tempering' was seen as an essential in men and a bonus in women. Role models of *zakalivanie* (for instance, Lenin or the nineteenth-century radical Nikolai Chernyshevskii) were all men; adventure stories for children (for example, Arkadii Gaidar's famous *Timur and his Team*, 1939) included a token girl or two, but it was always boys who exercised leadership and authority.[8] And the cult of toughness seems to have had a much larger following among male historical subjects than it had among their female contemporaries, at least to judge by memoirs. The 1930s diarist Leonid Potemkin, who relished 140-mile hiking trips, took part in Universal Military Training, and spent his spare time nurturing an earnest interest in Beethoven and Heine, reveals the association of *zakal* and masculinity in his concept of a suitable Soviet romance: 'With the living image of my brunette constantly on my mind, I [have been] overcome with an even more powerful drive to become a grown man in all senses [so as] to act firmly and confidently for her sake, to be a commander in the broad sense of the word, morally and physically. To speak beautifully and forcefully, not losing my dignity in any situation or conditions. I've become even more enamored of physical exercise.'[9]

The concept of *zakal* was vital to the governing early Soviet myth of a society led by supremely fit and committed citizens and as a component of the state-sponsored modernization program, which promised that in time all Soviet citizens would become 'steely'. However, not only the concept itself, but also its association with manliness and with the health of the nation, can be traced back well before the Revolution. What I intend to do here is examine the pre-history of *zakal* in the ideals of male behavior prevailing during the early years of the twentieth century, before returning to look briefly at the history of *zakal* under Soviet power. I shall show how the concept of the courageous, resolute, and unflinching male moved from being one of several alternative possibilities for men before the Revolution, to being the preferred ideal of male behavior in the 1920s and 1930s, before again becoming marginalized after the Second World War, and will hypothesize some reasons for these shifts in models of masculinity over the years.

Zakal was the Russian term for the quality known in English as 'backbone', 'character', 'moral fiber', or 'strength of will'.[10] The roots of the concept (which has connections with the northern European Romantic celebration of a northern barbarism that was contrasted to effeminate southern softness) lay in western sources as well as Russian ones, and in mass-market printed books as well as literary and philosophical texts (Schopenhauer, Nietzsche, Chernyshevskii, Dostoevskii). If 'highbrow' examples of manly resolution (for example, Robert Bage's hero Hermsprong or Chernyshevskii's Rakhmetov) were usually Romantic natural geniuses of moral fiber, drawing their authority from innate gifts (an idea raised also in Dostoevskii's hero Raskol'nikov's theory of the 'two classes' [*razryada*] of human beings, those made to lead and those to follow),[11] popular representations tended to emphasize the imitability of the character types they hymned. Brochures under titles such as *The Education of the Will, Shyness and How to Cure It*, and *The Fight with Idleness* began pouring from Russian mass-market presses in the late 1880s to instruct readers on how to become run-of-the-mill supermen, while exercise manuals, such as J. Müller's *My System* or D. Edwards' *The Culture of the Body*, both translated into Russian in 1909, laid down the methods by which men could attain *zakal* in the physical sense.[12] Just as after the Revolution, physical and mental control went hand-in-hand. Authors of exercise manuals emphasized that mere muscle-building was not enough, while authors of manuals on 'educating the will' asserted the triumph of mind over matter, even insisting that nocturnal emissions could be controlled through strong-mindedness.[13]

This last detail indicates the explicitness with which strength of will and masculine physiology were identified at this era. To be sure, the Russian intelligentsia's tradition of gender egalitarianism, which went back to the 1860s, sometimes meant that the rigid gender divisions of French, German, or English originals were softened in translation. In this context, it is interesting to note that the (female) translator of Jules Payot into Russian, in contrast to her (male) American counterpart, rendered a passage near the beginning of the book in gender-free terms. The English-language version reads: 'The real obstacle to work lies in a fundamental ever-present state of mind which may be called *effeminacy*, apathy, idleness, or laziness' (p. 4: my emphasis). The Russian, on the other hand, speaks of *'osnovnoe, prisushchee nam sostoianie dukha, kotoroe nikogda ne preryvaetsia, i kotoroe zovetsia vialost'iu, apatiei, len'iu, prazdnost'iu'* (p. 1: my emphasis). The gender-specific 'effeminacy' contrasts with the non-gender-specific *vialost'* (feebleness, flabbiness).[14] But such tentative attempts to preserve gender balance were undermined because translators faithfully reproduced many western manuals' insistence that women had separate and complementary roles. As a translated pamphlet called *The Secrets of Self-Control* put it: 'To demand self-control from women would not only be cruel, it would represent a total misunderstanding of their nature and destiny. The activity of a man takes place outside the home; the woman is occupied by domestic matters and the better she copes with this the more calmly she responds to the surrounding world.' In such sources, Russian readers were exposed to an especially rigid variant of the 'ideology of separate spheres', one that not only confined women to the home (as had been traditional for centuries in any case), but which permitted men only the most marginal role in domestic space (something that was rather more novel).[15]

The 'masculine' resonance of 'education of the will' and of *zakalivanie* was enhanced by the existence of a separate tradition of hygiene manuals for women, which stressed above all the need to regulate the female body's potential for pollution and insanitariness.[16] Equally, though texts aimed at women sometimes presented material on the desirability of efficiency (a piquant example was a set of guidelines on 'American behavior' set out for readers of *Ladies' World* in 1915),[17] such material was scanty and marginal compared with the quantities of brochures on 'educating the will' for men.

Given that the Russian book market was swift to respond to new interests on the part of its readers (the new craze for motoring, for instance, was humored almost immediately by the appearance of guides such as *The Automobilist*), it is reasonable to assume that the arrival of these self-help manuals reflected concerns and anxieties circulating in the public at large, an assumption also supported by the fact that several of them went through repeated editions. Particular popularity was enjoyed by a Russian translation of Jules Payot's *L'Education de la volonté*, reprinted at least nine times by 1917.[18] But what were the implications of 'educating the will', and exactly why did it become so popular in the early twentieth century?

According to their authors, self-help manuals of this kind were aimed at a specifically modern malaise: as summed up in Paul Lévy's *L'Education rationelle de la volonté*, 'the worst illness of our time is weakness of will'.[19] Payot, in similar vein, emphasized to his readers that a slough of sloth always threatened to overwhelm modern man: 'Our passiveness, thoughtfulness and dissipation of energy are only so many names to designate the depths of universal laziness, which is to human nature as gravity is to matter.'[20] As these examples suggest, pseudo-scientific terminology was ubiquitous, and undertones of Social Darwinism were often evident. In the words of one author, 'Thanks to the persistent struggle for survival, along with competitiveness and the sense that everyone has an equal right to life's benefits, a mass of inner sufferings and passions has come into being. Happy anyone who has been gifted by nature with a strong character! [*sil'nyi dukh*].'[21]

Treatises on educating the will showed those not so 'gifted by nature' how to come out winners in the 'struggle for survival', and how to cope with the psychological upheaval and pressure that were held to be side-effects of modern life. By learning to exercise will, it was proclaimed, readers would learn to take charge of their own lives.[22] The need for optimism was paramount: 'When we get up in the morning, we should always make ourselves believe: "Today is the most wonderful day of the rest of my life."'[23] (In the 1920s, Pollyanna-ish advice of this kind was to acquire its own mantra, supplied by Dr Emile Coué, whose readers were supposed to recite to themselves daily the formula 'Every day in every way I am getting better and better'. Coué's *Auto-Suggestion* was translated into Russian in 1928.)[24]

Admiration for self-assertion had its limits, however. Egotism was as much to be guarded against as pessimism. As their emphasis upon conformity made clear, the guides were aimed not so much at entrepreneurs, as at readers in white-collar employment who needed to learn how to make an impression upon subordinates, superiors, and colleagues in large organizations. In Russia, this advice was especially relevant, since hierarchical relations in private companies lacked the clarity they had in the Russian civil service, whose notoriously inflexible Table of Ranks ruled out speedy promotion for able social outsiders. The meritocratic egalitarianism of guides to acquiring 'strong will', their emphasis on the need to impose authority by personal qualities rather than by preascribed social rank, made them quite different from the treatises upon appropriate behavior for men published in Russia in the late eighteenth and early nineteenth centuries. These had also emphasized diligence and efficiency and the need for self-respect, but had asserted the importance of accepting social station as given, of deferring to superiors and condescending to inferiors.[25]

At one level, then, the cult of 'educating the will' pointed to a sea-change in perceptions of masculine honor (*chest'*), completing the move from a 'feudal' perception of identity, based on birth and family status, to a 'bourgeois', individualist one, emphasizing personal qualities, that had begun to be set in train during the Enlightenment. But this was not the only or perhaps even the main significance of the new manliness. As Robert Nye points out in his 1998 study, *Masculinity and Male Codes of Honor in Modern France*, a major preoccupation of 'new masculinity' propagandists was military success; they concerned themselves with 'the education of courage in particular, a quality additionally useful to the nation'.[26] Like France, Germany, and Britain, Russia was, at the beginning of the twentieth century, a major military power, with ambitions for territorial expansion and for the exercise of further geopolitical authority. In the wake of the humiliating defeat of the Russian Army by Japan in 1905, some of Payot's admonitions to his audience of post-Franco-Prussian-War Frenchmen must have struck a particular chord: 'A few years ago the power of the French artillery was mediocre, now it is stronger. Why? Because the shell used to explode when it struck the obstacle and would go off without doing any great damage, but now, by the invention of a special detonator, the shell, after it has struck, continues to move for a few seconds, penetrating right into the very heart of the place of attack.... In our practical education we have forgotten to add a detonator to the mind.'[27] But concern with Russia's military capacity was only part of the complex background to the reception of books on 'backbone', which in several important respects was different from that in France (if one credits Nye's description of the latter).

To begin with, the cult of manliness in Russia was more diverse and divided than was the cult of manliness in France. Nye argues for the essential endurance of a code of honor going back to medieval times, which 'survived the destruction of the Old Regime in 1789 by accommodating its practices and usages to the unique sociability and legal arrangements of bourgeois civilization'. This code of honor was remarkably constrictive: 'The men who submitted themselves to the sexual prescriptions and the social rituals of the honor code felt themselves enmeshed in a fatally narrow circle of alternatives.' One result was that duels continued to be taken seriously in France for considerably longer than they did in comparable countries (Britain or America): 'The passion for duelling increased after 1850 when the nation made democratic and libertarian advances that far outpaced other continental countries that conserved the duel.' In a culture which saw the duel as a contribution to the defense of the nation as well as a demonstration of personal valor, and where duels were used against political opponents, as a response to supposed slights by journalists, and even as a way in which French Jews could defend themselves against charges of being unfit for public life, a failure to respond to a challenge was something that only bohemian eccentrics, such as the writer Joséphin Péladan, could afford without cost to their reputation.[28]

In Russia, on the other hand, the practice of duelling had a much more ambiguous status. It was not simply another expression of the same code of 'manliness' that treatises upon 'educating the will' sought to inculcate. To be sure, some commentators on duelling in Russia have argued exactly along Nye's lines and have asserted that, while the participants in duels may have changed, regard for the custom did not, remaining very high even in the early twentieth century. In the words of Irina Reyfman, 'duelling did not disappear even when its original proponents, the nobility [that is, the *dvorianstvo*] had forfeited the cultural foreground. The duel's high status, established at the beginning of the nineteenth century, survived almost intact until 1917 and, in a certain sense, until the present.'[29] But interpretations of this kind ignore the fact that the duel's persistence into the twentieth century was partly the result of a *revival* of the practice in the late nineteenth and early twentieth centuries. The background to this was the tsarist administration's attempt to broaden the social base for the recruitment of army officers while at the same time preserving intact the ethos of the 'officer and gentleman', an attempt that was entirely characteristic of the contradictory commitment to economic modernization on the one hand and political conservatism on the other, which characterized the governments of Alexander III and Nicholas II. The egalitarian impact of D. A. Miliutin's military reforms in the 1860s, which had emphasized the importance of education and training, was averted by a policy 'promoting norms of officer behavior that were at least theoretically "aristocratic"'.[30] One of these norms was duelling. In 1894 it became incumbent upon officers to fight duels (despite the fact that these were still forbidden by criminal law)[31] in defense of their 'military honor', and tribunals of senior officers (*ofitserskie sobraniia*), later known as courts of honor (*sudy chesti*), were mandated to regulate the practice and to determine when a duel was necessary. Duels were obligatory 'even where the officers concerned did not feel that their honor had been insulted'.[32] Failure to fight a duel when one was ordered by a court of honor was punishable by dismissal from the service.[33]

This is not to say that duelling was a sort of cultural 'dead letter', a proof of valor recognized in the mind of the Russian military and bureaucratic establishment, but nowhere else. An indication to the contrary is the case of Aleksei Suvorin, the editor of the conservative newspaper *Novoe vremia*, who, in 1911, was incited to fury when a general whom he had attempted to call out was decreed not subject to challenge by the General Staff.[34] Given that the concept of 'challengeability' (*pravosposobnost'* or *duelesposobnost'*) was now thought by most commentators to be determined by a man's level of 'culturedness' (*kul'turnost'*) rather than by his social status (the estate, *soslovie*, to which he belonged), duelling had a democratic propensity that it had lacked in early nineteenth-century Russia and still lacked in contemporary Germany.[35] However, even officially sponsored duels involving army officers were not particularly common. Between 1894 and 1910, about 20 per year were fought (a total of 322 in 16 years), not a significant number given that there were over 35 000 officers on active duty.[36] Cases when officers risked dismissal by failing to fight duels, or subverted the process by fighting sham duels, were fairly numerous, and the fact that more than 27 percent of duels ended in serious injury or death undermined the authorities' pedagogical purpose from a different direction (the imposition of duelling as a corporative responsibility had been meant to produce responsible and comradely officers, not invalids or dead heroes).[37]

Official sponsorship, then, was less than wholly successful in popularizing the well-regulated form of duelling (a test of valor rather than a fight to the death) that the military high command had in mind. The proper procedures – the need to consult courts of honor, to maintain minutes (*protokoly*) of meetings between antagonists, to agree upon precisely which duelling code (*duel'nyi kodeks*) was to be used, and, not least, to be punctual upon all occasions – were long drawn out and laborious.[38] It is reasonable to suppose that the promotion of officers' duels in this bureaucratic form did little to enhance the status of the duel among educated civilian Russians opposed to the regime, who took the perniciousness of bureaucratic regulation for granted. Oppositional intellectuals were in any case heirs to a tradition of suspicion of, or even contempt for, duelling stretching back to at least the 1840s. The unease with regard to duelling that is evident in Lermontov's *A Hero of Our Time* (in which the hero Pechorin's honor is called into question by the fact that his opponent is so nonentious) had, by the late nineteenth century, been transformed into a widespread conviction that the practice was shameful and preposterous.[39] To be sure, literary figures occasionally indulged in duels (most famously in the case of Maksimilian Voloshin and Nikolai Gumilev, who fought over the pseudonymous poetess 'Cherubina de Gabriak'); but this was a peculiar and marginal phenomenon, derived from these writers' cult of the Pushkin era, upon whose mores they self-consciously modeled themselves, rather than an expression of intelligentsia passions more generally.[40] More typical was Kuprin's 1905 story *The Duel*, an excoriation of cynicism, brutality, and corruption in the Russian army, where refusal to fight was represented as a more honorable mode of conduct than compliance with the stipulations of the ridiculous 'court of honor'; or a lurid painting by Il'ya Repin, showing an injured man tended by friends, his opponent quivering to his right, while a haughty young blood, clearly the galvanizing force behind the encounter, smoked defiantly in the background.[41]

Rather than assimilating the new cult of 'backbone' into earlier models of valor, then, the typical Russian intellectual drew a sharp division between the old and the new. An intriguing illustration of this comes in Chekhov's play *Three Sisters* (1901). One of the opponents in the fatal duel that takes place in Act IV, Solenyi, is a grotesque caricature of the early nineteenth-century *bretteur* (ardent duellist); the other, Baron Tusenbach, is the most spineless, if also the most amiable, of the male characters. The fact that it is precisely the unmanly Tusenbach who has a valorous death thrust upon him calls into question the association between duelling and honor that was essential to the military cult of the practice. For official apologists of the duel, such as I. Mikulin, the custom was an external manifestation of internal honor, or 'conscience'.[42] Intelligentsia critics, on the other hand, invoked a distinction between 'honor' in an external sense (status, as preserved by the duel) and 'honor' in an internal sense (conscience) that had been central to western arguments against duelling since at least the seventeenth century.[43]

Hostility to the duel was exacerbated by the determination of early twentieth-century Russian *intelligenty* to jettison established practices that were seen as exemplifying the country's 'backwardness' (*otstalost'*). Conversely, the tendency to perceive self-transformation on the part of workers as a prerequisite of economic success (or, as Nye has put it, to understand the 'corporeal economy' as 'a metaphor for the larger problem of the vitality and prospects of the industrial order')[44] was fostered by the widespread tendency to perceive unmasculine flabbiness and pernicious self-indulgence as Russian national characteristics. For example, L. A. Zolotarev, in his *The Battle with Idleness*, argued that the most 'cultured' (*kul'turnye*) nations (Britain, France, Germany, and the Jewish community in Russia) were also those characterized by the highest levels of hard work. This industriousness was incompatible with a penchant for alcohol or illicit sexual activity, to both of which, he implied, Russian readers were sadly prone.[45] It was frequently argued that qualities such as 'empty dreaming' (*mechtatel'nost'*) or 'passivity' (*passivnost'*) must be jettisoned if society was to be remodeled – as in an essay by Zinaida Stolitsa on the 'fight with pessimism', that singled out the 'characterlessness' and 'instability' of Russian life as factors inhibiting the development of 'joy in life' and contributing to social malaise, as manifested, for instance, by the high rate of suicide among young people.[46]

Anxieties over Russian social passivity were nothing new in themselves: from the 1840s, they had crystallized in the literary cliché of the superfluous man (*lishnii chelovek*). But the *lishnii chelovek* took on a new lease of life and a new resonance during the late nineteenth century. Where earlier generations had seen 'superfluity' as the product of social forces (an illustration of the indolence fostered in the Russian *dvorianstvo* by serfdom), by the turn of the century it was usually perceived as a manifestation of a typically 'Russian' innate slothfulness. In the words of D. A. Ovsianniko-Kulikovskii:

> 'The superfluous man' is created by the interaction of two factors which can be present anywhere and under very different conditions of social life. The first is a person's poor psychic organization, whether inherited or acquired, which is expressed in an insufficiency

> of spiritual energy, flabbiness [*vialost'*] of feeling and thought, in an incapacity for steady and well-directed work, in an absence of initiative. . . . The second factor is an intellectual and moral disharmony between the individual personality and his environment. . . . Sometimes just one of the above factors is enough to make a man 'superfluous'. But it seems that the interaction of the two is essential if a whole group or type of 'superfluous men' is to come into existence. . . . A man who has large quantities of spiritual energy will find it possible to live an intellectual existence even if he is wholly out of harmony with his environment.[47]

To be sure, the pervasiveness of anxieties about 'poor psychic organization' and the widespread adulation directed at 'spiritual energy' did not mean that *zakal* was a universally accepted ideal. The British historian Bernard Pares, a frequent visitor to Russia in the 1910s, recorded in his memoirs, with a degree of humorous condescension, that the Russian intellectuals whom he met often felt hostile towards the success ethos, and demonstrated their attachment toward 'personal self-respect' everywhere, even on the tennis court:

> Anyone who was successful in so bad a world, nearly all of which was directly or indirectly official, was concluded to be inevitably mean and time-serving. The respect of the public went to those who lived in constant protest. . . . There was an amazing lack of what we regard as the main elements of character – stability, purpose, consistency. Again, mood dominated, and judgment went by whether the mood was 'noble'. One never ceased to hear this word 'noble' (*blagorodno*). Where no public standards were accepted, the individual felt that he must have his personal self-respect. This, no doubt, is simple enough, but it took forms that were at once childlike and absurd. A boy playing tennis served every other ball into the net because a soft service would not be 'blagorodno', but he did not happen to have thought that this was hardly 'blagorodno' to his partner.[48]

'Stability, purpose, consistency' were, then, sometimes considered part of a rather vulgar, success-driven ethos alien to Russian society; the celebration of conformist goal-orientation to be found in depictions of 'willpower' could provoke an assertion of 'personal honor' in the sense of grand gestures of self-sacrifice. The behavior depicted in Pares's anecdote had a more elevated counterpart in the assertion, among some of the Russian Symbolists, of the same 'empty dreaming' inveighed against by propaganda for backbone.[49]

Yet whatever their protective feelings about their own right to passive contemplation and to self-abnegation, adult men were often determined that boys, at least, should be exposed to new behavior patterns and absorb the virtues of a new kind of manhood. Though a book on the 'education of character' translated into Russian in 1888 argued that a father should take care to be gentle ('It is bad when children fear their father'), it also argued that he should at all costs bear in mind the need to inculcate manliness: 'One must make use of every opportunity in order to teach him [i.e. one's son] genuine virile courage [*istinnoe muzhestvo*].' Essential were 'exercises in order to temper him like steel [*uprazhneniia v zakalenie*]', the target of which was to 'stamp out the natural instinct of cowardice'.[50] An example of a native Russian text adopting this sort of pedagogical attitude is a poem written by the tsarist schoolmaster and modernist poet Innokentii Annenskii to his step-grandson Valerii Khmara-Barshchevskii, then aged about 12:

> Wherever you stand on the ship,
> By the mast or in the bows,
> Always serve your motherland well:
> She reared and raised you.
>
> Our road is hard, our road is uneven.
> Whether we have waves or ruts to cross
> Be patient and be valorous,
> But never crow over the weak.
>
> Having begun the fight, do not retreat,
> If you must make payment, do so,
> And if you have to sing, do so like a bird,
> Freely, musically, and bravely.

There is a striking contrast between the calm didacticism with which Annenskii sets out this 'Victorian' code for his schoolboy step-grandson and his use elsewhere in his verse of a lyric voice characterized by hesitancy and uncertainty, a 'decadent' persona. It is partly explicable by a polarization (typical in early twentieth-century Russian social commentators) between a *fin-de-siècle* despair over the capacities of adults, who were supposedly too exhausted to achieve serious social change, and an optimistic conviction of the promise offered by young people, who were destined to be the salvation of the *nachalo veka* (beginning of the century, but also, dawn of the new age). Whatever their personal distaste for 'backbone', many middle-aged Russians were determined to see it inculcated in the younger generation and most particularly in male members of that generation.

After the Revolution, commitment to character-building became still more widespread. Not only was propaganda for *zakal* a central element in prophylactic health literature and in manuals of self-improvement, but official Soviet novels, such as Anna Karavaeva's *The Saw-Mill* (1927) often depended on facile polarizations between men of action and weak-willed *intelligenty* of the old 'dreamer' type. And while Maiakovskii's work includes some notably ironic treatments of the 'tough manhood' construct (for example, the opening of *I Love*, which pillories a middle-aged man, 'waving his arms like a windmill to Müller's instructions' [*muzhchina po-Miulleru mel'nikom mashetsia*]), such moments of hesitation or doubt were offset by vehement expressions of commitment to self-discipline and resolution (a striking example being the finale to Maiakovskii's elegy for a fellow poet, 'To Sergei Esenin' [1925]).[51] Now that *zakal* had become an expression of 'Soviet patriotism' and a manifestation of commitment to utopian collectivism, it was accessible to 'dreamer' intellectuals who would have found *zakal* unacceptable in a context of capitalist self-advancement. Soviet 'revolutionary romanticism', as expressed in, say, the cult of *turizm* (hiking and mountain-climbing), was a brilliant fusion of the Slavophile myth of Russia as a country of northern asceticism and capacity for endurance, peasant respect for toughness and physical strength, and ideas and techniques drawn from the hygienic and psychological literature on 'educating the will' that had filtered into popular culture before 1917.

There was a defensive coloration to this 'Soviet patriotism' too. The knowledge that the country had emerged from the First World War as a defeated power, and that Soviet rule had with difficulty survived a vicious and divisive civil war, ingrained the association between national self-assertion, military preparedness, and the inculcation of 'courage' and 'will' in the Soviet population.[52] Such a 'survivalist' understanding of *zakal* was characteristic of at least some Russian émigrés as well as Soviet citizens, expressing itself especially in the socialization of young boys. Illuminating, in this regard, is Nina Berberova's tiny vignette of life in the household of the famous writer Vladimir Nabokov:

> Nabokov took a huge boxing glove and handed it to [his son Dmitri], telling him to show me what he could do. The boy put the glove on and started to hit Nabokov on the face as hard as his childish

> strength would let him. I could see that Nabokov was in some pain, but he smiled and put up with it. It was physical and moral training [*trenirovka*] – for him and for the boy.[53]

Despite fervently abominating 'the notion that small boys, in order to be delightful, should hate to wash and love to kill',[54] Nabokov remained convinced that some other traditional attributes of masculinity – physical and mental toughness – were crucial goals of a male child's upbringing. This conviction was neither eccentric nor marginal; movements such as 'Sokol', clubs training young men in militaristically colored gymnastics, and Baden-Powell scouting had much greater weight in the Russian emigration than they had had before the Revolution.[55]

The tribulations that Russians endured during the second two decades of the twentieth century were not the only force behind the persistence of belief in *zakal*. During the First World War, shell-shock was not a 'cultural fact' in Russia in the same way that it was in the West. Though battle trauma was the subject of specialist discussions in psychiatric journals, its resonance in the arts and in intellectual discourse more generally was limited at best.[56] The ideal of the perfectly resolute male survived because there was not yet a sense of circumstances to which that ideal was inadequate. It was only when the Second World War brought 'total war' in the modern sense to Russian soil, and when success proved to emerge from a very different kind of endurance from that propagandized in 'willpower' literature,[57] that *zakalennost'* and the cult of backbone started to lose their dominance in Soviet life. Both during and after the war, mythology emphasized the role of civilians (including women and children) in combatting the enemy; after victory was achieved, the images used to commemorate it were statues of the suffering 'Mother Russia', or burnt-out tanks on pedestals, rather than the heroic male fighters with guns portrayed on revolutionary monuments or memorials to the Civil War. While still seen as a virtue in men, especially young ones, and as an essential of physical health, *zakal* was now allocated a much more constricted niche in Soviet culture generally, its loss of symbolic force both a symptom of and a contribution towards the 'de-Sovietization' of behavior models that was such a notable feature of the decades after Stalin's death.[58]

Conclusion

This chapter has argued for the pervasiveness of a cult of 'manly resolve' in late nineteenth- and early twentieth-century Russia and for the widespread acceptance of a model of masculine behavior that was quite different from the early nineteenth-century ideal of *chest'* (honor or *honnêté*). There were striking resemblances between Russian models of masculinity and those current in France under the Third Republic, Wilhelmine Germany, or indeed late Victorian and Edwardian Britain. Kipling's poem 'If'[59] had its counterpart (admittedly a fairly downbeat one) in the poem by Innokentii Annenskii quoted here. However, if the *content* of masculine behavior models – notably their emphasis upon 'strong will', 'character', and 'backbone' – was consistent across Europe, there were important differences in terms of the models' location within broader cultural patterns. In France and Germany, duelling continued to have social weight right up to the First World War; in Britain, it had all but vanished by the mid-nineteenth century; in Russia, official attempts to revive the practice in the late Imperial era were at best partially successful. And in Russia, unlike France, the cult of 'willpower' did not graft itself easily on to an earlier notion of valor, but became associated with a commitment to transforming the 'backwardness' held to characterize traditional Russian culture. If citizens managed to transform themselves, so the reasoning went, Russia would throw off her traditional 'flabbiness' and 'backwardness' and be ready to lead the world. This belief persisted into the Soviet period, at which point the ideal of 'manly resolve' began to be propagandized to a much wider audience and became directly associated with the authority of the new regime and of its servants. It was only after the Second World War, most particularly in the post-Stalinist era, when the cult of *zakal* began to retreat from symbolic centrality, a process linked with a muting of *zakal*'s moral associations in favor of its hygienic ones and also with a crisis of confidence among many Soviet men themselves.

Notes

I wish to express my gratitude to the British Academy, which has generously supported research for the larger project on which this essay is based, *Refining Russia: Advice Literature, Polite Culture, and Gender from Catherine to Yeltsin* (Oxford University Press, 2001) by means of a Personal Research Grant in 1996 and places on the Academic Exchange with the Russian Academy of Sciences in 1997 and 1998.

1. This socialization by means of institutions is depicted, for example, in Fedor Gladkov's novel *Cement*, while *zakalivanie* in the second sense is the subject of Nikolai Ostrovskii's Soviet classic *How the Steel was Tempered* (1935).
2. See, for example, *Soviet Preschool Education*, vol. 1 (Program of Instruction) (no translator credited), (New York, 1969), 52, 77–8, 136–7.

3. Not only teachers, but also parents, were supposed to inculcate this in children. See ibid., 38, 76–8, 103, and also the model daily schedules for children of various ages, 175–82.
4. See, for example, L. G. Gol'dfail', *Lechenie vodoi doma, na kurorte i v lechebnom uchrezhdenii* (Moscow and Leningrad, 1930); V. V. Gorinevskii, *Remont i zakalivanie organizma* (Moscow, 1925); A. N. Studitskii, 'Nauchnye osnovy zakalivaniia', *Rabotnitsa*, no. 6 (1947), 12–13.
5. A. K. Toporkov, *Kak stat' kul'turnym* (Moscow, 1929), 83.
6. See, for example, A. L. Mendel'son, *Zastenchivost' i bor'ba s neiu*, 4th edn (Leningrad, 1930); P. Razmyslov, 'O vospitanii voli u detei', *Rabotnitsa*, no. 3 (1948), 13; *Pamiatka turista: gigiena i samokontrol'* (Moscow, 1951).
7. See, for example, the character testimonial (*attestatsiia*) for P. N. Sokol'chuk in V. Zenzinov (ed.), *Vstrecha s Rossiei* (New York, 1944), 584–5; epitaph from grave of V. A. Kolosov (1925–1957).
8. A. Gaidar, *Timur i ego komanda*, in *Sochineniia* (Moscow, 1946), 265–98. For Lenin as a model of *zakal*, see, for example, Mikhail Zoshchenko's 'Stories about Lenin' (1940), and S. Mirev, 'Kogda zhe on spit?', *Rabotnitsa*, no. 1 (1947); on Chernyshevskii as a glorious example of 'resolute behavior and capacity to affect one's environment [*sreda*]' see, for example, A. Studentsov, *Chernyshevskii o samoobrazovanii* (Penza, 1928), 5–6.
9. See Véronique Garros, Natalia Korenevskaia, and Thomas Lahusen (eds.), *Intimacy and Terror: Soviet Diaries of the 1930s* (New York, 1995), 264; and J. Hellbeck, 'Fashioning the Stalinist Soul: the Diary of Stepan Podlubnyi', *Stalinism: New Directions* (London, 2000), 100: 'the New Man . . . was a politically inclined individual with a materialistic world-view, who in his character displayed firmness and determination'.
10. The term 'backbone' (*khrebet*) is apparently not used for moral toughness. By the late nineteenth century, *zakal* had come into use as an abstract noun. V. I. Dal', *Tolkovyi slovar' zhivogo velikorusskogo iazyka*, 2nd edn (Moscow, 1880–2), 1, 582, records the meanings 'quality' (of steel) and 'a person toughened by severe conditions'. Chekhov's story 'Neschast'e' uses the word in this meaning, for instance.
11. Robert Bage, *Hermsprong, or Man as he is Not*, 2 vols (London, 1794); N. Chernyshevskii, *Chto delat'?* (1862), ch. 3, sections 29–30 (see his *Sobranie sochinenii v 3 tomakh* [Leningrad, 1978], 1, 275–319; F. M. Dostoevskii, *Prestuplenie i nakazanie* (1866) in *Polnoe sobranie sochinenii v 30 tomakh* (Leningrad, 1972–90), vol. 6 (Leningrad, 1973).
12. P. Lévy [as Levi], *Ratsional'noe vospitanie voli: Prakticheskoe rukovodstvo k dukhovnomu samolecheniiu i samovospitaniiu* (St Petersburg, 1912) (from *L'Education de la volonté* [Paris, 1898]); A. L. Dugas [as Diuga], *Zastenchivost' i ee lechenie* (St Petersburg, 1899) (from *La Timidité, étude psychologique et morale* (Paris, 1898); L. A. Zolotarev, *Bor'ba s len'iu* (Moscow, 1907); J. P. Müller (as I. P. Miller), *Moia sistema: 15 minut ezhednevnoi raboty dlia zdorov'ia* (St Petersburg, 1909) (from the English version of the Danish original, *My System: Fifteen Minutes' Work a Day for Health Sake* [London, 1905]); D. Edvards, *Ideal'naia kul'tura tela. Naibolee vernye i deistvitel'no obezpechivaiushchie zdorov'e uprazhneniia dlia kazhdogo cheloveka* (St Petersburg, n.d. [c. 1910]).
13. Lévy, *Ratsional'noe vospitanie*, 174–5.
14. The original French has *mollesse* ('softness') (see J. Payot, *L'Education de la*

volonté [Paris, 1895], 3). At least two of the Russian translators of Kipling's poetic celebration of 'backbone', 'If' ('If you can force your heart and nerve and sinew/To serve your turn long after they are gone/And so hold on where there is nothing in you/Except the Will which says to them 'Hold on!'/ . . . Yours is the earth and everything that's in it/And – which is more – you'll be a Man, my son!') rendered the word 'man' as the gender-neutral *chelovek*. (See the versions by M. Lozinskii and by S. Marshak in R. Kipling, *Stikhotvoreniia* [St Petersburg, 1994], 423–5, 468–9.) And women writers (for example, Zinaida Stolitsa in her brochure *Razvitie u detei zhizneradostnosti i bor'ba s pessimizmom* [St Petersburg and Moscow, 1912]) contributed to the stream of texts pronouncing on the need for backbone (for Stolitsa, too, the children who were to be 'cured' of pessimism included girls as well as boys).

15. *** Berndt [no first name given], *Sekret samoobladaniia, ili lechenie strastei i dushevnykh stradanii*, trans. Dm. Kriuchkov (St Petersburg, 1910), 44. The earliest domestic manuals all over Europe were addressed to men. See, for example, *The Goodman of Paris*, trans. Eileen Power (London, 1928) (the sixteenth-century Russian *Domostroi* accords with this tradition). But later manuals advocated a division of responsibilities within the household, an appreciation that was evident in late eighteenth- and early nineteenth-century translations from French and German into Russian (see, for example, V. Levshin, *Polnaia khoziaistvennaia kniga, otnosiashchaiasia do vnutrennego domovodstva kak gorodskikh, tak i derevenskikh zhitelei, khoziaev i khozaek. V desiati chastiakh, s risunkami. Sochinenie Vasil'ia Levshina* [Moscow, 1813]). Nationalist conservatives such as the so-called Slavophile group were later to make the domestic idyll based upon a division of labor a foundation stone of their eulogisation of *russkii byt* (Russian daily life). For a discussion of this, see ch. 2 of my *Refining Russia*.
16. On this see ch. 2 of *Refining Russia*.
17. See *Kalendar' 'Damskii mir' na 1915 god* (St Petersburg, 1915), 255.
18. This information is based on the General Catalog of the Russian State Library in Moscow, which has the fullest holdings of Russian advice literature anywhere.
19. Lévy, *Ratsional'noe vospitanie*, 101.
20. J. Payot, *The Education of the Will: the Theory and Practice of Self-Culture*, trans. S. E. Jeliffe (from the 30th French edn) (New York, 1909), 3; Payot [as Zh. Peio], *Vospitanie voli*, trans. M. Shishmareva, 6th edn (St Petersburg, 1910), 1.
21. Berndt, *Sekret samoobladaniia*, 5.
22. Lévy, *Ratsional'noe vospitanie*, 133.
23. T. Maingard, *Lichnoe vliianie, ili zakony dukhovnogo obladaniia. Sila vnutri nas. Rukovodstvo k pribuzhdeniiu i pol'zovaniiu tainstvennymi dushevnymi silami (piat' chastei prakticheskoi psikhologii dlia sovremennogo delovogo cheloveka)*, 11th edn (Saratov, 1910), 48.
24. E. Coué [as Kue], *Shkola samoobladaniia putem soznatel'nogo (prednamerennogo) samovnusheniia* (Nizhnii Novgorod, 1928).
25. See, for example, J. Grabiensky, *Conseils d'un ami à un jeune homme qui entre dans le monde* (Berlin, 1760), translated into Russian as *Druzheskie sovety molodomu cheloveku, nachinaiushchemu zhit' v svete*, 2nd edn (Moscow, 1765).

26. Robert A. Nye, *Masculinity and Male Codes of Honor in Modern France*, 2nd edn (Berkeley, 1998), 224.
27. Payot, *The Education of the Will*, 17; Payot, *Vospitanie voli*, 7. Note that 'the French artillery' is rendered in the Russian as '*nasha artilleriia*', that is, '*our* artillery'.
28. Nye, *Masculinity*, 8, 11, 135.
29. Irina Reyfman, 'The Emergence of the Duel in Russia: Corporal Punishment and the Honor Code', *Russian Review*, 54 (1995), 26. See also the same writer's *Ritualized Violence Russian Style: the Duel in Russian Culture and Literature* (Stanford, 1999).
30. W. C. Fuller, Jr., *Civil-Military Conflict in Imperial Russia, 1881–1914* (Princeton, 1985), 22–3.
31. Penalties for participation in duels ranged from 3 to 7 days for issuing a challenge, through 3 weeks to 3 months for fighting a duel if no injury took place, up to 2 to 6 years for the surviving participant if he killed his opponent. These penalties were significantly lighter than those imposed for murder, which, from 1871, carried a penalty of up to 20 years if premeditated and at least 4 years whatever the circumstances. (See *Entsiklopedicheskii slovar' Brokgauza i Efrona* vol. 34 [St Petersburg, 1902], 400.) According to I. Mikulin, *Sud chesti i duel' v voiskakh Rossiiskoi Imperii. . . . Nastol'naia kniga dlia ofitserov vsekh rodov oruzhiia*, 2 parts, 2nd edn (St Petersburg, 1912), 1, 77, after 1868 (when there had been inconclusive discussions about reducing the penalties for duelling) the authorities often avoided imposing the punishments that existed. The process in Germany went exactly the opposite way: a ruling of 1897 discouraged officers from duelling, and from that date courts of honor generally did their best to reconcile antagonists, rather than commanding them to fight. (See M. Kitchen, *The German Officer Corps, 1890–1914* [Oxford, 1968], 55.)
32. Paul Robinson, 'Always with Honor: the Code of the White Russian Officers', *Canadian Slavonic Papers*, 41, no. 2 (June 1999), 121–41. My thanks to Dr Robinson for letting me have a copy of this paper in advance of publication.
33. See *Polnoe sobranie zakonov Rossiiskoi Imperii*, 10618, 13 May 1894, vol. 14, 258–9; *Voinskii ustav o nakazaniiakh i Ustav distsiplinarnyi*, 3rd edn (St Petersburg, 1906), 170, supplement to article 130. The basic brief of the *ofitserskie sobraniia* was to try 'officers who have been found out in unbecoming behavior, or in acts which, though not forbidden by criminal law, are not in harmony with the concepts of military honor and the personal honor [*doblest'*] of an officer, or which reveal in an officer an absence of respect for the rules of moral and noble behavior'. See ibid., article 130, 163; P. A. Shveikovskii, *Sud chesti i Duel' v voiskakh Rossiiskoi Armii: Deistvuiushchee zakonodatel'stvo so vsemi kommentariiami. Nastol'naia kniga dlia ofitserov vsekh rodov oruzhiia*, ed. N. P. Vishniakov, 3rd edn (St Petersburg, 1912), 17–18; Mikulin, *Sud chesti*, 1, 97.
34. Suvorin had duelled with General Pykhachev of the Border Guards when the latter took exception to a letter in which Suvorin accused Pykhachev's brother officer General Martynov of *korystnye mery* (self-interest, a euphemism for bribery). Both participants were punished, Suvorin by a week in prison for 'intemperate language' (*rezkie vyrazheniia*), Pykhachev by a fine. Unable to bring Martynov to book by other means, Suvorin then challenged

him; the two agreed to duel but were prevented when the military command decreed that for generals 'honor was a personal, not a corporative, concept'. (See A. A. Suvorin, *Duel'nyi kodeks* [St Petersburg, 1912], 198–263.) Suvorin himself was challenged to a duel around this time by the impeccably liberal politician V. D. Nabokov, who had been enraged by a 'scurrilous piece' in *Novoe vremia* and called out the editor because he considered 'the well-known rascality of the actual author of the article made him "non-duelable" (*neduelesposobnyi*).' This duel, however, was averted by Suvorin's apology. (See Vladimir Nabokov, *Speak, Memory* [Harmondsworth, 1969], 147: the identity of Suvorin, not given here, is clear from the Russian edn of the text, *Drugie berega*.)

35. V. V. Durasov, *Duel'nyi kodeks*, 4th edn (St Petersburg, 1912), 13, article 4, stated, 'Duels are only possible between people of equal, which is to say gentle [*blagorodnoe*], birth.' However, Suvorin, *Duel'nyi kodeks*, 36, article 138 (1), related 'challengeability' to a man's 'cultural levels'; banned from duelling were 'persons who do not have a sufficient level of culturedness, according to the demands of today's society'. And Mikulin, *Sud chesti*, part 2, 28, article 100, made a man's 'level of culture' (*uroven' kul'tury*) and his 'position in society' (*polozhenie v obshchestve*) equally important. The appendix of sample decisions for courts of honor included several cases involving an imaginary 'Dvorianin B', who was deemed challengeable in most circumstances, but not, however, if he happened to be in some abject form of employment ('Dvorianin B, working as a doorman at the Bol'shaia Morskaia Hotel', 135), or still worse, discreditably unemployed ('Dvorianin B, a street tramp and beggar' [ibid.]). On the persistence of rigid notions of *Satisfaktionsfähigkeit* in Germany, see Kitchen, *The German Officer Corps*, 54.
36. See Mikulin, *Sud chesti*, Appendix to vol. 1, 177–203, Tables 1 and 2. For the size of the officer corps, see Fuller, *Civil-Military Conflict*, 25.
37. There were 15 deaths 1894–1910, meaning that nearly 1 duel in 20 had a fatal outcome. See Mikulin, *Sud chesti*, Appendix to vol. 1, 177–203, Tables 1 and 2.
38. See the duelling codes on all these. However, A. Vostrikov, *Kniga o russkoi dueli* (St Petersburg, 1998), goes too far in the note to plate 6 (after 64), showing Durasov, *Duel'nyi kodeks*, where he comments: 'Let us not forget that those who engaged in duelling did not read these books', since at least some certainly did use them. For instance, Suvorin records (*Duel'nyi kodeks*, 207) that he and General Martynov agreed to use the Durasov code for their meeting.
39. Take, for instance, Turgenev's *Fathers and Children* or Chekhov's story 'The Duel'. It was not only liberal commentators of this kind who rejected duelling. Conservatives such as the Slavophiles considered the practice foreign to Russian culture (see Aleksei Khomiakov's comment on Pushkin's duel, 'there was no decent cause for it': letter to N. M. Iazykov, February 1837, quoted in V. Veresaev (ed.), *Pushkin v zhizni* [Moscow, 1984], 636). Among women conservatives, the employment of the practice as a way of defending women's honor was seen as endorsing female self-indulgence (as in Karolina Pavlova's narrative poem *Quadrille*, 1859).
40. Reyfman, 'The Emergence', 26, n. 1, argues that 'the curiously enthusiastic treatment given to it by modern Russian historians' is 'one sign of the duel's

lasting prestige'. I would argue that, on the contrary, this 'enthusiasm' is the product of two factors of local significance in Soviet cultural history of the Thaw period, the first of which is the cult of the early nineteenth century that began in the 1960s, initiated by writings such as Okudzhava's novels and the semiotic studies of Iurii Lotman, and the second of which is the search for alternative models of masculinity that was provoked by official Soviet propaganda against deviant male behavior. For a more detailed exposure of these two points, see Chapter 5 of my *Refining Russia*.

41. See A. Kuprin, *Poedinok*, in *Sobranie sochinenii v 7 tomakh* (Moscow, 1964), 4, 5–231; the Repin canvas, *Duel'* (1913), is in the Muzei chastnykh sobranii in Moscow.
42. See Mikulin, *Sud chesti*, 15.
43. See, for example, Trotti de la Chetardie, *Instructions pour un jeune seigneur ou l'idée d'un galant homme* (Paris, 1683) (translated into Russian by Ivan Murav'ev as *Nastavlenie znatnomu cheloveku, ili Voobrazhenie o svetskom cheloveke* [St Petersburg, 1778]).
44. Nye, *Masculinity*, 222. See also Anson Rabinbach, *The Human Motor: Energy, Fatigue, and the Origins of Modernity* (New York, 1990); A. Gastev, *Trudovye ustanovki* (Moscow and Leningrad, 1924).
45. See L. A. Zolotarev, *Bor'ba s len'iu* (Moscow, 1907), esp. 35, 45, 46, 100.
46. See Stolitsa, *Razvitie u detei zhizneradostnosti*, esp. 43.
47. D. A. Ovsianniko-Kulikovskii, *Istoriia russkoi intelligentsii: Sobranie sochinenii*, vol. 7, part 1 (St Petersburg, 1914), 91. Contrast, for example, N. Dobroliubov, 'Chto takoe oblomovshchina', *Sobranie sochinenii v 10 tomakh* (Moscow and Leningrad, 1962), 4, 307–43.
48. Bernard Pares, *My Russian Memoirs* (London, 1931), 41.
49. See, for example, Andrei Belyi's journal *Zapiski mechtatelei*, whose first issue (published in 1919) carried an editorial statement asserting that the basis for a new reality would be 'a collective of dreamers'.
50. See A. Marten, *O vospitanii kharaktera*, trans. V. Reviakin (Moscow, 1888), 398.
51. On Maiakovskii and masculinity, see esp. C. Cavanagh, 'Whitman, Mayakovsky, and the Body Politic', *Rereading Russian Poetry*, ed. Stefanie Sandler (New Haven, 1999), 202–22.
52. One could compare the rise of militaristic aggressive manliness in 1930s Germany, where, as in Russia, the health and body cult had an ideological centrality that it did not in Britain or France. In these last two countries, it was institutionalized largely in the construction of open-air swimming pools and other comparatively 'frivolous' sites of physical culture and was often the preserve of marginal social groups, many of a radical or libertarian coloration.
53. N. Berberova, *Kursiv moi: avtobiografiia* (Moscow, 1996), 375.
54. Nabokov, *Speak, Memory*, 233. On the writer's horror when a biographer suggested he had told his son to 'spit on the flowers that look like Hitler faces', see letter to A. Field of 8 August, 1973 in V. Nabokov, *Selected Letters 1940–1977*, ed. D. Nabokov and M. J. Bruccoli (London, 1991), 517.
55. This argument is advanced by M. Raeff in *Russian Abroad: a Cultural History of the Russian Emigration, 1919–1939* (New York, 1990), 54; for brief details of these movements and the Vitiaz group, see M. Gorboff, *La Russie fantôme* (Paris, 1995), 114–15.

56. On shell shock in the West and its detrimental effects upon traditional views of masculine identity, see Elaine Showalter, 'Rivers and Sassoon: the Inscription of Male Gender Anxieties', *Behind the Lines: Gender and the Two World Wars*, ed. Margaret Higonnet et al. (New Haven, 1987), 61–70; Eric Leed, *No Man's Land: Combat and Identity in World War One* (Cambridge, 1979). On the psychiatric literature concerning battle trauma in Russia, see C. Merridale, 'The Collective Mind: Trauma and Shell-Shock in Twentieth-Century Russia', *Journal of Contemporary History*, 35, no. 1 (2000), 41–2. Merridale points out that even psychiatric discussion ceased soon after the Russian Revolution; I am not aware of a single significant Russian work of art (comparable, say, with the poetry of Wilfred Owen or Georg Trakl) inspired by the experience of shell shock.
57. Merridale, 'The Collective Mind', 48–50, convincingly argues for the importance to the Soviet consciousness of a myth of 'unshakable moral resilience' as a reason for war victory. However, this is not the same thing as *zakal* in the sense of machine-like efficiency and unreflective resolution.
58. For instance, a manual for Soviet conscripts, *Poleznye sovety voinu*, 3rd edn (Moscow, 1975), 347–9, has a section on 'self-tempering', and so do men's health books such as S. B. Shenkman, *My – muzhchiny*, 2nd edn (Moscow, 1980). Marginalization of *zakal* led eventually to an upsurge of anxiety about 'failed masculinity' in the 1960s and 1970s, as expressed, among other things, in anti-alcohol propaganda, in literature, and in films such as Kira Muratova's *The Asthenic Syndrome* (1991). For a more extensive discussion of this process and of post-Stalinist behavior models in general, see Kelly, *Refining Russia*, chapter 5.
59. See note 14 above.

9

The Disappearance of the Russian Queen, or How the Soviet Closet Was Born

Dan Healey

The historiography of modern homosexuality acknowledges that the association of effeminacy in men with same-sex love is a feature of recent constructions of homosexual identity.[1] This association appears both in constructions of homosexuality produced by medicine and by male homosexuals themselves. Gender behavior that transgresses masculine norms was not a compulsory component of the homosexual identity in the modern West, especially after homophile movements and gay liberationists took up the language of identity in the twentieth century. Yet from the early eighteenth century, effeminacy features in descriptions of a significant minority of the men who formed homosexual subcultures in northwestern European cities. Effeminacy was not simply an imitation of feminine styles, gestures or speech, but an ironic appropriation that some men-loving men used to proclaim affiliation and facilitate contact.[2] In a few infamous taverns in eighteenth-century London, 'mollies' staged raucous mock-birthing and wedding rituals to amuse knowing audiences of 'sodomites'. In Paris in the same era, men who sought sex together in public squares and parks knew each other by a repertoire of aliases drawn from women's names and aristocratic titles.[3] In Imperial Russia, the 'birth of the queen' came later than in western Europe. Evidence of the arrival of a distinctly Russian homosexual subculture, with an argot structured around playful and sometimes effeminate ritual, appears from the 1870s and 1880s, abounding in medical, legal, and parodic texts into the twentieth century, but diminishing rapidly from the mid-1920s. Tracing the late birth, precocious adolescence, and sudden silencing of the Russian 'queen' between 1861 and 1941 makes visible a significant boundary between normative (and eventually, explicitly heterosexual) manliness and transgressive homosexual masculinity in this modernizing society.

Before the 1870s, sex between Russian males did not bear a particular gender stigma, but belonged to a patriarchal masculinity that saw subordinate men and boys as sexually accessible. It would be anachronistic to interpret this indulgence of mutual masculine eros as proof of a more 'tolerant' approach to 'homosexuality' in Russian culture. Religious and popular sanctions had long been present. They were, however, less effective than in societies where Roman Catholic and Protestant clergy, abetted by more powerful state machinery, were able to impose a calculus of sexual sin through confession, religious education, and secular (often capital) penalties. In Russia, sex between men traditionally found expression in the patron–client relations of the extended household, the monastery, workshop, bathhouse, prison, and urban street.[4]

The diary of a third-guild merchant (by birth a peasant) of the 1850s and early 1860s speaks about same-sex relations without betraying gender anxiety.[5] Instead, Pavel Medvedev frequently worried about the moral and spiritual implications of his indulgence of 'lustfulness' (*sladostrastie*). The significant distinctions in sexual acts his diary records did not concern the gender of partners, but the patriarchal relationships (as husband, householder, client of female prostitutes, or as merchant and employer) that they occurred within and potentially disrupted. He noted, for example, in 1860 that he often masturbated with an 18-year-old 'boy' in his household, probably a servant or apprentice. 'Naturally, it is my overwhelming passion,' he wrote to justify his actions, 'but why do I train the young boy (albeit a grown up one) in this?'[6] For Medvedev, the answer lay not in a deviant masculinity, but in his 'passionate temperament and lustful impulses' that got the better of him, especially when he was downhearted and weakened by alcohol. Same-sex eros, within the conventions of homosociability and the cult of vodka, was not unmanly. On drunken sprees with his male companions, Medvedev recorded episodes of sex with coachmen ('You can almost always succeed with a 50-kopek coin, or 30 kopeks, but there are also those who agree to it for pleasure') and bathhouse attendants.[7] After a very inebriated and only partially successful attempt to seduce a friend, Medvedev voiced regret for having committed 'a foul thing' (*gadost'*). The foulness of the episode lay in the merchant's temporary loss of patriarchal dignity and in the moral qualms he felt at leading a man of equal status into temptation. Seeking 'mutually to produce lust by means of masturbation [*onanizm*]', Medvedev and his friend passed out in a muddy corner of Sokol'niki Park; both men were covered in dirt and the companion lost various pieces of clothing. Still drunk, the merchant left his friend 'sleeping like a dead man' and walked home at 3 a.m., 'in a disgusting state, with passersby looking at me like a monster. . . . In my years, and in my position, to do such foul things and unwittingly draw others into onanism using lustful tales.' Medvedev excused himself on the grounds that his unhappy marriage drove him to alternative outlets for his 'passion'.[8]

This picture of traditional masculine sexuality directed to the subaltern youth or man was replicated in numerous settings. The servants, apprentices, and bathhouse attendants figuring in Medvedev's adventures also appeared in textbooks for forensic medical practitioners and in legal records. Provincial gentrywoman Anna Kazakova's petition for separation from her husband, examined by the tsar in 1893, presented revealing depositions from peasant servants.[9] A coachman and another manservant had submitted to Konstantin Kazakov's sexual advances, earning the disapproval mostly of the female staff. 'The master commits sin with *muzhiki* using them in the backside [*v zadu*]', a peasant woman in the household reported. Yet both the coachman (who also got Anna pregnant) and the manservant admitted to these trysts (with vodka as an excuse), accepted three to five rubles for each episode, and ignored warnings about 'sin' from their co-workers. Urban apprentices also received the sexual attentions of men in authority. In one Moscow workshop, a 26-year-old craftsman was notorious for his sexual advances to apprentice boys, and his unmasking in 1892 initially provoked laughter rather than opprobrium.[10] The same year saw the trial of a baker, Chelnokov, whose sexual involvement with his apprentices aroused the ire of a Moscow charity.[11] Pedagogic arrangements were similar sites for abuse. One student, a victim of his 55-year-old teacher, explained in court in 1881, 'I came not long ago to Petersburg from the village and not knowing the customs here did not complain, because I thought that's the way things were with every master.'[12]

Relations of this type persisted into the twentieth century and may well continue today in the brutalized single-sex regimes of Russia's prisons and army.[13] Yet in the 1870s, as Russian cities expanded and commerce and industry grew, a new, 'homosexual' identity appeared alongside more traditional relations. Men identified by forensic doctors and by respectable critics as *tetki* (singular, *tetka*, meaning literally 'auntie', but translatable as 'queen') frequented specific notorious territories of St Petersburg and Moscow. The *tetki* of Russia's capitals used a repertoire of gestures and signals, ostensibly innocent but with a concealed meaning for initiates, to make contact with sexually available men. This pattern of relations marked a distinct break with older, patriarchal forms of male sexuality, for encounters took place beyond the patron–client nexus of the household or workshop. Now a sexual marketplace evolved, with a new hierarchy of values and a new symbolic order.[14] The 'little homosexual world' (*gomoseksual'nyi mirok*)[15] became a feature of Russia's largest cities.

The label '*tetka*' for the man devoted to same-sex love had obvious gender-inverting intent, emasculating the man thus labeled, while also making him seem elderly, frivolous, and perhaps unsophisticated. Before the appearance of this new meaning, in popular and peasant speech *tetka* was in wide use as a deprecating term for any woman older than the speaker. The newer, more specialized use was in all likelihood a foreign borrowing. It circulated among both observers and denizens of Russia's homosexual milieu and appears to have shifted in meaning. The analogue '*tante*' was used in mid-nineteenth-century French to designate the male prostitute, but by the end of the century, it more usually referred to men-loving men in general.[16] It was in the first sense that St Petersburg doctor Vladislav Merzheevskii had used its Russian variant in his 1878 manual on forensic gynecology.[17] Ten years later, Peter Tchaikovsky was already using *tetka* in the more generalized, second sense, with its nuances of preening lubriciousness, in his diary.[18] In a similar fashion, an anonymous denouncer who penned an elaborate and extremely informative indictment of St Petersburg's *tetki* in the late 1880s or early 1890s generally used the word to refer to the clients of men and youths who sold sex.[19]

Who were the *tetki*? Hostile observers identified their interest in sex acts with other men as the primary badge of membership. The denouncer of St Petersburg's sodomites defined six subtypes of *tetki* based on the sexual acts and postures adopted, including oral and intercrural connections, but it was anal intercourse that sustained this observer's curiosity. Most of these men, he noted, 'use' each other 'in the anus' (*upotrebliaiut . . . v zadnii prokhod*). This vocabulary of 'use' conformed to widespread nineteenth-century ideas of the phallus as the sole source of sexual desire (insertive partners 'actively' took this role 'as a result of sexual arousal'), while those who adopted the receptive posture were described as 'passively' enjoying or permitting others to 'use' them. According to this phallocentric logic, the anus was only dimly (if ever) perceived as a locus of pleasure and receptive partners could only be comfortably imagined as 'passive' and therefore emasculated.[20] The denouncer distinguished between the *tetka*'s 'vice' as something possibly derived from 'sexual satiety' and disgust with women on the one hand, and the opportunistic 'pederasty' of the 'impoverished, young . . . victims serving to satisfy' them.[21] In this view, the *tetka* was predominantly an affluent character, tempting victims into sex acts they otherwise found repugnant with the lure of easy money and luxury. It is unlikely that all partners of the *tetka* were so repulsed by same-sex acts; undoubtedly, as in the case of Medvedev's coachmen, 'some agree[d] to it for pleasure' alone and did not seek payment. The actual class profile of these identities also remains sketchy, although most sources present the objects of the *tetka*'s 'exploitation' as young men newly arrived from the countryside, working as apprentices in workshops or commerce, living rough on the street, studying, or enlisted as soldiers or sailors. Circulating through the homosexual subculture, these men and youths confronted the prospect of a gradual life-transition from desirable 'commercial catamite' to aging *tetka*, a perhaps unpalatable career sweetened by hopes of material advancement. A loyal patron might offer the young 'pederast for money' the opportunity to leave the sexual marketplace and form a partnership of sorts. Meanwhile those with steady occupations (such as military recruits) who engaged in more casual forms of male sexual exchange and prostitution abandoned this trade when age reduced their appeal, or when military service took them from the city.[22] Unlike the very visible persona of the *tetka*, the boys and men who sold sexual favors did not acquire a stable subcultural label in Russian. This eloquent silence perhaps testifies to the transitory nature of their participation. It also signals the discomfort the masculine sex-trade provoked and the concealment that participants felt was necessary. Outsiders might refer to these sexually available men as 'pederast-prostitutes', 'commercial catamites', and later on, as 'homosexuals', but their apparent refusal to name themselves underlines their tenuous claim to masculine respectability that rested on keeping their sexual activity hidden.

The *tetki* and the men they attracted employed public space to construct a sexual marketplace, the new nexus of a homosexual identity. Many of these sexualized territories were marginal spaces in the heart of the city or places where leisurely strolling or outright loitering could appear comparatively innocent. While there, participants feigned interest in blameless activities to hide the real purpose of their presence from passersby. Gestures, signals from clothing and comportment, and the rituals of masculine sociability enabled participants to identify each other and become acquainted. Information about this subculture is more prolific for St Petersburg than Moscow, suggesting that the new capital saw an earlier and more elaborately developed homosexual presence.

The St Petersburg streetscape had acquired a homosexual geography by the 1870s. Especially notorious was the Passazh (Passage), a covered gallery completed in 1848 that connected the busy Nevskii Prospekt with another contact-point, Mikhailovskaia (now Iskusstvo) Square. This arcade of shops proved ideally suited, especially in the winter, for the discreet pursuit of same-sex liaisons. By the 1860s, the Passage was already attracting blackmailers who preyed on *tetki* seeking youths in its upper reaches.[23] The Mikhailov gang, a group of accomplished extortionists caught in 1875, was well known to the operators of nearby Dominic's restaurant and of the billiard hall located inside the Passage itself.[24] The city's anonymous denouncer of pederasty observed that 'On Sundays in the winter *tetki* stroll in the Passage on the top gallery, where cadets and schoolboys come in the morning; at around six in the evening, soldiers and apprentice boys appear.'[25]

By the late 1880s, the pavements of Nevskii from Znamenskaia Square to Anichkov Bridge (both locations where public toilets were used for making contacts) and on toward the Public Library and the Passage, formed a promenade visible to initiates. This was apparently the city's most enduring homosexual cruising ground, with participants reporting encounters into the 1910s and 1920s. Wednesdays saw a gathering of upper-class *tetki* at the Mariinskii Theater for the ballet. A similar class patronized restaurants, with their private dining rooms discreetly (if sporadically) serving as meeting-places for 'pederasts'.[26] Saturdays were reserved by some seeking 'apprentice boys' or poorer youths at the more plebeian amusements of the Cinizelli Circus.[27] The embankments of the Fontanka Canal and the gardens adjoining the Circus, remained hubs of male prostitution into the 1920s.[28]

By 1908, one jaundiced critic was able to map the daily routine for 'an entire band of suspicious young people', the male prostitutes he judged to be part of the 'little homosexual world'. They gathered in the dog-exercising garden by the Circus in the mornings, moved on to Nevskii Prospekt and the Café de Paris in the Passage during the afternoon, and returned to the Fontanka Embankment, or the Tauride Gardens, to attract clients in the evening.[29] The critic's observations about the availability of male lovers (some for hire) in the latter Gardens are confirmed by correspondence between the famously homosexual poet Mikhail Kuzmin and Val'ter Nuvel'.[30]

In Moscow, the Boulevard Ring furnished an arena for the subculture that combined the necessary circulation of bodies with a plethora of excuses for leisurely sociability. Medvedev's diary of the 1850s–60s says nothing about a culture of street-cruising, but a surviving sodomy trial of 1888 indicates that by then, men could find 'devotees' of same-sex love on the old capital's streets. Townsman Petr Mamaev was arrested on Prechistenskii Boulevard after a drunken dispute with a younger man named Agapov. Suspected of 'sodomy', Mamaev eventually confessed, 'For the past eight years I have been committing sodomy with different, unknown persons. I go out to the boulevard at night, strike up a conversation, and if I find a devotee (*liubitel'*), then I do it with him. I cannot identify whom I did it with. . . . I attempted to do just the same with Agapov, without money, without any exchange of money in mind, just to obtain pleasure for myself and for him.'[31] A chance encounter on the same boulevard transformed the life of 17-year-old peasant 'P.', a shop assistant recently arrived from Smolensk province. There he met '*svoi liudi*' (his own people, or his own kind), in 1912 and began his career as a male prostitute.[32]

Codes of mutual recognition in gesture and speech imbued these locations with significance for the homosexual subculture. The rituals that are best documented in the sources were practiced primarily in the world of male prostitution and public sex. The single most important gesture of discreet self-proclamation by men seeking lovers on the streets was the significant glance. The anonymous denouncer of St Petersburg's sodomites commented, 'The *tetki*, as they call themselves, recognize each other with one glance, by signs unnoticeable to passers-by, yet by these experts can even define the category of *tetka* we are dealing with.'[33] An exchange of sustained eye contact, especially in a notorious location, established participation in the subculture. Soldiers and *tetki* performed this ritual in the vicinity of the public toilets of the Zoological Gardens, as did rent boys and their clients outside a facility by the Cinizelli Circus, as noted in 1908.[34] The rituals of requesting, offering, and lighting cigarettes were favored, although 'hooligan' male prostitutes dispensed with such niceties. Their clients, commented a prerevolutionary critic, could be recognized by their 'nonchalantly thrown glance' and the 'particular, specific mask of desire' on their faces.[35] This set of signals did not change after 1917. A sailor arrested in 1921 at a 'pederastic party' in Petrograd admitted he was aware of the sexual intentions of those present: 'I saw it in their glances, conversations and smiles.'[36] The prostitute P. claimed that between 1925 and 1927, he had 'seen in person, met somewhere, [or] recognized as one of his kind' no less than 5000 homosexual men in Moscow.

Effeminate gesture and dress, or simply conspicuous clothing, were considered by critics and subcultural denizens alike to be marks of the *tetki* and the 'commercial catamites' they consorted with. Blackmailers understood effeminate manners and garish outfits as part of the code.[37] The anonymous denouncer of the capital's *tetki* produced a lengthy list of suspects, characterizing many of them by their feminized traits. Some were said to be flamboyantly effeminate in public, and a few had nicknames such as 'Dina' and 'Aspaziia'. A 'very beautiful' banker, the 20-year-old son of a senator, was supposedly 'considered a courtesan of the highest grade' (*kokotka vysshei marki*). One Zaitsev, 'recently arrived from Moscow' and 'startlingly resembling a woman', exploited this 'effeminacy' (*zhenopodobnost'*) to appear 'at public balls and private receptions in women's clothing'. Another young 'courtesan' appeared at such functions 'in women's costumes [tailored] down to the finest details'.[38] The denouncer labeled many of his subjects 'ladies' (*damy*), apparently because they enjoyed the receptive role in anal intercourse.[39] Post-1905 parodies of the subculture were laden with images of distorted femininity and exaggerated class pretensions. Aliases as baronesses, duchesses, and *baby* (peasant women) proliferated among the male prostitutes based near the Cinizelli Circus, echoing the professional names adopted by female brothel workers. Color codes supposedly distinguished 'homosexual' men. The coquettish sported 'their bright red cravats, a kind of homosexual uniform, and some have a bright red handkerchief blazing from the pocket'. *Tetki* and male prostitutes sometimes also wore makeup in the street. A German hairdresser wandered the town after he closed his shop 'to catch a pederast' by wearing rouge, 'so that they'll see I'm a girl'.[40]

In contrast to these vivid and perhaps unusual figures, the soldiers, sailors, and schoolboys who offered themselves for commercial and unpaid sex prowled the territories of St Petersburg's homosexual underworld in their distinctive official uniforms, redolent of an exemplary masculinity. Outwardly forced to conform to the tsarist standards of self-control and sobriety required by their clothing, they nevertheless found it a convenient camouflage for their participation in the subculture. It was also a masculine style with erotic potential when viewed through the eyes of sexual dissidents. Linked to these idealized manly images was another subcultural label which circulated in both capitals, that of the 'woman-hater' (*zhenonenavistnik*). 'Balls of women-haters' (*baly zhenonenavistnikov*, with some men attending in drag) were reportedly staged in Moscow before the Great War, while a Petrograd sailor, interviewed after his arrest at the 1921 'pederasts' party', said he enjoyed sex with men, 'especially when a woman-hater came his way, someone of a masculine appearance who did not make himself up to be a woman'.[41] The term apparently invoked a masculinist solidarity to banish the effeminacy and perhaps the ruralizing nuances audible in the label '*tetka*'.[42] Our sense of the interaction between these characters, the *tetka*, the 'pederast for money', and the 'woman-hater', remains obscure because of the fragmented sources at our disposal. At a superficial level these roles resemble the pre-1945 system of 'fairies', 'punks', and 'wolves' that prevailed among American men in New York City and that has been richly described by George Chauncey. Available evidence is still too modest to support this kind of historical anthropological account for Russia.[43]

The advent of a visible homosexual subculture evoked reactions against the perceived corruption of young men and the spread of male prostitution that were relatively moderate by comparison to the politicized press frenzies that accompanied England's Oscar Wilde trials and the Prince Eulenberg scandal in Germany. Russian jurists revising the criminal code retained the prohibition against 'sodomy' dating from 1835, but their 1903 draft law acknowledged the existence of young male prostitutes who had no 'innocence' to exploit, and suggested milder penalties for sex with such knowing teenagers.[44] Satirical depictions of the subculture played on the anxiety that the numbers of such youths were on the increase as wealthy and 'cynical' *tetki* lured boys into sexual slavery. The *succès de scandale* of Kuzmin's novel *Wings* (published in 1906, and the first modern European 'coming-out' novel with a happy ending) brought praise from those who backed its defense of a 'common culture' of homosexuality and condemnation from others who saw in it the importation of western depravity.[45] European advocates of homosexual emancipation took note of the appearance and character of Russia's subculture and circulated their observations and recommendations for experts and tourists alike. Yet despite the worry about corrupted youth, the light policing of same-sex love in Russian cities barely disturbed the *tetki*'s underworld in the last peacetime decade of tsarist rule. Indeed, capitalists were now taking the Russian *tetka* and his friends seriously, running bathhouses, bars, and 'balls of women-haters' that catered discreetly to this clientele. Statistics show a sharp increase in convictions for 'sodomy' only in cities of the Caucasus. In Russia's Orient, local patterns of male prostitution (such as the Central Asian *bachi*, who were feminized dancing boys kept in troupes to sexually service male clients, and boy-abduction and rape, said to be persistent in the Caucasus) attracted intensified attention from officials apparently bent on 'civilizing' the imperial periphery.[46]

Surprisingly, despite the seven-year hiatus of war, revolution, and civil war that concluded in 1921, much of the male homosexual underworld that existed before 1914 reconstituted itself in the early years of the New Economic Policy. Street cruising and male prostitution returned to Moscow and Petrograd, with the same toilets, parks, and boulevards providing arenas for the market in both paid and unpaid sex between men. Soviet Russia's new rulers allowed an aura of ambiguity to hang over the question of homosexual emancipation. In Russia, Belorussia, and Ukraine, they scrapped the tsarist prohibition of 'sodomy' in a thoroughgoing modernization of the definition of sexual offenses. Soviet Russia was by far the most significant power since the French Revolution to decriminalize male same-sex relations, while Britain and Weimar Germany continued to prosecute homosexuals. Soviet health authorities courted the left-leaning sex reform movement headed by Berlin sexologist and homosexual rights campaigner Magnus Hirschfeld. Biologists and doctors chiefly sponsored by the Commissariat of Health began to investigate homosexuality as a scientific and medical phenomenon, often from sympathetic perspectives that were in comparative terms markedly advanced. Yet at the same time, clerical 'pederasty' was rooted out and exposed in show trials staged by Bolshevik antireligious campaigners. More ominously, as Soviet power expanded southward and eastward, 'sodomy' and the keeping of *bachi* were outlawed in the Soviet Union's new republics of Azerbaijan (1923), Uzbekistan (1926), and Turkmenistan (1927).[47] In Uzbekistan, the sexual harassment of men was made a crime, in language that mirrored the Russian republic's pathbreaking 1923 statute protecting women from the same offense.

Whatever the ambiguities presented by Bolshevik actions, Soviet police and some jurists quickly judged effeminacy linked to homosexuality to be an intolerable defect in men. A raid on a 'pederastic party' in Petrograd on 15 January 1921 resulted in the arrest of 98 sailors, soldiers, and civilians, many of them dressed in drag. They had staged a mock wedding ceremony and celebrated the occasion with waltzes and minuets. Other guests wore 'Spanish costumes' or 'white wigs', and there was a 'flying post' for sending messages; one lucky sailor got notes saying 'I fancy you' and 'I'd like to get to know you'.[48] A lone Justice Commissariat lawyer argued that this raid was justified despite the decriminalization of sodomy, for public displays of 'homosexual tastes' endangered suggestible personalities. He proposed prosecuting such overt demonstrations of these tastes as 'hooliganism'. No subsequent hooliganism charges based on cross-dressing or public displays of homosexuality have come to light. Few other jurists advocated such a criminalizing approach, and most explained the absence of a sodomy ban as a feature of the sexual revolution.[49] There is no doubt, however, that the exuberant visibility of the male homosexual subculture declined; Kuzmin's diary lost its playful tone as he looked back to 1906–7 as 'a merry time' in contrast to the cautious tenor of Soviet existence.[50] Commercial spaces which had previously sheltered same-sex intimacies (such as bathhouses and pubs) were now under bureaucratic supervision if not outright public ownership, and the homosexual subculture's purchase on these sites became fleeting and ephemeral.[51]

Psychiatrists, keen to 'sovietize' their discipline, explored male effeminacy and female masculinization as aspects of a medical definition of homosexuality. Despite the Party's prevailing suspicion of women who evaded their 'natural' reproductive role, some doctors allowed that masculinization imbued the lesbian with strength, public presence, and skillfulness, all politically admirable attributes. Male femininity, on the other hand, rendered men soft, frivolous, and obsessed with a cozy bourgeois domestic sphere.[52] By the late 1920s a clear public ethic against play and pleasure prevailed, influencing even sympathetic doctors to erase the male homosexual's ironic femininity from their case histories. Effeminacy continued to provide a coded language for the increasingly clandestine homosexual subculture, but official discourses abhorred any mention of men's refusal of the masculine. Doctors were responding to the increasingly negative and confined approach to sexual expression that began to dominate Party pronouncements and sexological research during the 1920s; an aspect, as Eric Naiman has shown, of Bolshevik anxieties about their precarious grip on power.[53]

Even behind closed doors sympathetic psychiatrists and other scientists recoiled from the prospect of effeminacy. In a 1929 discussion about 'transvestites' and the 'intermediate sex' conducted by the Expert Medical Council of the Commissariat of Health, women of the 'masculinized type' (cross-dressing army commanders, for example) were considered with fascination and indulgence.[54] These 'transvestite' women 'dressed up' as men; some demanded the 'right' to same-sex marriage. By contrast, this gathering of Russia's top neuropsychiatric specialists was virtually silent about 'feminized' males, men 'dressed up' as women, or same-sex marriages between male 'transvestites'. Femininity in men was a marker of backwardness. Experts spoke of effeminacy not in the Russian homosexual, but in the 'unfortunate *bachi* of Turkestan', boys of 'an utterly clearly defined masculine sex' who 'were dressed in feminine clothes and spoiled forever' by sexual and economic exploitation.[55] Male femininity could only be imagined as foreign, primitive, and tragic, while masculinization in women could (in carefully controlled circumstances) endow them with competence, authority, and, crucially, loyalty to the modernizing (and implicitly Russian) values of the Revolution.[56] After the 'Great Break' of the First Five Year Plan, with its increasingly militarized atmosphere and the use of coercion and violence to impose policy, the few psychiatric textbooks that mentioned homosexuality began to speak only of the foreign homosexual as effeminate.[57]

The crisis-laden early 1930s saw the fusion of anti-prostitution initiatives and campaigns to rid the newly socialist city of 'social anomalies'. 'Recidivist criminals', female prostitutes who refused to take factory jobs, and 'professional' beggars all had their own subcultures of the urban street that social workers, militia, and secret police studied and strove to eradicate with increasingly forceful measures. The recriminalization of sodomy in all Soviet republics in 1933–4 was a response to the persistence of the male homosexual subculture of the street, another 'social anomaly' incompatible with the new society.[58] Correspondence and early draft statutes reveal that the subculture, as a site for the 'recruitment and corruption of totally healthy young people' (men, in fact), was feared. The original draft law condemned 'sodomy . . . for payment, as a profession or in public', highlighting the subcultural aspects of the crime. Nothing explicitly described and condemned the effeminate homosexual, the Soviet *tetka*.

Yet in sodomy cases after 1934, police and court officials employed the language of 'active' and 'passive' sexual roles, of men 'using' other men sexually by penetrating them, to represent their perceptions of homosexual relationships. Since the law made no such distinction, condemning all parties equally, the persistent attention that authorities paid to sexual postures presents an eloquent redundancy. The obsession with 'active/passive' roles expressed Soviet officialdom's underlying expectations about power and gender. In one 1935 trial, much time was devoted to an examination in court of the romance between Pavlov, a 40-year-old bachelor, and Shelgunov, an ex-priest of 54. Wounded in the genitals during the civil war, Pavlov had been 'deprived of the ability to lead a normal sex life'. Incapable of an 'active sexual role', Pavlov was said to be 'the object of Shelgunov' and thus the receptive partner in sex. Yet emotionally, roles were reversed: Pavlov's 'active strivings' were expressed 'in his spiritual ties (*dukhovnye sviazy*) with Shelgunov, who on this level played the role of a woman (*igral rol' zhenshchiny*)'.[59] In documents recording confessions of three men associated with a theater school, all arrested in 1941, the defendants are represented as using this same language; perhaps they were responding to prompts from interrogators, or police secretaries transformed the crude argot of the cellblock into an acceptable bureaucratic formula.[60] Those men who 'played the role of a woman' were singled out; occasionally, such men were subjected to forensic medical examinations of their anuses to 'prove' a connection with 'active' partners. The 'passive' role was the 'woman's' role and men who willingly adopted it feminized and debased themselves in the eyes of the secret and ordinary police, whose knowledge of same-sex relations was undoubtedly dominated by perceptions of sexuality in Russia's prisons.

The trial documents give fragmentary evidence of the persistence of the homosexual subculture in the 1930s. Street-cruising, and public sex, especially in the vicinity of the Boulevard Ring, continued; the records recoil from much mention of ironic femininity. In November 1934 Bezborodov and Gribov (a 'ringleader' whose address-book fell into police hands) 'wishing to drink alcohol', visited the flat of one Petr 'by nickname "The Baroness", who kept an entire den of homosexuals'. The court designated this flat as a significant 'meeting place of pederasts', although the fate of the man grandly styled 'Baroness' and location of the gathering-spot he organized is unclear.[61] Toilets in Nikitskie Gates and Trubnaia Square were mentioned as sites for sexual encounters and police arrests. Homosexuals continued to share information about the subculture. One defendant confessed: 'In 1936 in the apartment where I lived, Afanas'ev, an artist of the ballet, moved in. . . . He showed me the places where pederasts meet – Nikitskii Boulevard and Trubnaia Square.' Another defendant said that in the early 1930s a friend 'told me that the chief places for pederasts were Nikitskii Boulevard, Trubnaia [Square], a bar on Arbat [Street], and the Tsentral'nye Baths'. Soldiers and sailors continued to display their uniformed bodies in these locales and the sexualized territories of other Soviet towns, making themselves sexually available to men for small gifts of food, alcohol, cinema tickets, or cash. Now, however, the stakes involved were becoming more drastic, with the earliest victims of the anti-sodomy legislation being sentenced to five years' imprisonment.[62]

Most of Moscow's recorded sodomy trials of the 1930s took place behind closed doors, effectively concealing the defendants within a judicial closet. Surrounded by secrecy and given little press coverage, the Stalinist anti-sodomy law took jurists, psychiatrists, and homosexuals by surprise. Yet men who loved men were not simply 'disappeared', but subjected to the full rigors of a legal process that involved the informed participation of innumerable secretaries, judges, lay assessors, criminal investigators, advocates, police, and jailers. These individuals witnessed the unmasking of the accused 'homosexual's' intimate life in police interrogations and courtroom testimony. Almost all defendants were successfully convicted; a handful, portrayed in court as married and 'normal', or 'family men', were acquitted after stage-managed alterations of testimony.[63] The fate of men branded as 'homosexuals' could not have escaped the attention of those around them, and it certainly did not escape the attention of homosexuals themselves, many of whom, according to their testimony, were aware of the arrests of their friends, lovers, and acquaintances.

Fear now marked their lives, and while the subculture of the streets and toilets was never eradicated, persecution drove many homosexual men toward deeper strategies of concealment. A few unnumbered sheets, stuffed inside a huge bound book of Moscow criminal court sentencing records, convey the claustrophobia of the Soviet closet, as experienced by a fortunate survivor of one sodomy trial. Three years after his 1938 conviction for sodomy in Moscow, Pavel Silvestrov wrote to a friend, evidently someone closely connected with the circumstances that led to his arrest, for assistance in obtaining the conviction records necessary to apply for a permit to travel to the capital. Silvestrov now lived in Ashkhabad, where he worked in a theater. The ex-Party member had received the minimum three-year sentence for sodomy, but on appeal, as frequently happened in these cases later in the 1930s, his sentence was suspended.[64] He was sent to the Turkmen republic and denied the right to return to Russia's major cities. In his plea to his unnamed correspondent, he wrote:

> Understand me correctly: I have no grounds to seek revenge upon you, I only find that experience I lived through, that so strangely brought me to the courtroom dock, unusually interesting. You can't write everything in a letter, but I very much would like to tell you the real heart of the matter; you would find it very useful in your work. Remember: it was 1937–38 and by nationality, I am Latvian . . . and if you still recall (what happened in 1938!!), that my nearest (*blizkie*) were in the courtroom, you would understand the contradiction of my behavior during the criminal investigation [. . .]
>
> I believe you will not refuse my modest request. I have no other way. The fact that I completed my education after the trial, and was sent off to responsible work gives me the right to hope that you will receive me as a human being.[65]

Now cringing and hoping to be treated 'as a human being' by an old acquaintance, Silvestrov nevertheless hinted at the possibility that he could pull this Moscow friend down with him, in revenge for some unspecified wrong. Some unspeakable truth lay behind this letter, one that could not be trusted to the monitored Soviet post, yet its author was able to allude clearly to the fear inspired by his personal ordeal of 1938. However Silvestrov 'strangely' came to find himself before the court in that year, and whatever the 'contradiction' of his deeds while the case was under investigation, his life and undoubtedly that of his 'nearest' friends had been irretrievably stigmatized. Not in show trials or noisy press campaigns, but in hundreds and perhaps thousands of personal tragedies like these, unmanly displays of pleasure-seeking and ironic effeminacy were erased. A disreputable and illegal masculinity was constructed around the subculture of the *tetka*, and his supposedly abnormal 'use' of the male body. The Soviet closet was born.

Notes

The author gratefully acknowledges financial support for the research in this chapter from the Social Sciences and Humanities Research Council (Canada), the University of Toronto Stalin-Era Research in the Archives Project, and the Wellcome Trust (grant no. 488142).

1. My work proceeds from the axiom that sexualities are socially constructed and historically contingent discourses, and not (for the historian's purposes) essential, universal, and timeless biological impulses. For post-essentialist guides to conceptualizing 'homosexuality' and the male 'homosexual' in history, see Edward Stein (ed.), *Forms of Desire: Sexual Orientation and the Social Constructionist Controversy* (New York, 1990); Jeffrey Weeks, *Against Nature: Essays on History, Sexuality and Identity* (London, 1991).
2. For a genealogy of effeminacy, see Alan Sinfield, *The Wilde Century: Effeminacy, Oscar Wilde, and the Queer Movement* (London, 1994). On irony as a constituent of modern gay identity, see Brian Pronger, *The Arena of Masculinity: Sports, Homosexuality and the Meaning of Sex* (London, 1990), 104–10; on the functions of male femininity in the homosexual subculture, see George Chauncey, *Gay New York: Gender, Urban Culture, and the Making of the Gay Male World, 1890–1940* (New York, 1994), 101–11. For a statement on the 'performativity' of normative and subversive gender roles see Judith Butler, *Gender Trouble: Feminism and the Subversion of Identity* (London, 1990).
3. On London, Randolph Trumbach, 'The Birth of the Queen: Sodomy and the Emergence of Gender Equality in Modern Culture, 1660–1750', *Hidden From History: Reclaiming the Gay and Lesbian Past*, ed. Martin Duberman, Martha Vicinus, and George Chauncey, Jr. (New York, 1989); on Paris, Michael Rey, 'Parisian Homosexuals Create a Lifestyle, 1700–1750: the Police Archives', *'Tis nature's fault: Unauthorized Sexual Behavior During the Enlightenment*, ed. Robert P. Maccubbin (New York, 1985).

4. Dan Healey, 'Moscow', *Queer Sites: Gay Urban Histories since 1600*, ed. David Higgs (London, 1999).
5. Jeffrey Burds, trans. and ed., 'Dnevnik moskovskogo kuptsa Pavla Vasil'evicha Medvedeva, 1854–1864 gg.' (in progress). I am grateful to Professor Burds for providing me with a transcript of the diary; references here use his transcript's pagination. The diary is held in Tsentral'nyi istoricheskii arkhiv g. Moskvy (TsIAM), f. 2330, op. 1, dd. 984, 986. For an introduction, see A. I. Kupriianov, '"Pagubnaia strast" moskovskogo kuptsa', *Kazus: Individual'noe i unikal'noe v istorii*, ed. Iu. L. Bessmertnyi and M. A. Boitsov (Moscow, 1997).
6. Burds, *Dnevnik moskovskogo kuptsa*, 144.
7. Ibid., 152, 156.
8. Ibid., 132.
9. Rossiiskaia Gosudarstvennnyi Istoricheskii Arkhiv (RGIA), f. 1412, op. 221, d. 54, ll. 29–37 and passim. I am very grateful to Gaby Donicht for sharing these data with me.
10. TsIAM, f. 142, op. 2, d. 433. The craftsman was acquitted of sodomy with minors. Note also the case of Kniazev, son of a workshop owner, convicted of raping an 11-year-old apprentice in 1874; ibid., f. 142, op. 3, d. 233.
11. Ibid., op. 1, d. 172. See also A. F. Koni fond, Gosudarstvennyi Arkhiv Rossiiskoi Federatsii (GARF), f. 564, op. 1, d. 260, ll. 92–100.
12. V. M. Tarnovskii, *Izvrashchenie polovogo chuvstva. Sudebno-psikhiatricheskii ocherk* (St Petersburg, 1885), 70.
13. Eros and sexual violence between men have been a constant feature of Russian prison life since documentation of the phenomenon began in the late nineteenth century. Soviet Gulag and prison life have invested mutual male eros and sexual violence with powerful meanings. On these themes, see Lev Samoilov, 'Puteshestvie v perevernutyi mir', *Neva*, no. 4 (1989), 150–64; Dan Healey, 'Homosexual Desire in Revolutionary Russia: Public and Hidden Transcripts, 1917–1941' (Ph.D. diss., University of Toronto, 1998), chapter 6; V. K. and Nikolai Serov, 'Letters about Prison Life', *Out of the Blue: Russia's Hidden Gay Literature*, ed. Kevin Moss (San Francisco, 1996). In the military an analogous sexual culture exists; on hazing employing sexual violence (*dedovshchina*) see Catriona Kelly and David Shepherd (eds), *Russian Cultural Studies: an Introduction* (Oxford, 1998), 328; on male rape by Russian soldiers in Chechnia, see Ian Traynor, 'Tales of torture leak from Russian camps: escaped Chechen victims tell of rape, beating and humiliation', *The Guardian*, 19 February 2000, 17.
14. Historians of western men's same-sex love generally accept that the transformation of city life by capitalism facilitated the appearance of a subculture with mechanisms for homosexual affiliation beyond traditional patriarchal relationships. There is less agreement on when this transition occurred in various settings, which is logical given uneven development across Europe. See John D'Emilio, *Making Trouble: Essays on Gay History, Politics, and the University* (New York & London, 1992), chapter 1.
15. The subject of a sardonic series of sketches in V. P. Ruadze, *K sudu! . . . Gomoseksual'nyi Peterburg* (St Petersburg, 1908).
16. Claude Courouve, *Vocabulaire de l'homosexualité masculine* (Paris, 1985), 207–9. German used the word in a similar fashion.

17. V. Merzheevskii, *Sudebnaia ginekologiia. Rukovodstvo dlia vrachei i iuristov* (St Petersburg, 1878), 205.
18. He fleetingly described a gathering of such men: 'Russian *tetki* are repulsive.' See P. I. Chaikovskii, *Dnevniki 1873–1891* (Moscow-Petrograd, 1923, reprint 1993), 203 (13 March 1888); the word retains this generalized sense today. See Vladimir Kozlovskii, *Argo russkoi gomoseksual'noi subkul'tury: Materialy k izucheniiu* (Benson, Vt., 1986), 69.
19. RGIA, f. 1683, op. 1, d. 199, ll. 1–13. The denunciation is reprinted in full in V. V. Bersen'ev and A. R. Markov, 'Politsiia i gei: Epizod iz epokhi Aleksandra III', *Risk*, no. 3 (1998), 105–16; it was discovered and partially published by Konstantin Rotikov [pseud.], 'Epizod iz zhizni "golubogo" Peterburga', *Nevskii arkhiv: istoriko-kraevedcheskii sbornik*, no. 3 (1997), 449–66. Bersen'ev and Markov argue that the undated denunciation was written in the early 1890s, while Rotikov dates it from 1889. Rotikov uses it extensively in his cult-success guide to the 'gay' history of St Petersburg, *Drugoi Peterburg* (St Petersburg, 1998). For critical evaluations of this work from the perspective of western histories of sexualities, see Evgenii Bershtein, 'Goluboi Peterburg', *Novoe literaturnoe obozrenie*, no. 1 (1999), 403–6; Brian James Baer, 'The Other Russia: Re-Presenting the Gay Experience', *Kritika: Explorations in Russian and Eurasian History*, 1, no. 1 (2000), 183–94.
20. Queer theorists regard the 'active/passive' interpretation of gay men's anal sexuality as a function of the dominant sex/gender system. See for example, Guy Hocquenghem, 'Towards an Irrecuperable Pederasty' and Leo Bersani, 'Is the Rectum a Grave?' in *Reclaiming Sodom*, ed. Jonathan Goldberg (New York, 1994). Russian forensic doctors in different eras have expressed a nervous awareness of the ambiguous power of the supposedly 'passive' partner in men's same-sex contacts. Such men's 'ability through exercise to govern this muscle [the sphincter] at will' troubled A. Shvarts, in 'K voprosu o priznakakh privychnoi passivnoi pederastii (Iz nabliudenii v aziatskoi chasti g. Tashkenta)', *Vestnik obshchestvennoi gigieny, sudebnoi i prakticheskoi meditsiny*, no. 6 (1906), 816–18 (quote at 818). For late Soviet techniques to unmask 'passive homosexuals' by measuring sphincter control mechanically, see I. G. Bliumin and L. S. Gel'fenbein, 'Ob odnom diagnosticheskom priznake pri ekspertize polovykh sostoianii muzhchin', *Voprosy travmatologii, toksikologii, skoropostizhnoi smerti i deontologii v ekspertnoi praktike. Vypusk 3* (Moscow, 1966).
21. Bersen'ev and Markov, 'Politsiia i gei', 109.
22. Fragmentary evidence hints at these life transitions, suggested in the Petersburg denunciation (ibid.). Homosexual sponsorship promoted the careers of the male protégés of Prince Meshcherskii; see W. E. Mosse, 'Imperial Favorite: V. P. Meshchersky and the Grazhdanin', *Slavonic and East European Review*, 59 (1981), 529–47. In a Soviet psychiatrist's case history of a Moscow male prostitute in his thirties, the prostitute related how his engagement in the sex trade was interrupted during extended periods of sponsorship in first an aristocrat's and then an industrialist's household: V. A. Belousov, 'Sluchai gomoseksuala-muzhskoi prostitutki', *Prestupnik i prestupnost'. Sbornik II* (1927), 309–17. For career structures of male prostitution in England of the same era, see Jeffrey Weeks, 'Inverts, Perverts and Mary-Annes: Male Prostitution and the Regulation of Homosexuality in England in the Nineteenth

and Early Twentieth Centuries', *Hidden from History*, eds M. B. Duberman, M. Vicinus, and G. Chauncey.

23. On 6 January 1869, a 56-year-old Dane met a young Petersburger while buying eau-de-cologne in this gallery. After sex with the Dane in his flat, the young man tried to blackmail him; Merzheevskii, *Sudebnaia ginekologiia*, 254.
24. A. F. Koni, *Na zhiznennom puti*, 3 vols (St Petersburg, 1912), 2, 154–5; Tarnovskii, *Izvrashchenie polovogo chuvstva*, 72.
25. Bersen'ev and Markov, 'Politsiia i gei', 109.
26. The young Tchaikovsky escaped scandal when the Chautemps Restaurant was exposed in the press; see Alexander Poznansky, *Tchaikovsky's Last Days: a Documentary Study* (Oxford, 1996), 10. Another scandal forced the closure of a restaurant around 1893; see P. V. Ushakovskii [pseud.], *Liudi sredniago pola* (St Petersburg, 1908), 6.
27. Bersen'ev and Markov, 'Politsiia i gei', 109.
28. Ruadze, *K sudu! . . . Gomoseksual'nyi Peterburg*, 55–6, 102–3. For a Soviet report that the 'vicinity of the Cinizelli Circus with its little benches' continued to function as a 'meeting place', see Belousov, 'Sluchai gomoseksuala-muzhskoi prostitutki', 314.
29. Ruadze, *K sudu! . . . Gomoseksual'nyi Peterburg*, 102–3.
30. John E. Malmstad and Nikolay Bogomolov, *Mikhail Kuzmin: a Life in Art* (Cambridge, Mass., 1999), 107; for the correspondence, see N. A. Bogomolov, *Mikhail Kuzmin: Stat'i i materialy* (Moscow, 1995), 229.
31. Mamaev's wife and children lived in distant Ekaterinburg; TsIAM, f. 142, op. 2, d. 142, l. 148.
32. Belousov, 'Sluchai gomoseksuala-muzhskoi prostitutki'.
33. Bersen'ev and Markov, 'Politsiia i gei', 109. See also Tarnovskii, *Izvrashchenie polovogo chuvstva*, 62.
34. Male prostitutes lined the pavement leading to the facility and followed potential customers into it. 'They became acquainted with the intimate details of their bodies, and then came to an agreement on where to go and for how much.' Ruadze, *K sudu! . . . Gomoseksual'nyi Peterburg*, 103.
35. Ibid., 105–6, 108.
36. V. M. Bekhterev, 'O polovom izvrashchenii, kak osoboi ustanovke polovykh refleksov', *Polovoi vopros v shkole i v zhizni*, ed. I. S. Simonov (Leningrad, 1927), 170.
37. Merzheevskii, *Sudebnaia ginekologiia*, 254; Koni, *Na zhiznennom puti*, 154.
38. Bersen'ev and Markov, 'Politsiia i gei', 111–14.
39. For example, one Obrezkov, a 60-year-old senior civil servant in the Ministry of Foreign Affairs, was described as 'A lady, loves to be used by persons with large members', ibid., 114.
40. Ruadze, *K sudu! . . . Gomoseksual'nyi Peterburg*, 55–6, 90, 105, 108, 109. On the red necktie as a turn-of-the-century signal in America, see Chauncey, *Gay New York*, 3, 52, 54.
41. Belousov, 'Sluchai gomoseksuala-muzhskoi prostitutki'; V. P. Protopopov, 'Sovremennoe sostoianie voprosa o sushchnosti i proiskhozhdenii gomoseksualizma', *Nauchnaia meditsina*, no. 10 (1922), 49–62. See also 51, case no. 5.
42. In Wilhemine Germany, these two ideals of male homosexuality found expression in the gender inversion-based theories of Magnus Hirschfeld,

which were countered by the masculine supremacist arguments of Benedict Friedländer and his Community of the Special. See Eve K. Sedgwick, *Epistemology of the Closet* (Berkeley, 1990), 88–9. Variations on 'women-hater' as sexual identity (including 'stratophiles', devotees of sex with military men) circulated in pre-1914 Europe; see Xavier Mayne [Edward I. Prime-Stevenson], *The Intersexes: a History of Similsexualism as a Problem in Social Life* ([Naples], 1908), 198, 212–23.

43. On the 'boundaries of normal manhood' implicit in the relations between 'wolves' (masculine men) and 'punks' (the youths they had sex with), and 'fairies' (as feminized and very visibly transgressive men open to sex with other men), see Chauncey, *Gay New York*, 47–97.
44. On these points, see Dan Healey, *Homosexual Desire in Revolutionary Russia: the Regulation of Sexual and Gender Dissent* (Chicago, 2001), chapter 4.
45. Novels exploring the homosexual predicament appeared in major European languages in the two decades before 1914, but most resolved their plots with melodrama, suicide, or dismal self-hatred, while the young hero of *Wings* achieves a joyful acceptance of his sexuality; ibid. On the novel's reception, see Simon Karlinsky, 'Death and Resurrection of Mikhail Kuzmin', *Slavic Review* 38, no. 1 (1979), 92–6.
46. Healey, *Homosexual Desire in Revolutionary Russia*, chapter 3. On the *bachi*, see I. Baldauf, *Die Knabenliebe in Mittelasien: Bačabozlik* (Berlin, 1988).
47. Soviet Georgia, but not Armenia, also had an anti-sodomy statute; Healey, *Homosexual Desire in Revolutionary Russia*, chapter 6.
48. On this raid and reports about it, see ibid., and V. M. Bekhterev, 'O polovom izvrashchenii, kak osoboi ustanovke polovykh refleksov', *Polovoi vopros v shkole i v zhizni*, ed. I. S. Simonov (Leningrad, 1927).
49. G. R., 'Protsessy gomoseksualistov', *Ezhenedel'nik sovetskoi iustitsii*, no. 33 (1922), 16–17; Healey, *Homosexual Desire in Revolutionary Russia*, chapter 4.
50. Note too his comments on German homosexual emancipationist Hirschfeld (then on a disappointing pilgrimage to the USSR), whom he described as 'naive and pompous' after a 'deadly dull' official meeting in June 1926 (Malmstad and Bogomolov, *Mikhail Kuzmin*, 348).
51. Healey, 'Moscow', 49–57.
52. See the profiles of the male and female homosexual in L. G. Orshanskii, 'Polovye prestupleniia. Analiz psikhologicheskii i psikhopatologicheskii', *Polovye prestupleniia*, ed. A. A. Zhizhilenko and L. G. Orshanskii (Leningrad-Moscow, 1927). Health Commissar Semashko, a physician sympathetic to homosexual emancipation, found it necessary nevertheless to condemn the 'masculinization' of women as a vulgarization of revolutionary ideals; see N. A. Semashko, 'Nuzhna li "zhenstvennost'"? (v poriadke obsuzhdeniia)', *Molodaia gvardiia*, no. 6 (1924), 205–6.
53. Eric Naiman, *Sex in Public: the Incarnation of Early Soviet Ideology* (Princeton, 1997). On sexology see also Frances Bernstein, 'What Everyone Should Know About Sex: Gender, Sexual Enlightenment, and the Politics of Health in Revolutionary Russia, 1918–1931' (Ph.D. diss., Columbia University, 1998).
54. GARF, f. A482, op. 25, d. 478, ll. 85–7.
55. Ibid., l. 86.
56. These specialists, having acknowledged the value of the 'masculinized type'

of women in the Red Army, suggested that female 'transvestites' after psychiatric tests might receive the 'right' to same-sex marriage, ibid.

57. V. P. Osipov, *Rukovodstvo po psikhiatrii* (Moscow-Leningrad, 1931), 574–5.
58. This argument is developed in Healey, *Homosexual Desire in Revolutionary Russia*, chapter 7.
59. Tsentral'nyi Munitsipal'nyi Arkhiv Moskvy (TsMAM), f. 819, op. 2, d. 11, ll. 241–2. All names from TsMAM documents have been altered.
60. 'I gave in to him and we committed a sexual act. First I took the role of a woman, then he did', TsMAM f. 819, op. 2, d. 51, l. 16; 'We became close and then committed acts of sodomy. . . . First he used me, and then I him', ibid., ll. 57–8; see also ll. 29, 57 ob., 100, 108 ob.
61. Ibid., d. 11, l. 241.
62. Healey, *Homosexual Desire in Revolutionary Russia*, chapter 8.
63. Nowhere in these documents (which used 'homosexual' freely) was the word 'heterosexual' used. Men whose sexuality was judged respectable were labelled as married (*zhenatyi*) or family men (*semeinyi*; *sem'ianin*). Modern concepts of heterosexuality, like the term itself, were developed after discourses of homosexuality; see Jonathan Ned Katz, *The Invention of Heterosexuality* (New York, 1995).
64. For a discussion of the treatment of sodomy cases by the Moscow city courts, including an assessment of the severity judges accorded this crime compared to heterosexual rape and child abuse, and the dynamics of sentencing policies through the Great Terror, see Healey, *Homosexual Desire in Revolutionary Russia*, chapter eight.
65. TsMAM, f. 819, op. 2, d. 30, unnumbered sheets following l. 47.

10

Masculinity and Heroism in Imperial and Soviet Military-Patriotic Cultures

Karen Petrone

Don Cossack Koz'ma Kriuchkov was the first First World War soldier to be awarded a St George's Cross for single-handedly defeating eleven German cavalry officers on 12 August 1914. The text of a poster depicting his 'heroic battle' thus described the scene: 'The Germans struck with lances and first he repulsed them with his rifle; when his rifle gave out, then he began to fell them with his saber, and then he wrested a lance from a German and put it to use.'[1] Twenty-five years later, on 18 July 1939, an official speaking at the All-Union Physical Culture Parade on Moscow's Red Square recounted the individual exploit (*podvig*) of Hero of the Soviet Union, Deputy Politruk Bamburov at Lake Khasan: 'In a engagement with Japanese robbers, he alone stood against tens of samurai. The courageous Komsomol mowed down the enemy with machine gun fire, threw hand grenades at them, and when his ammunition ran out, he hurled himself at the Samurai with the barrel of his gun.'[2] The remarkable similarity of these two passages suggests that, changes in military technology aside, the trope of the outnumbered hero who succeeded through raw courage and determination was virtually identical in 1914 and 1939.

In the first four decades of the twentieth century, Europeans experienced profound challenges to nineteenth-century hierarchies of class, gender, and nationality. War, socialist revolution, nationalist uprisings, and the rise of the 'New Woman' precipitated crises of masculinity, national identity, and political power. Nowhere was this more the case than in Russia, where the failures of the Old Regime led to revolution and the introduction of a radical new ideology that embraced gender equality and rejected traditional notions of patriotism. How, then, can we explain the persistence of this military-patriotic trope and the strong continuity between Russian and Soviet conceptions of military-heroic masculinity? By exploring the attributes of Russian heroism and valor (*muzhestvo*, which in the Russian language is etymologically connected to 'manliness'), this essay will consider both continuities and transformations in depictions of heroic masculinity between 1904 and 1939.

This essay focuses on one type of modern masculine archetype – the soldier-hero. Attributes of the soldier-hero such as 'aggression, strength, courage, and endurance' have made this image 'one of the most durable and powerful forms of idealized masculinity within Western cultural traditions since the time of the Ancient Greeks'.[3] A critical masculine quality that the ideal soldier also possesses is self-control.[4] He must be able to control his will and his passions as he sacrifices himself for the cause. In depictions of the ideal soldier, hysteria and fanaticism, both the results of an excess of passion, are belittled as feminine and negative traits.

Military-heroic masculinity is intimately connected with modern nationalism, for to be a soldier-hero is to be willing to fight and die for one's nation. In the Russian Empire, the ideal military hero went into battle 'with "the cross of Christ before his eyes". Such men were always ready to die, and if they had to bury fallen comrades, they would not weep.'[5] The stoicism of the ideal Russian soldier in the face of death was a product both of his self-control and of his belief in a heavenly reward. In the Soviet Union, ideal soldier-heroes gave their lives with the ultimate goal of communism rather than 'the cross of Christ' before their eyes. Nevertheless, both Russian and Soviet soldier heroes faced death to defend their countries.

Neither the Russian Empire nor the Soviet Union was a homogeneous nation-state. They both encompassed a large number of different nationalities arranged in hierarchical relationships. Russia, as a multinational empire, was profoundly conscious of the dangers it faced from movements for national autonomy and self-determination and responded, in Benedict Anderson's words, by 'stretching the short, tight, skin of the nation over the gigantic body of the empire'.[6] In the Soviet period, the problems of creating an inclusive patriotic identity in the face of great ethnic diversity persisted. It is not coincidental, therefore, that depictions of Russian and Soviet heroic masculinity often sought to articulate national unity at the same time that they maintained ethnic difference.

In the process of building patriotism, military-heroic masculinity often minimizes the distinctions among the male citizens of a country. Bravery, sacrifice, and self-control in battle are portrayed as tearing down barriers among men and producing a camaraderie that unites men of different classes. Indeed, hierarchies of social status tend to disappear in accounts of heroic masculinity. In the Russian Empire, however, this leveling theme was not as strong as it was elsewhere in Europe. [7] This essay explores the tension between the assertion of military hierarchies and the celebration of male camaraderie in Russian and Soviet patriotic culture. It examines as well the ways in which ethnic and class hierarchies shaped the articulation of Russian and Soviet military-heroic masculinities.

To highlight the interaction of masculinity and ethnicity in the depiction of Russian and Soviet soldier-heroes, this essay focuses primarily on the depiction of military campaigns against an ethnically and racially distinct enemy, the Japanese. There were three such confrontations between Russian/Soviet and Japanese forces between 1904 and 1939. The first, the Russo-Japanese War of 1904–5, began when Japan, fearing Russian territorial expansion in the Far East, made a surprise attack on the Manchurian city of Port Arthur in February 1904. In the ensuing war the Japanese destroyed the Russian navy and besieged Port Arthur. The dismal performance of the Russian Empire against a minor power like Japan was one of the causes of the Russian Revolution of 1905.

The second episode came during the Russian Civil War (1918–20). In early 1918, shortly after the Bolsheviks took power, they were confronted with military opposition from pro-tsarist forces, socialist opponents, nationalists demanding autonomy, and anti-Soviet peasants. Soviet Russia also faced foreign invasion by the French, British, Americans, and the Japanese, who sent 100000 troops to the Soviet Far East in the interest of territorial expansion at Soviet expense.[8] By 1922, the Soviet military had succeeded not only in defeating internal opponents but in securing the withdrawal of all foreign troops from Soviet soil.

The Lake Khasan incident of 1938 was also a military success for the Soviet Union. Once again the Japanese and the Soviets fought over the definition of the Soviet borders. The Japanese army, then occupying Manchuria and most of eastern China, moved troops onto a hilltop on the Soviet side of the Soviet–Manchurian border, 70 miles southeast of Vladivostok. After two weeks, the Red Army expelled the Japanese and, as the Soviet sources put it, 'the inviolability of the sacred borders of our country" was affirmed without the loss of "even one *vershok* of Soviet land'.[9] Ignoring the significant disparity in casualties (Soviet troops had suffered 3400 casualties in comparison to Japan's 1400),[10] Soviet ideologues and propagandists celebrated the heroes of Khasan by publishing a wide array of books, pamphlets, and articles. That the Soviets exaggerated the importance of this event makes the rhetoric about Lake Khasan even more revealing of the transformations in military-patriotic culture in the late 1930s.[11]

One of the most striking similarities in Imperial and Soviet military and patriotic culture is one of genre. The ideologues of both the Russian Empire and the Soviet Union used short vignettes and longer fictional accounts about exemplary individual heroes to inspire their citizens.[12] It is well known that the Soviets frequently adopted the forms of tsarist discourses while radically reshaping their content. In this case, however, Soviet publicists employed both the genres and the theme of individual heroes that had characterized prerevolutionary military discourse, even while claiming that "Soviet heroism is a collective endeavor."[13] Because of the continuing power of individual heroes to inspire the population, Soviet ideologues were willing to employ a traditional model of individual heroism that contradicted Soviet commitments to the value of the collective.

The first section of this chapter analyzes Russian and Soviet depictions of the Japanese so as to explore the ways in which masculine ideals of bravery and self-control interacted with notions about race and social status in the first third of the twentieth century. Transformations and continuities in these values illuminate Russian and Soviet attempts to create unity and patriotic identification with the nation. The second section compares the mythologizing of military heroes in the Russian Empire and the Soviet Union.

Bravery, passion, masculinity and race

In the Russo-Japanese War, the Civil War, and the Lake Khasan incident, the Imperial and Soviet armies fought the Japanese. How Imperial and Soviet publicists depicted these enemies reveals a great deal about their understanding of both masculinity and racial difference in their multi-ethnic and multiracial states. Characterizations of the behavior of both Russian and enemy troops in battle revealed a tension between two concepts – courageous self-control and passionate bravery. In a February 1904 lecture to benefit the Red Cross at St Vladimir University in Kiev, Professor I. A. Sikorskii claimed that 'in war, the yellow race easily becomes fanatical because of the property of its mind, and gives itself over to feelings and passions, and not intellect and reason.'[14] The white race, on the other hand, was superior because of its 'measured, symmetrical development of the mind, will and feelings'. Sikorskii also argued that because of their 'simplicity and naturalness', Russians made superior soldiers; they 'look[ed] straight into the face of death', while Japanese were incapable of doing so.[15] In Western thought, masculine self-control has often been contrasted to feminine emotion. Sikorskii played on this tradition to affirm the racial and masculine superiority of the Russians, expressed by their remaining calm when in mortal peril. The Japanese, members of an inferior race, were susceptible to female passions.

This simplistic view of the Japanese was soon challenged by the enemy's overwhelming success on the battlefield. As the Japanese proved their prowess, Russian authors described them in increasingly masculine terms. A 1905 article admitted the strength of the Japanese army and attributed this power to 'an unwritten code of military honor, worked out by the former military caste of the samurai. The union of popular ethics with the rules of knightly morals created an imposing force.'[16] This definition of the victorious Japanese affirmed their masculinity by acknowledging their moral consciousness. By arguing that a noble or knightly ethos led to Japanese success, this author suggested that class and gender had overcome racial inferiority. His tacit comparison of the ability of Russian and Japanese nobles to shape the ethics of non-nobles (that is, enlisted men) was also a somewhat veiled reference to the failure of Russian Imperial officers to create a unity of purpose among their men. The key factor in the defeat of the Russian army, in this observer's view, was the inability of the nobility to imbue their soldiers with 'the rules of knightly morals' or to create a manly camaraderie that would ease the distinctions between nobles and peasants. In fact, the Japanese had been more successful than the Russians in building national unity, but the author ascribed their victory not to these successes, but to what he imagined to be the still vital ethics of a long-vanished warrior class.

The author also cited other, less admirable aspects of the Japanese national character to explain their success in battle, including, 'an innate ability to be secretive, outstanding self-possession, bravery bordering on contempt for death, persistence, perseverance, all of which was tightly interwoven with malice, deceit, base unscrupulousness, brutality, and mass suicide if it was impossible to fall with honor'.[17] This author granted the Japanese many of the traits of the soldier-hero – bravery, persistence, self-possession, and brutality – and distinguished them from the Russians not by their lack of manliness but by their extremism in pursuit of victory.

Racial and ethnic stereotypes also influenced the ways in which non-Russian soldiers from the Russian Empire were portrayed in discussions of the Russo-Japanese War. Depictions of military heroism distinguished between two types of bravery – the one spontaneous and passionate and the other reasoned and conscious. Non-Russian soldiers of the Russian Empire were seen by journalists and other writers on the Russo-Japanese War as tending toward the former while Russians excelled at the latter.[18] The author of an article about military scouts explained the differences among Siberian Cossacks in terms of their ethnic 'blood':

> The descendants of Ermak and Polushkin are the best scouts; those in whom there is more Buriat and settlers' blood are cold, indecisive and lazy. Tea is worth more than anything to them; but such people were not accepted into the division of scouts. The mountain people of the Caucasus are full of a wild ardor. It is difficult for them to understand the situation when they do not know the language, but their bravery and impetuosity sometimes bring immense benefit.[19]

This article emphasized the inequality of the Empire's ethnicities and articulated a clear hierarchy of ethnic groups in the military. Only those soldiers descended from Slavic ancestors combined the consciousness and the bravery necessary to be good scouts. Other Imperial nationalities had bravery without consciousness. The spontaneous Caucasians, for example, could be effectively utilized by the army if they were firmly under the direction of Cossacks and Slavs. The Imperial army could thus employ its more passionate, 'wild' nationalities to combat passionate Asian enemies.

This passage clearly reveals the dilemmas of a multiethnic Imperial army that simultaneously affirmed the superiority of Russians and other Slavs, yet depended on the participation of many different nationalities in their military efforts. Overt racism that implied that the non-Russian soldiers of the Empire had more in common with the enemy than with the Empire clashed with a discourse about the non-Russian soldier's unswerving loyalty to the Empire. Praise of the admirable qualities of non-Russian soldiers collided with a deep conviction of their essential difference from Russians. Asians and Caucasians in the Empire were ambiguously both brave and passionate, members of the Empire, yet potentially treacherous.

A literary sketch of a loyal Ossetian in the *Illiustrirovannaia letopis' Russko-iaponskoi voiny* illustrates the complicated attitudes of publicists toward the non-Russian heroes of the Russo-Japanese War. Bitsko Torchinov, a loyal and brave soldier in the retinue of the Commander-in-Chief is depicted as willing to 'shield the commander from enemy bullets with his own body'. He is called 'the best representative of a knightly tribe, an Ossetian'.[20] Here we see the ways in which Imperial publicists sought to bridge the gap between Russians and other nationalities in the military and administration of the Empire. By praising the noble ancestry of the Ossetians, the author confirmed that this soldier belongs in an Imperial army in which noble blood is crucial to status. Just as one author tried to explain Japanese victories by pointing to the knightly morals of the officer corps, this celebrant of noble Ossetian blood affirms the importance of class over ethnicity or race.

When Torchinov prevents the Commander-in-Chief from going into enemy fire, his superior reveals his assumptions about the inferior masculinity of the non-Russians and calls him a coward. Not offended, Torchinov replies, 'No. I am not a coward. . . . I will go wherever you want me to. But I will not let you pass because you are needed for Russia.'[21] Here Torchinov addresses the commanding officer in the familiar form and gives him orders. The safety of the commander is more important to him than obeying orders or defending himself from insult. It is arguable that the Ossetian in this situation is behaving more rationally than his hotheaded Russian commander, but the author of the portrait does not draw this conclusion from his own evidence. Rather, he emphasizes the passionate quality of Torchinov's attachment to his superior, 'to whom he gave himself body and soul'. Torchinov's devotion to Russian commanders also acknowledges Russian hegemony, for by loyally serving the Empire, he proves its legitimacy.

The description of Torchinov does not stop there, however. After retelling tales of the Ossetian's bravery, the author moves to his limitations. When the Commander-in-Chief asked Torchinov to describe the battle site from which he has just returned, 'he completely lost his ability to express himself clearly'.[22] He cannot tell the Commander-in-Chief anything about the number of casualties on the battlefield. While the author claims that this reticence is useful, since Torchinov will never reveal military secrets, he is in fact emphasizing the spontaneous spirit of the Ossetian while denying his intellect. Torchinov lacks the consciousness and intelligence of his Russian superiors but his difference from the Russians enhances rather than reduces his contribution to the army.

The author also distinguishs between Slavic and Ossetian masculinity. Describing Torchinov's appearance, he mentions that even though he is no longer young, 'his waist . . . was like a girl's, so slender and graceful'.[23] This explicit feminization of Torchinov is part of a long-standing European tradition of feminizing the Orient in order to express its otherness and to assert the superior masculinity of the European male.[24] Torchinov is brave because of his passionate devotion to his commander, an emotion implicitly feminine and therefore negative. This sketch of Torchinov claims that he belongs to the Imperial army, but its feminizing representations define him as fundamentally different from his European counterparts.

Because the Japanese army defeated Russian forces in 1904 and 1905, Imperial publicists were forced to acknowledge Japanese manliness and bravery. They emphasized the effectiveness of Japanese morale and male camaraderie in order to suggest that reforms were needed in the Russian army. The Red Army in the Civil War suffered no such public humiliations at Japanese hands, and this may explain the fact that Soviet propagandists recognized the positive qualities of their enemies far less frequently. Some Civil War depictions written in the 1920s acknowledged the superior military power and potent masculinity of the Japanese but criticized their morality and ethics. In Aleksandr Fadeev's *The Rout* (written in 1925–6 and sometimes titled in translation *The Nineteen*), the Japanese appear as strong but brutal enemies who rape Russian women, are rumored to be using poison gas, and are capable of wringing Red partisans' necks 'like chickens'.[25] The partisans stand in awe of the Japanese advance, which is likened to 'an iron boot fashioned by death pitilessly scattering ant heaps'.[26] While Japanese strength is described as 'confident, intelligent, and yet somehow blind', the partisans remain unable to capitalize on this blindness and do not defeat the Japanese.[27]

In Vsevelod Ivanov's novella *Armored Train 14–69*, written in 1922, the Japanese are portrayed not so much as strong military aggressors but as a breed apart from the Red partisans. The leader of the partisan detachment and hero of the story, Nikita Vershinin, is open-minded about other soldiers, considering both a Chinese man who fought with the partisans and even an American interventionist to be 'the same kind of peasants, like us', who 'till the land and all of that'. Vershinin's sense of international class solidarity does not extend to the Japanese, however: 'But the Japanese man, what does he do? Stuffs his face with rice, and you've got to talk to him differently.'[28] Vershinin also likens the Japanese to savage predators: 'A Japanese man is worse than a tiger for us. Before devouring a Chinese man, the tiger will pull off his clothes, let him air out. But a Japanese man won't stop to take stock.

He'll devour you boots and all.'[29] The wild beast is thus seen as more discriminating than the Japanese man. Throughout the novella, the Japanese are demeaned as 'short people', 'cheap people', 'light . . . a piece of muslin', and 'cowards'.[30] The Japanese are simultaneously feminized and dehumanized in this account. Their small stature, lack of bravery and insubstantial nature point to the absence of manly qualities. Their wild brutality also reveals their lack of humanity. Despite Soviet assertions about unity of workers and peasants across all borders, Ivanov does not acknowledge the possibility of good laboring Japanese.

While the 'yellow' Japanese are excluded from the international community of toilers in the novella, the 'yellow' Chinese character Sin-Bin-U becomes a hero and martyr for Soviet power. [31] Although throughout he speaks a comic pigeon Russian and is portrayed as the target of the Red partisans' jokes, Sin-Bin-U offers his life to the revolution. To stop an armored train so that they can ambush it, the partisans decide that someone must lie down on the tracks. After the Russian paymaster Vaska Okorok decides to make this sacrifice, Sin-Bin-U joins him, saying in broken Russian that Vaska is lonely. Sin-Bin-U demonstrates his desire to be part of the partisan community by asserting his comradeship with Vaska. Once they are both stretched out on the tracks, however, Vaska loses his nerve, jumps up, and runs away. Sin-Bin-U remains alone in his martyrdom. Even at this moment of great heroism, though, there is ambiguity in the way that Sin-Bin-U is portrayed. On the train track, Sin-Bin-U's head is 'flat and emerald-eyed like that of a cobra', it 'felt the ties, tore itself off of them, and wavering, lifted itself up above the rails. . . . It looked around.'[32] Ivanov describes Sin-Bin-U as a wild animal just as he compares the Japanese to tigers. Sin-Bin-U is thus dehumanized and held apart from the men of the Soviet community. Although he demonstrates more discipline than the Russian, Sin-Bin-U's self-control also wavers as the train approaches and he shoots himself so that he will be sure to stop the train. The meaning of Sin-Bin-U's suicide remains unclear; was it heroism, a protest against his exclusion from the partisan community, a failure of his manly will to remain on the tracks, or evidence of his fanatical, unreasoned devotion to the cause? Like non-Russians in the Imperial Army, Sin-Bin-U is not granted a fully masculine or fully heroic status.

Soviet publicists celebrated the inclusion of brave non-Russians, including Maslims and Jews, as had their Imperial predecessors. In *Chapaev*, Dmitrii Furmanov's famous Civil War novel, the narrator describes a Soviet Muslim regiment made up of fourteen different nationalities that 'performed deeds of unheard-of valor and heroism'.

However, these childlike troops needed the tutelage of the Communist Party more than other regiments since 'they matured slowly and were unable to grasp at once the causes and the scope of the social struggle that was in progress'.[33] These soldiers have manly valor but not manly intellect. With proper education, received mostly from Russian communists, these non-Russian soldiers can attain Soviet consciousness and become fully masculine.

Ten years later, in the rigid rhetoric of the Stalin era, no aspect of the enemy's existence could be presented in a favorable light. The Lake Khasan vignettes demeaned and discounted Japanese military power at every turn. Japanese soldiers were not strong, brave, or manly in any way; they revealed their cowardice by panicking, becoming confused and retreating in disorder in every battle. Their military equipment was inferior to the Soviets' and they were very poor marksmen. They only had enough nerve to go into battle when they were drunk. This rejection of Japanese valor created a logical problem for Soviet ideologues. The only way to create heroes when one had declared the enemy so inferior was to find situations in which valiant Soviet soldiers were severely outnumbered. In using this fantasy trope of the folkloric superhero who took on ten enemy soldiers, Soviet ideologues consciously or unconsciously reproduced the swaggering rhetoric of the early days of the First World War, rhetoric produced before German military superiority became clear.[34]

The rhetoric of Lake Khasan reflected Soviet culture of the 1930s as well. The politics of the 1930s created a relatively coherent discourse about internal and external enemies and the images of the Japanese fit easily within this discourse. As Victoria Bonnell has recently pointed out in her analysis of Soviet posters, descriptions of the enemy in the 1930s used a language of dehumanization.[35] In depictions of battles at Lake Khasan, the Japanese were consistently denied human form. They were instead represented as locusts, reptiles, vultures, swine, rabbits, cats and other creatures. While the tactic of dehumanization existed in prerevolutionary and early Soviet war rhetoric, the particular features of the Lake Khasan enemies were drawn directly from the vocabulary of the 1930s.

Soviet discourse naturally differed from Imperial discourse in its representations of class and rank. While nobility carried positive connotations in patriotic rhetoric before 1917, in the Soviet Union the meaning of nobility was exclusively negative. Descriptions of the heroes of Khasan often dwelt on their humble origins and occupations before they joined the ranks of the Red Army. In this manner, the essential unity of people and army was affirmed. The enemy army, on the other hand, was represented as imperialist, capitalist, and fascist, with no organic ties to oppressed Japanese workers and peasants. Lake Khasan thus became a class war of the Soviet proletariat versus the Japanese nobility. By consistently referring to the Japanese soldiers as 'samurai', propagandists defined all members of the army as members of the feudal nobility, while denying all of the attributes of manly honor and bravery that such a term could connote. As in the Civil War, Soviet ideologues avoided addressing the vexing contradiction that the ranks of the Japanese army were filled with the oppressed workers and peasants whose fate they bemoaned. By emphasizing that the Japanese military ethos stemmed from the noble traditions of the samurai, the Soviet propagandists echoed the rhetoric of the Russo-Japanese war, but they stripped nobility of its manly connotations.

The Soviet government publicly renounced the racism of the pre-revolutionary government and asserted the equality of all nationalities, both inside and outside of the Soviet Union. Despite this official rejection of racialist thinking, elements of pre-revolutionary racism re-emerged in the military-patriotic discourse of the late 1930s. The new racism was not nearly as widespread as the vilification of the Japanese as animals or capitalist-imperialists, but it nonetheless made its mark in the discourse of Lake Khasan. As in the pre-revolutionary period, the Japanese were described as deceitful and morally deficient. A description of the exploits of Sergei Bamburov written by F. Leonidov, for example, called the sneak attack by the Japanese a 'trick' that was perpetrated because of the enemy's 'home-bred Asiatic cunning'.[36] A senior company political leader described the Japanese as having 'revolting mugs with narrowed, malicious eyes'.[37] As in the Imperial period, a cornerstone of Stalinist racism was the denial of Japanese masculinity. The Japanese soldier was feminized, becoming 'hysterical' when the Soviets attacked.[38] In a description of hand-to-hand combat, one Soviet author described how a Japanese officer jumped 'like a female cat' onto the back of a Soviet lieutenant.[39] These images affirmed the racial and gender inferiority of the unmanly Japanese.

The most racialized images of the Japanese came not in the literary descriptions of the war, but in pictorial and satirical representations of the enemy. Japanese soldiers were usually portrayed as corpulent, a sure sign of enemy status in the Soviet period. What racialized this image was his features, which often included glasses, eyes squinting to make up for poor vision, gaping mouths like monkeys, and buck teeth. These caricatured characteristics of the Japanese, which denied them both manliness and humanity, were ubiquitous in the Soviet images of the late 1930s, a visual shorthand by which Japanese could be designated enemies.[40]

The Soviet Union's use of racial discourse was complicated, as the Imperial propagandists' had been, by the fact that the army enlisted soldiers of many ethnicities. The propaganda trope of the friendship of peoples in the 1930s had at its heart the same contradiction that had caused difficulties for the Imperial army: how was the Soviet government to depict the non-Russians as a part of the whole while the control of the country was predominantly in the hands of Slavs? The Soviet solution to this problem was not unlike the Imperial one. Just as the Imperial Russians could use their consciousness to tame and utilize the wild Caucasian mountain peoples and Siberian Cossacks, Sovietized and Slavic Red Army soldiers could tutor non-Russians and make them Soviet. In one vignette, the Soviet Captain Bochkarev was stopped by a wounded Kazakh soldier who told him to retreat because 'death is there [ahead]'. Bochkarev replied, 'We Bolsheviks are not afraid of death' and continued forward. A few minutes later, the Kazakh announced that despite his wound he would accompany the captain, and he repeated, 'We Bolsheviks are not afraid of death.'[41] Soviet heroism had been transmitted from officer to soldier and from Slav to Kazakh. The unmanly nature of the non-Russian soldier had been transformed by his interaction with a model of Soviet masculinity.

This analysis of depictions of social status, race, and gender in patriotic culture has demonstrated strong continuities between Imperial and Soviet military-patriotic discourses. Both the Russian Empire and the Soviet Union differentiated between Europeans and other races by feminizing the non-Europeans, and contrasting their weakness to the true masculinity of the mostly Slavic Europeans. Both before and after the Revolution, characterizations of the enemy's masculinity depended as much on his success or failure in battle as on the government's position on racial or gender equality. Non-European enemies who proved their strength were granted more masculine and positive qualities than those whom the Russians defeated. This tactic allowed the defeated Russians to assert their own army's masculine heroism. Representations of interactions between Slavic and non-Slavic soldiers fighting on the same side also remained constant. Non-Slavic heroes do not reach the full masculine and heroic stature of Slavic heroes and often require the tutelage of Slavic mentors to accomplish heroic deeds.

From heroic to mythic masculinity

Now that we have explored continuities in depictions of the enemy, we will turn to an analysis of the attributes of Russian Imperial and Soviet heroism. The behavior of the wounded soldier was one way of measuring valor in battle in both periods, for a wounded man had especially dramatic opportunities to display perseverance and self-control. During the Russo-Japanese War, officers were praised for remaining at their posts and continuing to fight after sustaining grievous injuries. For example, 'mortally wounded Staff-Captain Isaev threw himself on the parapet and shot all of the cartridges left in his revolver at the Japanese who encircled him with bayonets'.[42] The dying Isaev gained heroic stature by making a desperate effort to destroy the enemy with his last strength. Russian soldiers were also celebrated when they successfully returned to their own lines in spite of injuries, evading capture by the Japanese: 'Noncommissioned officer Makurin was wounded by a bullet, received a bayonet wound, was again caught by a bullet in the leg, and nonetheless crawled back to his own.'[43] Others were praised for risking their own lives as they carried wounded comrades and officers out of battle.[44] Brave actions that were taken under fire, when wounded, and during a battle that was already lost defined Russian military heroism.

While the participants in the Russo-Japanese War were depicted as heroic men, they were still generally portrayed as men with human weaknesses. In the early days of a far more perilous war, the First World War, Imperial military heroes were built up into supermen; an example is Koz'ma Kriuchkov, who reportedly suffered sixteen wounds when he battled single-handedly with eleven German cavalry officers.[45] Civil War heroes shrank from these mythic proportions. The partisans fight bravely and tenaciously but when they are outnumbered or surprised, they sustain heavy losses. Individual Civil War heroes succumb to bullets in the usual way. Their heroism is not fully developed and they struggle to learn consciousness, discipline, and manliness. The most mythic of the Civil War heroes, Chapaev, was praised for enduring in total silence an 'excruciating operation' to remove a bullet from his skull, but in general the Furmanov novel celebrates Chapaev's military tactics and inspirational leadership rather than his physical strength.[46] The narrator of the novel explicitly denies that Chapaev had any 'superhuman' abilities. Instead, he asserts that Chapaev was 'extremely human, even lacking in many valuable qualities'.[47] The entire plot of the novel revolves around the attempts of the communist political officer Fyodor Klychkov to cure Chapaev of his many faults, chief among them impetuosity, a violent temper, and a hatred of 'headquarters'.[48] Like Bitsko Torchinov, Chapaev also has feminine qualities; his hands are 'delicate, almost feminine' and he has 'a strangely lithe and sinuous way of moving, like a girl'.[49]

The Stalinist period dispensed with such nuanced heroes and instead exaggerated the capabilities of the New Soviet Man so as to construct a mythic hyper-masculinity. Consequently, the Soviet heroes of Lake Khasan were more like the warriors of the early days of The First World War, in that they were portrayed as possessing untold reserves of strength and stamina. Whereas the heroic officers of the Russo-Japanese War handed over their commands to the next in line when they were wounded,[50] Soviet commanders such as the Hero of the Soviet Union Captain Levchenko stay with their troops. Levchenko 'twice wounded and contused, did not tell anyone about his injuries and, clenching his teeth in pain, once again led his troops in an attack. His eyes grew dull from loss of blood, his wounded shoulder burned, but he remained at his post.'[51] Officers of the Russo-Japanese War and Civil War partisans, with the possible exception of Chapaev, were described simply as strong and brave men; Stalinist officers were mythic heroes, to whom it was virtually impossible for ordinary Soviet men to measure up.

One of the most critical attributes of the military hero in a democratic age is his relationship with his subordinates. He is expected to foster unity of purpose and camaraderie, that is, build a male community in which differences of rank become insignificant. The heroes of both the Russo-Japanese War and the Civil War could be celebrated even if they failed to construct this kind of community. Because of the low morale and difficult conditions of the Russo-Japanese War, an officer was sometimes considered heroic even if his men did not follow him into battle. In an article entitled 'Individual Heroes', the exploit of one Russian lieutenant was praised in spite of the fact that when he 'threw himself forward' against the Japanese, 'only two soldiers followed him'.[52] In an army plagued by class conflict, the bravery of an officer was more important than whether he commanded the obedience of his men.

When the literature of the Russo-Japanese War deals with the theme of camaraderie directly, it reveals the extreme divisions that plagued the Imperial army. Even in idealized depictions of Russian camaraderie, the bonds between soldiers and officers are portrayed as deeply affected by their consciousness of rank. Lieutenant Dmitriev, who blew up a Japanese minesweeper, told of the atmosphere on board ship after he had set off the explosion: 'The squad, forgetting discipline, pulled my sleeve in order to share their impressions. . . . We extracted our cognac and drank straight from the bottle, first Morozov and I, then we passed the bottle to the squad. How much vigor a single gulp instills!'[53] The victory brings the team closer to its leaders, but it is impossible for anyone to forget the hierarchy of command. Spontaneously touching a superior is recognized by Dmitriev as a breach of discipline, and even the convivial sharing of cognac has a hierarchical form as the commanders drink first. Heroism could not be articulated without attention to hierarchy.

Soviet authors portrayed Civil War leaders as complicated figures who have to struggle with themselves in order to be better commanders of others. The plots of the novels revolve around the central characters' acquisition of manly discipline and self-control. For example, the hero of Fadeev's novel *The Rout* is a Jewish partisan commander named Levinson who feels estranged from the men he leads. He considers himself 'a hostile force raised above the company'; he feels fear and loss of control over events in battle; he makes a mistake and leads his men to their deaths in a bog.[54] At several critical points in the novel, Levinson fails to create the camaraderie that would reduce the distance between him and his men. Much more introspective than any of the other military figures discussed here, Levinson also constantly questions his own decisions and actions.[55]

In the Soviet period, the ability to create male camaraderie became a much more important trait for the hero. Soviet publicists of both the Civil War and Stalinist eras used lyrical images to depict how the spiritual unity of the soldiers and their devotion to a leader transformed the individual members of the unit into a whole greater than the sum of its parts.[56] Dmitrii Furmanov's description of the relationship between Chapaev and his men during the Civil War became canonical for later Soviet literature. Chapaev was legendary in his ability to mobilize his men into a battle-ready community. His partisans think, 'He is one of us, to be sure, but he's something out of the ordinary; you can't put him quite on a level with us,' and they treat him with 'love and respect'.[57] Their regard for Chapaev, not his rank (he had been an enlisted man in the Imperial army), raise him above them as leader and their devotion to him and to one another made them a powerful fighting force. Chapaev's partisans gain status and masculinity from their egalitarian heroic comradeship and loyalty to their commander.

Civil War literature also emphasized the strong bonds between men, often by portraying a relationship between two heroes. In *Chapaev*, Furmanov focuses on the relationship between Chapaev and his mentor, the political commissar Klychkov. In the course of the novel, Chapaev learns party discipline from Klychkov and Klychkov gains courage and battle skills from Chapaev. They love each other and neither wants to part when Klychkov is reassigned.[58] In partnership, the two men form a powerful military force, both spontaneous and disciplined.

In *The Rout*, Levinson, despite his failures in leadership, is able to forge bonds of love and affection with his men. He is particularly fond of his young second-in-command, Baklanov; Baklanov, for his part, so admires Levinson that he imitates his mannerisms.[59] Between battles, the men engage in horseplay together, pinching and wrestling with one another.[60] When Baklanov tries to express his feelings to Levinson, Levinson cuts him off abruptly and they go to bathe bare-chested in the river.[61] When Baklanov is killed in battle, Levinson breaks down: 'he sat huddled up in the saddle, slowly blinking his long wet eyelashes, and the tears ran down his beard'.[62] The last words of the novel articulate a model for masculine leadership and self-control: '[Levinson] ceased crying; it was necessary to live and a man had to do his duty.'[63] The powerful emotional bonds of Levinson's partisan detachment had been broken by death, but the true leader would continue on to forge more bonds and fight again.

Just as it was impossible for Soviet enemies to be granted any positive qualities in the Stalinist period, Soviet heroes at the battle at Lake Khasan had few, if any, negative qualities. Failures of leadership could not be admitted in the 1930s for two reasons: first, because the Soviet censors did not permit the realities of war to impinge on depictions of heroic action in battle; secondly, because the unity of the masculine community of soldiers, commissars, and officers was the defining feature of the ideal Soviet army, setting it apart from all 'imperialist' armies. The Stalinist hero, therefore, did not waver and always earned the loyalty of his troops.

A typical example is the memoir 'Threatening Attacks', in which Red Army soldier L. Antipov recounts his experiences at Lake Khasan.[64] This work is more fiction than autobiography and includes the interior monologues of characters other than the author. Antipov was in the same unit as one of the most celebrated martyrs of the Lake Khasan battle, the Commissar Ivan Pozharskii. On the eve of the battle, after the commander and commissars brief the troops on the next day's engagement, the entire unit goes swimming together. Commissar Ivan Pozharskii, around whom the unit has coalesced, jumps in the water and swims vigorously, 'in great strokes, as they do in the Volga', while the rest of the soldiers laugh, shout and receive 'enormous satisfaction'.

One soldier then climbs onto the shore and begins to sing about how 'all of nature invites us to be her guests'.[65] This image of naked men frolicking together in nature before meeting the enemy reveals a great deal about the imagined source of Soviet heroism. It was in this homosocial and potentially homo-erotic environment that the bonds that united men of all ranks were forged and it was because of those bonds that ordinary men became capable of becoming great heroes.[66]

Their ultimate test comes, of course, in combat. In 'Threatening Attacks', Antipov focuses on the personal tie between the commissar Pozharskii and a promising young Red Army soldier named Panchenko. As the Soviet advance at Lake Khasan is about to begin, Pozharskii calls, 'Well, come on lads, let's go', and Panchenko 'felt that a warm wave approached his heart . . . so loving did the words of Pozharskii sound in the chaos of continuous explosions and the rattle of machine-gun fire'.[67] It is the personal, emotional, and, one might even suggest, romantic attachment of Panchenko to Commissar Pozharskii that gives him the strength to fight. Both Panchenko and Pozharskii are killed in the battle that ensues.

While differences of rank existed in the Soviet army, their meaning was blurred by publicists, as it had been in at least some prerevolutionary literature, by assertions that the soldier obeyed his superior because of affection rather than coercion. Chapaev, Pozharskii, and, to some degree, Levinson were portrayed as effectively leading men in battle because of their love and affection for their soldiers and their soldiers' love for them, not because of their superior rank. The battle scenarios also reveal another striking difference between Soviet and Russian patriotic tropes. The ideal Soviet relationship between leaders and soldiers was never cemented over a drink. Instead it was personal interaction and communion with nature that forged the special relationship between a Soviet leader and his men. Never would it even be hinted in a 1930s depiction of battle that valor came from a bottle. Only the Japanese enemy used liquor to embolden cowardly soldiers to take part in a unjust and senseless battle. Soviet soldiers were motivated by Bolshevik spirit rather than vodka or cognac. Unlike the discourse of the Russo-Japanese War and the Civil War, which acknowledged the complexities of human motivation and human interaction, Stalinist literature minimized the intricacies of human nature.

While masculine courage was a key factor in the rhetoric of all wars, in the Soviet period manliness took on new meaning. Men's relationships with one another were portrayed as charged with emotion, and these relationships were seen as fostering a communal heroism that was distinct from the bravery of 1905 and 1914. The source of individual acts of heroism was a Soviet camaraderie, a masculine community that gave the New Soviet Man new strengths. However, it was only after Stalin came to power that the Soviet male hero was consistently depicted as larger than life and without blemish.

Tsarist military-patriotic rhetoric appealed to Soviet ideologues for a variety of reasons. The first reason was practical. Since one had to have a clear command structure in the army, it became inevitable that Soviet discourse would heroize commanders and encourage the loyalty of soldiers to their superiors, just as Imperial discourse had done. Imperial military-patriotic rhetoric also appealed to Soviet authors because of underlying continuities between Imperial Russian and Soviet worldviews. Despite the diametrically opposite values they assigned to noble status, both Russians and Soviets considered nobility more important than race. Nonetheless, in both worldviews, the perceived otherness of the non-Slavic nationalities created contradictions in the rhetoric of Empire. Imperial and Soviet authors therefore employed a narrative of tutelage simultaneously to include non-Russians in the Empire, yet to deny them full status as men and citizens.

Other similarities in Imperial and Soviet patriotic rhetoric were structural and related to popular tastes. Individual heroes were more stirring than collective ones, and the Soviet desire to mobilize the population led to an adoption of heroic genres that recapitulated the patriotic discourse of a confident Russian Empire. Soviet patriotic discourse thus owed far more to its pre-revolutionary predecessors than it was willing to admit. One area in which Soviet discourse remained distinct from the Imperial discourse of the Russo-Japanese War was in the depiction of heroic masculinity. While the trope of the courage of the individual hero in battle persisted over time, portrayals of a masculine community of Soviet heroes spurring each other to bravery revealed a more egalitarian conception of heroic masculinity that began in the Civil War period, but was developed more fully in the 1930s. Because it downplayed the significance of differences in social status and rank, the new Soviet conception of military-heroic masculinity was much closer to contemporary western European military-heroic masculinity than to Imperial ideals.

Soviet masculinity did incorporate some aspects of tsarist masculinity, however. One of these was the denigration of the enemy by feminization and dehumanization. Despite official policy to the contrary, Soviet male identity, like Imperial identity, was in part constructed in relation to racialized 'others', some of whom could never become part of the Soviet family. Soviet boundaries were permeable to some extent, as were boundaries in Imperial Russia, and notions of Soviet masculinity were formed through a web of 'imperial' hierarchical relations with both pro-Soviet and anti-Soviet non-Russians. An important aspect of Soviet maleness was to have the power to transform oneself, one's comrades, and inferior 'others' into more perfect Soviet beings in order to crush the enemies who could not be transformed.

The New Soviet Man represented a new definition of masculinity, one that based identity on the comradeship of male heroes, who were often soldiers but could as well be Stakhanovite workers engaged in the struggle to industrialize the nation. While both men and women embraced the new roles and egalitarian ideals that revolution and Civil War afforded them, while both men and women could be Stakhanovites or soldiers, male comradeship, often expressed in military terms, was the central theme of the discourse of the hero in the early decades of the Soviet Union. Because of his pre-eminence, the New Soviet Man undermined the revolutionary rhetoric of gender equality in the Soviet Union.

Notes

I would like to thank the participants of the Midwest Russian History Workshop, meeting at Ohio State University in October 1998, David Hoffmann, Matthew Payne, Kenneth Slepyan, and the editors of this volume for their thoughtful comments on this article.

1. 'Geroiskaia bor'ba kazaka Koz'my Kriuchkova s 11 nemtsami' (Odessa, 1914), Hoover Institution on War, Peace, and Revolution, Stanford University, Poster Collection (hereafter Hoover), RU–SU 162.
2. Tsentral'nyi Khranenie Dokumentov Molodezhnykh Organizatsii, Fond 1 (Tsentral'nyi Komitet Komsomola), op. 23, d. 1363, l. 104.
3. Graham Dawson, *Soldier Heroes: British Adventure, Empire, and the Imagining of Masculinities* (London, 1994), 1.
4. George L. Mosse, *The Image of Man: the Creation of Modern Masculinity* (New York, 1996), 32.
5. Catherine Merridale, 'The Collective Mind: Trauma and Shell-shock in Twentieth Century Russia', *Journal of Contemporary History*, 35, no.1 (January 2000), 41.
6. Benedict Anderson, *Imagined Communities: Reflections on the Origin and Spread of Nationalism*, rev. edn (London, 1991), 86.
7. This kind of male comradeship and bonding was widespread among western European soldiers at the beginning of the twentieth century. See George L. Mosse, *Nationalism and Sexuality* (New York, 1985), 80; Paul Fussell, *The Great War and Modern Memory* (New York, 1975), 272.
8. John J. Stephan, *The Russian Far East* (Stanford, Calif., 1994), 144.

9. 'Predislovie', *Kak my bili iaponskikh samuraev: sbornik statei i dokumentov*, compiled by Iu. Zhukov (Moscow, 1938), 18.
10. David M. Glantz and Jonathan House, *When Titans Clashed: How the Red Army Stopped Hitler* (Lawrence, Kan., 1995), 14. Though precise figures are not available, one analyst estimated that by the end of the conflict approximately 20000 Soviet troops had been mobilized, as compared to 7000 Japanese troops. (*The Changkufeng Incident: a Study in Soviet-Japanese Conflict*, 1938 [Lanham, Md., 1988], 126–7.)
11. For a detailed discussion of the military significance of this battle, see Alvin D. Coox, *The Anatomy of a Small War: the Soviet-Japanese Struggle for Changkufeng/Khasan*, 1938, Contributions to Military History, no. 13 (Westport, Conn., 1977).
12. See 'Sluchainosti voiny', *Illiustrirovannaia letopis' Russko-iaponskoi voiny*, 11 (1905), 57; 12 (1905), 96; *V ogne: Boevie vpechatleniia uchastnikov voiny* (Petrograd, 1914); *Nashi chudo-bogatyri v voine 1914 goda* (Petrograd, 1915); *Boevye epizody: Sbornik statei i materialov o sobytiiakh u ozera Khasan* (Moscow, 1939); *Geroi Khasana: Sbornik statei* (Moscow, 1939).
13. 'Predislovie', *Kak my bili iaponskikh samuraev*, 10. The heroes of both the 1920s and the 1930s differed sharply from those of the First Five Year Plan. The literature of that time celebrated unnamed 'little heroes'. See Katerina Clark's seminal article, 'Little Heroes and Big Deeds: Literature Responds to the First Five-Year Plan', *Cultural Revolution in Russia, 1928–1931*, ed. Sheila Fitzpatrick (Bloomington, 1978), 189–206.
14. I. A. Sikorskii, *Kharakteristika trekh osnovnykh chelovecheskikh ras – chernoi, zheltoi i beloi – v sviazi s voprosami Russko-iaponskoi voiny* (Kiev, 1904), 7.
15. Ibid., 10, 11.
16. 'Kharakteristika iaponskikh voisk', *Illiustrirovannaia letopis' Russko-iaponskoi voiny*, 15 (1905), 63.
17. Ibid.
18. For a discussion of spontaneity and consciousness in the Soviet context see Katerina Clark, *The Soviet Novel: History as Ritual* (Chicago, Ill., 1985), 3–24.
19. 'Divizion razvedchiki', *Illiustrirovannaia letopis' Russko-iaponskoi voiny*, 12 (1905), 98.
20. 'Bitsko Torchinov – Osetin', ibid., 11 (1905), 69.
21. Ibid.
22. Ibid., 70.
23. Ibid.
24. See Edward W. Said, *Orientalism* (New York, 1979), for a discussion of European depictions of the Orient.
25. A. Fadeyev, *The Nineteen* (Westport, Conn., 1973), 108. See also v, 48, 98.
26. Ibid., 132.
27. Ibid., 134.
28. Vsevelod Ivanov, *Armored Train 14–69*, in *Russian Literature of the Twenties: an Anthology*, ed. Carl R. Proffer et al. (Ann Arbor, Mich., 1987), 164. I have modified the translation of the words 'iaponets' and 'kitaets', which the translator rendered as 'Jap' and 'Chinaman'. I do not see any evidence for the pejoratives in the original Russian. See Vsevelod Ivanov, *Bronepoezd No. 1469*, in *Povesti velikikh let* (Moscow, 1932), 7–110.
29. Ivanov, *Armored Train 14–69*, 158.

30. Ibid., 159, 168, 210.
31. Ibid., 171, 195.
32. Ibid., 195.
33. Dmitrii Furmanov, *Chapayev* (Westport, Conn., 1973), 61.
34. For a discussion of First World War propaganda see Hubertus F. Jahn, *Patriotic Culture in Russia During World War I* (Ithaca, 1995); Karen Petrone, 'Family, Masculinity, and Heroism in Russian War Posters of the First World War', *Borderlines: Genders and Identities in War and Peace*, ed. Billie Melman (New York, 1998), 95–119.
35. Victoria E. Bonnell, *Iconography of Power: Soviet Political Posters under Lenin and Stalin* (Berkeley, 1997), 217–21.
36. F. Leonidov, 'Sergei Bamburov', *Za rodnuiu zemliu: U ozera Khasan na granitse* (Leningrad, 1939), 73.
37. 'Geroicheskie epizody', *Za rodnuiu zemliu*, 94.
38. *Boevye epizody*, 186.
39. 'Geroicheskie episody', *Za rodnuiu zemliu*, 88.
40. Western depictions of the Japanese during World War II employed similar images. See John Dower, *War Without Mercy: Race and Power in the Pacific War* (New York, 1986).
41. *Geroi Khasana*, 52.
42. 'Gibel trekh russkikh batarei', *Illiustrirovannaia letopis' Russko-iaponskoi voiny*, 11 (1905), 59.
43. 'Otdel'nye geroi', ibid., 13 (1905), 76.
44. 'Gibel trekh russkikh batarei', 60–1.
45. Hoover RU–SU, 134.
46. Furmanov, *Chapayev*, 349.
47. Ibid., 262.
48. Ibid., 255.
49. Ibid., 73, 77.
50. 'Otdel'nye geroi', 76.
51. *Geroi Khasana*, 32.
52. 'Otdel'nye geroi', 76.
53. 'Minnyi kater bronenostsa "Retvizan", *Illiustrirovannaia letopis' Russkoiaponskoi voiny*, 13 (1905), 83.
54. Fadeyev, *The Nineteen*, 154, 246, 272–3.
55. At the first Soviet Writers' Union plenum in 1932, V. Kirpotin criticized Fadeev for 'too much exploration of the inner man and his doubts'. Quoted in Clark, *The Soviet Novel*, 30.
56. For actual relations between commanders and soldiers during the Soviet period see Mark von Hagen, *Soldiers in the Proletarian Dictatorship: the Red Army and the Soviet Socialist State, 1917–1930* (Ithaca, N.Y., 1990); Roger R. Reese, *Stalin's Reluctant Soldiers: a Social History of the Red Army, 1925–1941* (Lawrence, Kan., 1996).
57. Furmanov, *Chapayev*, 77.
58. Ibid., 397–8.
59. Fadeyev, *The Nineteen*, 135.
60. Ibid., 49–50.
61. Ibid., 229.
62. Ibid., 292.

63. Ibid., 293.
64. L. Antipov, *Groznye ataki* (Moscow, 1939).
65. Ibid., 12.
66. While it was possible to represent this kind of lyrical comradely love between men in the late 1930s, after the recriminalization of sodomy in 1934 any hint of erotic relationships among men was defined as 'class-alien' and suppressed. Male comradeship could blur differences of rank in a retelling of a military campaign, but it did not threaten to overturn power hierarchies as homosexual relations could have done.
67. Ibid., 17.

11

Socialism in One Gender: Masculine Values in the Stalin Revolution

Thomas G. Schrand

Between the years of 1929 and 1941, Soviet society experienced what might be described as a gender-quake, a seismic shift in sexual divisions of labor produced by the largest national peacetime expansion of women's employment in world history. As a result of this rapid industrialization campaign, over 10 million women began wage-labor in the industrial and service sectors of the Soviet economy, raising their percentage of the non-agricultural workforce from 24 percent to 39 percent.[1] The Soviet government actively recruited women for industrial employment, created affirmative action programs to train female technicians and skilled workers, and greatly expanded childcare and cafeteria facilities to free working women from some of their domestic obligations. Examining this transformation in the deployment of women's labor power inevitably raises questions about men and masculinity: if gender systems are constructed around oppositions, then a change in one side of the gender equation should produce an equivalent response in the other side. How did male gender roles change to accommodate the dramatic expansion of women's participation in the industrial economy?

The answer, perhaps not surprisingly, is that the mobilization of women's productive labor was accompanied by an elevation of men's status in Soviet society. The mass recruitment of women into paid labor during the 1930s certainly affected the sexual division of labor in the Soviet Union, but due to the 'double burden' which resulted for women, it did not necessarily represent an improvement in women's social status and occurred in such a way as not to threaten the dominant position of men in Soviet society. Because it resulted from the widespread labor shortages generated by the First Five Year Plan, the expansion of women's employment was never accompanied by widespread male unemployment. Consequently, women's entry into the wage economy did not lead to the major change in traditional gender roles or produce the male anxiety that Friedrich Engels describes (and exhibits) in *The Condition of the Working Class in England.*

> Very often the fact that a married woman is working does not lead to the complete disruption of the home but to a reversal of the normal division of labour within the family. The wife is the bread-winner while her husband stays at home to look after the children and to do the cleaning and cooking.... In Manchester alone there are many hundreds of men who are condemned to perform household duties. One may well imagine the righteous indignation of the workers at being virtually turned into eunuchs.[2]

The entry of women into the Soviet labor force did not seriously alter their traditional domestic obligations and thus Russian men's conceptions of masculinity were never challenged by the need to participate in household labor.[3] In fact, by the 1930s, the Communist Party had approached women's employment from two distinct ideological perspectives, and both of them involved privileging identities and social spheres that were gendered 'masculine'. The first approach, developed by the Party's Women's Department (Zhenotdel), intended to liberate women by releasing them from private domestic work and admitting them into paid productive labor on equal terms with men. The second approach, shaped by Stalin's doctrine of 'socialism in one country', mobilized women for wage labor without truly freeing them from their traditional household labor obligations. The ideological and socio-economic conditions that accompanied this latter strategy may not have raised the status of most individual Soviet males, but it did heighten the cultural and symbolic value of masculine roles and activities while effectively restricting women's progress toward social equality.

The first of these two approaches developed during the pre-Stalin era, when Marxist ideology inspired Bolshevik feminists to seek to emancipate women by integrating them into the largely masculine sphere of public work and industrial production. As formulated by Zhenotdel activists such as Alexandra Kollontai and Inessa Armand, this blueprint for achieving gender equality would free women by creating communalized social services – cafeterias, childcare centers, public laundries – that would liberate them from domestic labor and allow them to enter productive work on an equal basis with men. The Zhenotdel's strategy of emancipation was designed not only to give women economic independence from men, but also to release them from the private sphere of reproductive labor. According to this feminist branch of Marxist theory, private housework, child-rearing, and other reproductive tasks were economically inefficient; socializing this work would bolster the new socialist economy by replacing the inefficiencies of individual women's household labor with economies of scale and would also raise productivity by shifting millions of new workers into Soviet industries. Just as importantly, this transformation would liberate women from a type of labor that Marxist theory condemned as 'ahistoric' and non-productive, contributing neither to human self-realization nor to the development of society as a whole. By abolishing the family and transferring women into the wage economy, Marxist feminism would liberate women by 'promoting' them to a new role as, essentially, honorary or surrogate men, while largely eliminating the 'feminine' sphere of private reproductive labor.

According to Eric Naiman, a similar impulse to erase the feminine appeared in Russian cultural traditions that otherwise had little in common with revolutionary feminism. In his quest to escape the world of the flesh and female sexuality, the pre-revolutionary spiritual philosopher Nikolai Berdyaev longed for a future androgynous society in which maternity 'would be "conquered"' and the problematic category of woman would be eliminated.[4] This type of antipathy towards the feminine could also be found within the Bolshevik Party, whose male members tended to identify women as backwards and counter-revolutionary. Women were associated with the private or domestic sphere, which the revolutionaries intended to destroy, and Bolsheviks often viewed family life as detracting from a Party member's devotion to the cause.[5]

Although Bolshevik feminists clearly did not share these misogynistic attitudes, the logic of the Zhenotdel strategy seems to have been aimed towards outcomes similar to those sought by Berdyaev: conquering maternity (or at least the obstacles it created for women's social equality) and creating a society that minimized gender distinctions. Although Soviet women would still be obligated to conceive and bear children for the socialist society, the Zhenotdel hoped to facilitate women's equality and freedom by providing collective childcare that, in its maximal variant, would completely replace individual parents as caregivers.[6] With this strategy of liquidating the family and private reproductive labor in favor of production and public life, the Zhenotdel approach to women's liberation tended to preserve and elevate 'masculine' roles while largely eliminating the private social spheres previously occupied by women. Viewed schematically, this emancipatory strategy seems to involve shifting women out of one set of gender roles, the traditionally feminine ones, and into another set long regarded as masculine that the Bolsheviks had left virtually intact and unchallenged. As the socialist revolution abolished the 'specific' limitations and spheres associated with the female gender, the new Soviet person would, by default, be oriented toward a 'universal' gender identity that most Soviet citizens understood as essentially masculine.[7]

Despite its endorsement of masculinist values, however, the Zhenotdel strategy had little appeal for most male (and even most female) Party members. From a male perspective, this strategy, in addition to the expenses and turmoil it would involve, threatened to weaken further the status of individual men by eliminating the social context for patriarchy, which modernization had already begun to undermine.[8] Without families, male heads of households would lose their remaining authority and prerogatives, a prospect that may partially explain the lack of enthusiasm among male Party members for the Zhenotdel and its activities. In the end, this controversial strategy for liberating women was defeated by an overpowering combination of factors, including economic underdevelopment, unfavorable political priorities, the economic structure of peasant households, and widespread opposition both from within the Party and from the population as a whole.[9]

As the Zhenotdel began its decline in the late 1920s, gender policies were increasingly influenced by a new ideological paradigm – Stalin's doctrine of 'socialism in one country' – that privileged the masculine in a second and entirely different way. The Zhenotdel approach to liberating women involved integrating them into a super-productive socialist economy that would be created following a global (or at least, continental) revolution. In this scenario, Russia would have access to the rest of Europe's technology and resources, which would allow it to modernize its economy and to invest in the infrastructure of nurseries, daycare centers, and other institutions that would make women's emancipation possible. Stalin began developing the idea of 'socialism in one country' during the mid-1920s, as it became clear that global revolution was not coming to the rescue of the Soviet economy. Rather than retreating from the goal of socialism, Stalin and his followers decided that the USSR would have to create the economic prerequisites for it in isolation, while surrounded by hostile capitalist powers. From this perspective, the campaign for industrialization and modernization became, among other things, a desperate struggle to arm the Soviet Union for the defense of socialism. New heavy industries would not only provide the foundation for a highly productive socialist economy, but were also essential to produce the military might necessary to protect the socialist homeland from its foreign enemies. 'Socialism in one country' would also involve internal class warfare, as the party confronted what it saw as the urban and rural enemies of socialism within Russia.

The rhetoric of Stalin and his supporters emphasized the contrasts between the 'socialist offensive' that the new policies entailed and the passive treatment of class enemies that they saw as characterizing the NEP. Historians have often noted the military terminology associated with Stalin's 'revolution from above', and have argued that it expressed a yearning among young communists, and in Stalin himself, for a 'new October' and the mythologized heroism of the civil war that followed.[10] By using imagery from and nostalgia for the Civil War to energize the Party for the 'revolution from above', the Stalin regime was drawing upon memories or fantasies of a homosocial experience that largely excluded women and the feminine.[11] The new doctrine appealed to male Party members by emphasizing activism, willfulness, and mastery over the physical and political environment. In contrast, the NEP was often gendered and criticized as feminine, characterized by demoralizing (and emasculating?) ideological compromises that the virile pursuit of 'socialism in one country' promised to sweep away.[12] Stalin himself personalized this analysis by questioning the manhood of his opponents in the inner-party power struggles of the 1920s. Robert Tucker has pointed out that at the 15th Party Conference in October 1926, Stalin described the Zinoviev-Kamenev-Trotsky opposition as

> 'a combination of castrated forces', explaining that to be castrated means to be 'deprived of power'. Now he was saying that the political eunuchs had a view of the Revolution which deprived it of its own internal, independent power and condemned it to a passive role in international relations. This was a frank appeal to the pride of political virility in the rising Soviet ruling class, its will to believe in the potency and world mission of the Russian revolution.[13]

You can almost smell the testosterone in the air as the Party girds itself for the socialist offensive. According to Victoria Bonnell, the resulting efforts to subordinate the agricultural sector to the demands of industrialization were also represented in strongly gendered terms, as poster art 'feminized the image of the peasantry as a social category'.[14] These images used 'gender differences to convey the hierarchical relationship between the worker (male) and peasant (female) and by implication, between urban and rural spheres of Soviet society'.[15] Perhaps the Stalin revolution was answering the male anxieties that the NEP produced within the Party by harkening back to masculinized episodes in Party history and symbolically subordinating the feminine to the masculine.

'Socialism in one country', however, did more than promote aggressive 'masculine' policies; it also created an economic context that systematically undermined efforts to emancipate women. By assigning so much urgency to rapid industrialization, Stalin's doctrine required all of the Party's resources to be focused on developing the heavy industries that would make further industrial and military growth possible. These investments came at the expense of the light industries, which not only employed many women, but also produced the consumer goods that might have lightened their domestic labor. The new priorities also restricted the construction of cafeterias, laundries, daycare centers, and other institutions necessary for Bolshevik-style women's emancipation.

Ultimately, 'socialism in one country' allowed the Party to sublimate the 'woman question' in order to pursue policies that had a more visceral appeal for the Party's membership. The Marxist blueprint for a workers' revolution had always assigned male activists to the 'heroic' and 'masculine' task of forcibly overthrowing a corrupt and repressive order. The emancipation of women following this violent revolution, however, was an entirely different process; it was outlined only vaguely in the Marxist canon and involved dismantling the remnants of a patriarchal order from which male workers themselves generally benefited. As interpreted by the Bolsheviks, this revolution involved building cafeterias and providing daycare for children, tasks which Party members tended to view as 'feminine' and less compelling than crushing the bourgeoisie.[16] Instead, the Stalin leadership chose to activate the Party's male rank-and-file to achieve 'socialism in one country' through a new round of class warfare, an offensive war against internal class enemies and a defensive war against the encircling capitalist powers. The result was a 'quasi-wartime mobilization' that placed a premium on masculine skills and activities.[17]

In this new rhetorical and political context, the full emancipation of women – previously theorized as an economic prerequisite for socialism – could now be viewed as a luxury to be pursued only after the immediate dangers had been overcome. This trend became increasingly clear in 1930, after the abolition of the Zhenotdel, as the First Five Year Plan created shortages of male labor that spurred the regime to begin recruiting more women into the paid-labor force. The Soviet government actually began developing a Five Year Plan for Women's Labor, but the effort to mobilize women was not accompanied by a commitment to freeing them from domestic labor. Although social services did expand somewhat during the 1930s, they did so within limits, and only to the extent necessary to recruit a certain number of women workers. As the Commissariat of Labor was drafting the Plan for Women's Labor in May 1930, it expressed both the new Stalinist priorities and the restrictions that would limit the liberation of women from their private reproductive responsibilities:

> The further socialization of everyday life will proceed according to the growth of the industrialization of the social economy and on the basis of the rise of the material circumstances of the nation. In the present, it is necessary to throw maximum resources into industrialization, into the development of tractors, combines, sowing-machines, etc., which permit the social adaptation of the countryside. It is impossible (*nel'zia*) to throw more than a fixed minimum of resources into the completion of the socialization of everyday life. But that minimum should be significant enough to guarantee the fulfillment of the female five year plan. . . .[18]

This 'fixed minimum' approach confirmed a traditional gender hierarchy within the industrial labor force. Despite the regime's reliance on women as workers, their incomplete emancipation would consign them to being a type of provisional, auxiliary labor force, rather than fully liberated and thus equal to men.

The leading status of male workers as the primary labor force was also reinforced by the health studies and protective legislation concerning industrial labor during the 1930s. The Commissariat of Labor (Narkomtrud) advised that studies be carried out to determine which industrial jobs were safe for the 'female organism'. The research and regulations that resulted showed an obsessive concern with women's reproductive organs and processes, as Narkomtrud studied the impact of heavy lifting and tractor driving upon women's uteri.[19] As a result, this legislation defined all women first as potential mothers, and consequently as a 'specific' type of labor power, restricted to jobs that did not threaten reproductive capacities. The 1936 abortion ban compounded this tendency by placing all women in jeopardy of becoming mothers, whether they chose to or not. Narkomtrud never examined the reproductive health of men, despite their many hazardous occupations in the early Soviet economy, thus leaving them defined as 'universal' workers, whose labor could be applied in any sector of the economy.

The distribution of skills within industry was another factor guaranteeing men a privileged status within the workforce. Despite the regime's formal commitment to equal pay and training for women, a variety of factors prevented women from obtaining skilled status. Diane Koenker has recently analyzed the hostility of male printing workers towards women workers during the NEP and described how these men defined skill as a masculine trait.[20] These attitudes made it difficult for women to enter into apprenticeships or establish the type of interpersonal relationships through which skilled status was transferred. This misogyny did not disappear with the NEP, of course, and Koenker even suggests that it might have intensified in the masculine reassertion of the Stalin revolution.[21] Certainly, many examples of shopfloor hostility toward women workers can be found during the 1930s, and they often took the form of questioning women's suitability for skilled work, or for industrial work in general. In 1931, a Belorussian factory committee member stated that, 'The only work for women is to wash windows and clear out boxcars.'[22] When the director of a ship-repair station in Archangelsk was asked about the recruitment of women, he replied, 'We don't need women. I intend to raise the issue of canceling these absurd directives. Women have not proven themselves and work worse than men.'[23] The supervisor of a furnace shop in the Urals flatly refused to accept female workers, announcing, 'You will not fulfill the Five Year Plan with women.'[24]

Despite these shopfloor attitudes towards women as skilled workers, the chronic labor shortages of the early 1930s motivated the regime to train women as specialists (especially because these jobs were considered less physically demanding and thus were better suited for the vulnerable 'female organism'). The quotas for training women in skilled professions, however, were consistently underfulfilled during the early 1930s, due to weak recruitment and high drop-out rates among female students. Throughout the 1930s, women workers were typically hired 'at the gate' and channeled into unskilled, low-paying and physically strenuous jobs, leaving men with a virtual monopoly on many skilled jobs.[25] All of these trends involving the integration (or segregation) of women within the industrial labor force ensured that the role of worker would be gendered as 'masculine,' just as it was in the poster art of the time.

Men's leading roles as the workers, producers, and engineers of Soviet society was also highlighted by the *obshchestvennitsa* movement, which attempted to involve the wives of managers and industrial specialists in volunteer work at their husbands' factories. While these women worked at improving the 'feminine' spheres of factory life – the cafeterias, dormitories, medical centers, and childcare facilities – they were instructed not to allow this work to interfere with their duties as wives to provide comfortable homes and good meals for their husbands.[26] By 1939, these expectations seemed to apply to all wives, even working-class women, as this quote from the journal *Obshchestvennitsa* suggests:

> Women should try to create at home for their husbands all of the conditions for fruitful work and cultured relaxation. Breakfasts and dinners that are prepared on time, cultured relaxation, a well-organized place at home for home-work and study – all of these are very effective measures in the struggle with tardiness, in the struggle to raise the culture of labor.[27]

The *obshchestvennitsa* phenomenon served a normative purpose by presenting elite wives as a role model for all Soviet women and publicly emphasizing the subservience of women to men. The movement reinforced male primacy by mobilizing and positioning women according to their husbands' occupations, rather than allowing them independent identities.[28] At the same time, the movement also portrayed wives as potentially interfering with their husbands' important responsibilities, an image that echoed earlier Bolshevik perceptions of women as 'dark'

and counter-revolutionary. The threat of idle, unhappy wives distracting their specialist-husbands from their work was a recurrent theme in descriptions of the benefits of the *obshchestvennitsa* movement:

> We have many newly-arrived employees. Often it turns out this way: the husband is working well in the factory, but he comes home – the wife is sitting on a suitcase and – in tears: 'Let's go to the capital! It's boring to me here! I'm vegetating here.' How easily do you think work goes for such an engineer?[29]

This image of a 'backward' wife undermining her husband's work echoes Lenin's own description of women as 'little worms, which . . . rot and corrode' men's 'joy and determination'.[30]

As the *obshchestvennitsa* movement indicates, the role of husband retained its privileges in the Stalin era, even as men were able to escape many of the responsibilities shouldered by prerevolutionary patriarchs. During the 1930s, the burdens of parenting were increasingly divided between women and the state, especially as employment migration, arrest, or male abandonment left many families headed by women.[31] Although collective childcare did not liberate Soviet women from family responsibilities, it did expand dramatically during the 1930s, allowing the state and Stalin to assume symbolically the role of father.[32] Meanwhile, the Stalin regime increasingly identified women as mothers even as it intensified women's reproductive responsibilities and labor. The abortion ban and the labor legislation have already been mentioned. By the mid-1930s such hortatory events as the celebration of Women's Day tended to emphasize women's roles as mothers and homemakers, rather than as workers and citizens.[33]

As the emphasis on women's roles as wives and mothers grew stronger, the responsibilities of men in family life were decreasing. In the pre-Soviet era, the peasant patriarch could be described as a 'responsible autocrat', a family leader who wielded great power, but was also responsible for organizing the work and consumption of the family.[34] In the Soviet era, these responsibilities gradually diminished with the rise of industrialization and urbanization, but cultural values that subordinated wives to husbands persisted and were even reinforced by the *obshchestvennitsa* movement. Analysts who attempt to explain the 'hyper-masculinity' of Soviet men point to the decline of male responsibilities in the family, which produced a matrifocal society in which the Soviet man strove 'desperately to hold on to the traditional prerogatives that most forcefully set him off as a man – namely the right to behave in a free and self-serving way in sexual life, drinking, and other matters'.[35] With bans on abortions and the sale of contraceptives, the Stalin regime clearly sought to intensify the reproductive labor and family obligations of Soviet women. For men, the Stalin revolution accelerated the erosion of patriarchal obligations and, in many cases, removed men from the family altogether. This, of course, was not always a positive trend for individual men, but traditional male freedoms and privileges did remain largely intact, even as male responsibilities declined.

More than anything else, the new configuration of male hegemony in the Stalin era derived from the perceived military threat from capitalist enemies, which in turn made the male role of soldier a primary element in the new masculine identity. Even while the Stalin regime was coming to see all women as potential mothers, it was treating all men as potential soldiers. By 1928, military conscription was universal for all male 'toilers' between ages 19 and 40, and Soviet men entered five years of active service at age 21.[36] Although tens of thousands of women had served in the Red Army during the Civil War, they had often encountered hostility and resistance to their combat roles and their participation produced little change in traditional views of women in the military.[37] Without entirely ruling out female participation during future wars, the Soviet government excluded women from the armed forces following the Civil War, citing the same health and reproductive concerns that governed female labor in industry: 'And if women are not enlisted into military service, that can be attributed to the sufficient quantity of male contingents in our nation, which makes it possible to free women from these heavy responsibilities, just as she is freed from a whole range of harmful industries.'[38] Meanwhile, military service qualified male recruits for educational opportunities, improved eligibility for Party membership, and training and connections for careers both within the armed forces and in the civilian economy.

Although the role of soldier offered disadvantages as well as advantages to the individual man, it contributed overall to the promotion of the 'masculine' within Soviet society. The ultimate goal of 'socialism in one country,' after all, was to make the Soviet Union strong enough militarily and industrially to defend itself against capitalist aggression. Mark von Hagen has described the development of a 'militarized socialism' during the 1920s, which was characterized by 'a bellicist world view and the predominance of national security values and military interests in the economic and cultural life of the country'.[39] A society centered so strongly around military security is likely to be oriented toward the 'masculine', and to value the interests and contributions of male citizens over those of female citizens. As Karen Petrone has pointed out in her study of Stalinist celebrations, the leading status of the Red Army, the pre-eminent masculine institution in Soviet society, was represented symbolically during these years by its leading position in holiday parades.[40]

During the first Five Year Plan, this concern with military strength contributed to the Party's efforts to recruit women into industry. The authors of the 'Five Year Plan for Women's Labor' noted its 'special military significance', explaining that in the event of war, it would allow officials 'to know how and where maximally to introduce female labor power. In addition, the female five year plan is directly a defensive measure, since the threat of war is inevitably growing.'[41] As the USSR began mobilizing for war in Poland and Finland in September 1939, the party instructed union, Komsomol and industrial organizations to support the so-called 'masculine professions' movement, which aimed to recruit women into fields that had previously been considered too skilled or physically demanding for women.[42] In anticipation of a military crisis that would drain off skilled male workers, industrial officials began encouraging women to work as locomotive engineers, engine machinists, open-hearth furnace workers, and to enter other occupations from which they had previously been excluded. Where the party had initially promoted women's employment in terms of its emancipatory effects, it now justified recruiting women as a means of freeing men for the more important tasks of defending the socialist homeland. In this same spirit, *obshchestvennitsy* used a military metaphor to describe their movement as 'work that strengthens the rear of production, which assures the uninterrupted and precise work of production itself'.[43] This metaphor privileges production as the military front where men make the essential contributions, while the wives fulfill an auxiliary role, assisting their husbands by working behind the lines. Likewise, the military crises that inspired the 'masculine professions' movement served as much to emphasize the significance and value of male roles as it did to raise the social status of the women involved.

The alterations of male and female roles during the prewar Stalin era produced a peacetime example of what Margaret and Patrice Higgonet have termed the 'double helix', an image they use to describe the reorganization of gender roles during massive wars such as the First and Second World Wars.[44] In these cases, women's status in society may improve as they are mobilized to replace conscripted men in industry and to assume auxiliary roles in the military. At the same time, however, total war raises men's status, for they become the physical defenders of their societies. The double helix refers to the fact that the temporary wartime improvement of women's status is only possible because of a corresponding and equivalent improvement in men's status; the gap between the two genders and the hierarchy within which women and men are ordered remain the same. The Stalin revolution produced a similar 'wartime' dynamic during the 1930s, as gendered priorities and policies worked to privilege masculine roles and values. Lest women's expanded role in the wage labor force threaten the equilibrium of gender relations in the new Soviet society, state policies and cultural initiatives restored the balance by bolstering the male side of the equation.

It has been argued here that the Zhenotdel strategy for emancipating women espoused, albeit implicitly, long-standing masculinist values. The doctrine of 'socialism in one country' made those values its fundamental credo. The Stalin revolution asserted male primacy at the expense of women's social equality, producing a cultural, social, and economic system that recast masculine hegemony for a new socialist context. As a program for creating a modernized, centralized, and 'cultured' society, 'socialism in one country' involved dismantling many of the socio-economic structures that empowered men as patriarchs and it offered at least some women opportunities that would have been unimaginable prior to 1917. In important symbolic and material terms, however, the Stalin revolution provided Lenin's famous query – *kto-kogo?* – with a gendered answer: *muzhskoi – zhenskogo.*

Notes

An earlier version of this essay was presented at the AAASS 29th Annual National Convention, 22 November 1997. I would like to thank Barbara Clements, Rebecca Friedman, and Dan Healey for their very helpful comments and assistance.

1. Gail Warshofsky Lapidus, *Women in Soviet Society: Equality, Development, and Social Change* (Berkeley, 1978), 166.
2. Friedrich Engels, *The Condition of the Working Class in England,* trans. and ed. W. O. Henderson and W. H. Chalover (Stanford, 1958), 162.
3. See Daniel Rancour-Laferriere, *The Slave Soul of Russia: Moral Masochism and the Cult of Suffering* (New York, 1995) for an interesting discussion of the strongly gendered cultural attitudes towards housework among Russians: 'In Russia domestic labor such as cleaning and cooking is semiotically loaded. It *signifies* femininity and low status. It is therefore a *threat* to masculinity and to male authority within the family' (169, italics in the original).
4. Eric Naiman, 'Historectomies: On the Metaphysics of Reproduction in a Utopian Age', *Sexuality and the Body in Russian Culture,* ed. Jane T. Costlow, Stephanie Sandler, and Judith Vowles (Stanford, 1993), 263.
5. Anne E. Gorsuch, '"A Woman is Not a Man": the Culture of Gender and Generation in Soviet Russia, 1921–1928', *Slavic Review* 55, no. 3 (Fall 1996), 636–60, emphasizes these attitudes among male Komsomol members. Lenin himself revealed similar suspicions toward women: 'The backwardness of women, their lack of understanding for the revolutionary ideals of the man, decrease his joy and determination in fighting. They are like little worms, which unseen, slowly but surely rot and corrode.' See Klara Zetkin, 'Reminiscences of Lenin', *The Family in the USSR,* ed. Rudolph Schlesinger (London, 1949), 78.
6. In a 1921 speech at Sverdlov University, Alexandra Kollontai emphasized women's productive role and described maternity as a social responsibility: 'The labor republic sees woman first and foremost as a member of the labor force, as a unit of living labor: the function of maternity is seen as highly important, but as a supplementary task that is not a private family matter but a *social* matter [italics in the original].' Alexandra Kollontai, 'The Labour of Women in the Revolution of the Economy', *Selected Writings of Alexandra Kollontai,* trans. Alix Holt (Westport, Conn., 1977), 143.
7. Wendy Z. Goldman, *Women, the State and Revolution: Soviet Family Policy and Social Life, 1917–1936* (Cambridge, 1993) also notes this tendency in Soviet family policies: 'If women were to be liberated economically and psychologically, they needed to become more like men, or more specifically, more like male workers' (11).

8. See S. A. Smith's paper in this volume for a discussion of the weakening of traditional patriarchal authority and the reconstruction of masculinity that resulted from rural–urban migration.
9. For the decline of the Zhenotdel and its emancipatory strategy, see Goldman, *Women, the State and Revolution* and her 'Industrial Politics, Peasant Rebellion, and the Death of the Proletarian Women's Movement', *Slavic Review*, 55, no. 1 (Spring 1996), 46–77.
10. The links between the Stalin revolution and the military context of the Civil War are discussed in Sheila Fitzpatrick, 'The Legacy of the Civil War', *Party, State, and Society in the Russian Civil War*, ed. Diane P. Koenker, William G. Rosenberg, and Ronald Grigor Suny (Bloomington, 1989), 395–7; and in Mark von Hagen, *Soldiers in the Proletarian Dictatorship: the Red Army and the Soviet Socialist State, 1917–1930* (Ithaca, N.Y., 1990), 331–43.
11. See Barbara Evans Clements, *Bolshevik Women* (Cambridge, 1997), 171–200, for 'the masculinist cast of Bolshevik political culture' during the Civil War.
12. For an intriguing discussion of the anxiety and threatening female imagery associated with the NEP, see Eric Naiman, 'Revolutionary Anorexia (NEP as Female Complaint)', *Slavic and East European Journal*, 37, no. 3 (1993), 305–25.
13. Robert C. Tucker, *Stalin as Revolutionary, 1879–1929: A Study in History and Personality* (New York, 1973), 388–9. The 'masculine' values associated with 'socialism in one country' are also readily apparent in the policies that it inspired. The industrialization 'campaign' demanded by the new doctrine was treated by the Party as a quasi-military mobilization and military metaphors abounded. See Stephen Kotkin, *Magnetic Mountain: Stalinism as a Civilization* (Berkeley, 1995), 33.
14. Victoria E. Bonnell, 'The Peasant Woman in Stalinist Political Art of the 1930s', *American Historical Review*, 98, no. 1 (February 1993), 79.
15. Ibid., pp. 79–80.
16. See Carol Eubanks Hayden, 'The Zhenotdel and the Bolshevik Party', *Russian History* 3, no. 2 (1976): 161, for examples of the disdainful attitudes towards the work and objectives of the Zhenotdel which male (and some female) party members exhibited in the 1920s. This mindset can also be seen in the widespread neglect of childcare and other social services by industrial officials during the 1930s. Even in cases in which abundant funds and construction materials were provided for these purposes, managers refused to utilize them, focusing instead on the battle for production in their enterprises. See Gosudarstvennyi Arkhiv Rossiiskoi Federatsii (GARF), f. 3316, op. 51, d. 7, 50–1; d. 3, p. 15; d. 2, 9.
17. Fitzpatrick, 'War and Society in Soviet Context: Soviet Labor Before, During and After World War II', *International Labor and Working-Class History*, no. 35 (Spring 1989), 37–52. Both Fitzpatrick and von Hagen (*Soldiers in the Proletarian Dictatorship*, 337) describe Soviet society during the 1930s as being mobilized for war in a way similar to what other Western nations experienced during the Second World War.
18. GARF, f. 5515, op. 13, d. 5, 21b.
19. Ibid., d. 13, 1–4; Ibid., f. 5451, op. 15, d. 357, 108.
20. Diane P. Koenker, 'Men against Women on the Shop Floor in Early Soviet Russia: Gender and Class in the Socialist Workplace', *American Historical*

Review 100, no. 5 (December 1995): 1438–64. In this volume, Smith describes a similar, prerevolutionary trend as male rural migrants, lacking the control of land or family members, redefined masculinity in terms of industrial skill, which led in turn to shop-floor misogyny.

21. Ibid., 1462–3.
22. GARF, f. 5451, op. 15, d. 362, 84.
23. Ibid.
24. *Istoriia industrializatsii Urala, 1926–1932gg.* (Sverdlovsk, 1967), 408.
25. For details on efforts to hire and train women workers during the 1930s, see Thomas G. Schrand, 'Industrialization and the Stalinist Gender System: Women Workers in the Soviet Economy, 1928–1941' (Ph.D. diss., University of Michigan, 1994).
26. Veronique Garros, Natalia Korenevskaia, and Thomas Lahusen, (eds)., *Intimacy and Terror: Soviet Diaries of the 1930's* (New York, 1995), 185. Recent evaluations of the *obshchestvennitsa* movement's goals and evolution include Mary Buckley, 'The Untold Story of *Obshchestvennitsa* in the 1930s', *Europe-Asia Studies*, 48, no. 4 (1996), 569–86; Sheila Fitzpatrick, *Everyday Stalinism* (New York, 1999), 156–63; Rebecca Balmas Neary, 'Mothering Socialist Society: the Wife-Activists' Movement and the Soviet Culture of Everyday Life, 1934–41', *The Russian Review*, 58 (July 1999), 396–412; and Schrand, 'Soviet "Civic-Minded Women" in the 1930's: Class, Gender and Industrialization in a Socialist Society', *Journal of Women's History*, 11, no. 3 (Autumn 1999), 126–50.
27. *Obshchestvennitsa*, January 1939, 25.
28. This trend of subordinating women's identities to those of their husbands reached its cruellest point during the Great Purges, when women were sent to labor camps because they were 'wives of traitors to the motherland'.
29. Rossiskii Tsentr Khraneniia I Izucheniia Dokumentov Noveishei Istorii (TsKhIDNI), f. 17, op. 120, d. 255, 8.
30. Zetkin, *Reminiscences of Lenin*, 78.
31. Fitzpatrick, *Everyday Stalinism*, 139–63, notes the prevalence of female-headed households and the various socio-economic difficulties created by men who abandoned or neglected their families during the 1930s.
32. See Naiman, 'Historectomies', 275–6.
33. Instructions for the 1935 Women's Day ordered local factory committees to inspect the institutions 'called upon to serve women and children: nurseries, daycare centers . . . maternity homes, hospitals, and also laundries, sewing and repair shops, cafeterias, etc.' (GARF, f. 5451, op. 19, d. 458, 1).
34. H. Kent Geiger, *The Family in Soviet Russia* (Cambridge, 1968), 243–4.
35. Ibid., 244. For the link between matrifocal societies and hyper-masculinity, see Rancour-Laferriere, *The Slave Soul of Russia*, 144.
36. D. Fedotoff White, *The Growth of the Red Army* (Princeton, 1944), 286.
37. See Clements, *Bolshevik Women*, 171–93.
38. *Spravochnik Osoaviakhim po podgotovke trudiashchikhsia zhenshchin k oborone* (Moscow, 1930), 10.
39. von Hagen, *Soldiers in the Proletarian Dictatorship*, 331.
40. Karen Petrone, '"Life Has Become More Joyous, Comrades": Politics and Culture in Soviet Celebrations, 1934–1939' (Ph.D. diss., University of Michigan, 1994), 35.

41. GARF, f. 5515, op. 13, d. 5, 6b–7.
42. See G. P. Anufrienko, 'K voprosu o vovlechenii zhenshchin v promyshlennosti v predvoennye gody', *Sbornik nauchnykh trudov Magnitogorskogo gorno-metallurgicheskogo instituta im. G. I. Nosova*, no. 79 (Magnitogorsk, 1970), 41–5.
43. *Vestnik Inzhenerov i Tekhnikov*, no. 1 (January 1936), 13.
44. Margaret R. Higgonet and Patrice L.-R. Higgonet, 'The Double Helix', *Behind the Lines: Gender and the Two World Wars*, ed. Margaret Randolph Higgonet, Jane Jenson, Sonya Michel, and Margaret Collins Weitz (New Haven, 1987), 31–50.

12

'If You Want to Be Like Me, Train!': the Contradictions of Soviet Masculinity

Julie Gilmour and Barbara Evans Clements

'If you want to be like me, train!' a Soviet athlete declaims in a 1950 sport poster (Fig. 5).[1] The message to the boy who sits beside him, looking admiringly at the man's massive biceps, is that he too can become a Soviet sportsman if he works properly and diligently. This was the predominant message of athletics to Soviet citizens throughout the postwar period. Athletes were presented to the public as exemplars of three principles. The first was that pre-eminence in sport was more a function of systematic training than of talent. Secondly, any Soviet citizen could achieve such pre-eminence and by doing so would contribute to the nation's greatness. And thirdly, it was the responsibility of Soviet men and women who did become sports heroes to serve as examples, especially to the younger generation.

Male athletes were also supposed to instruct Soviet youngsters and the readers of the nation's sports magazines in the essentials of masculinity, which included such 'healthy' behavior as hard work, physical exercise, service to profession and nation, and devotion to family. This masculine ideal, described in Russian as *kul'turnyi* or 'cultured', was juxtaposed in the sports press to a much criticized antithesis, *nekul'turnyi* or 'uncultured' male behavior. Uncultured masculinity valorized self-indulgence (typically expressed in smoking, drinking, and sexual adventures) and aggressive physical self-assertion both in relation to other men and to women. This latter ethos was not dreamed up by Soviet propagandists, of course; it included, in somewhat caricatured form, ideas about men that had been circulating in Europe for centuries. S. A. Smith has discussed its prevalence among the Russian working class in the late nineteenth century earlier in this book. The distinction between cultured and uncultured masculinity was a significant part of the rhetoric of Soviet sports, because it had long figured in Soviet attempts to trans-

Figure 5 'If you want to be like this – TRAIN!' Physical culture poster, 1950

form the men of the nation into model citizens. Women as well as men were urged to adopt many of these values; women too should be hard-working, self-disciplined, and responsible. But there were gender differences in the ways in which *kul'turnost'* (culturedness) was defined for women and for men that make it possible to identify the masculinity preached by Soviet sports in the post-war period.

Throughout the years from 1945 to 1960, *Sovetskii sport* frequently carried biographical sketches of elite athletes, a genre of article we will call here 'success stories'. They often begin with the early phase of an athlete's life, before he or she took up sports. Usually, these stories include a crisis or turning point when the future hero becomes involved with a coach who shows him or her how scientific training can lead to championships. A rational approach to skills development and an attendant work ethic make success possible in these stories, and the mentor who guides the fledgling athlete through his training is a frequent theme.[2] An account of the career of Nikolai Korolev, a champion boxer, is typical. The young man is attracted to sport through the influence of an older master. Rigorous training and the assistance of state coaches develop his natural talent and make a boxer out of him. Korolev leaves sport during World War II to fight for his country in the underground that operated behind German lines, an enormously dangerous assignment. He returns to the ring in peacetime and by 1950 has won eight national championships.[3]

To make Soviet boxers, wrestlers, and weightlifters seem larger than life and also to tap into (and build) nationalist sentiments, publicists often called them modern *bogatyry*. The *bogatyry* (singular, *bogatyr*) were mythical heroes from medieval epic poetry, characters of great courage, strength, and cunning who defended the Russian land against both foreign enemies and cowardly nobles.[4] Even non-Soviet athletes who lived up to this image of strength and courage, such as the American weightlifter Paul Anderson, were sometimes identified as *bogatyry*. A typical poster published in *Sovetskii sport* in 1955 drew on these old Russian themes to portray three Soviet medal winners in front of a traditional depiction of three *bogatyry*. The caption below read 'May glory always go to the *bogatyry* of [our] native and great land.'[5]

Influenced by the entry of the USSR into Olympic competition in the 1950s, reporters also likened Soviet champions to ancient Greek models of physical beauty and athletic prowess. In 1957, Iurii Vlasov, 'the heavyweight, Muscovite military man', began to set weigh-lifting records, inspiring *Sovetskii sport* to run an article under the headline 'Who is Iurii Vlasov?'[6] The answer was that the rising star was an army cadet studying in Moscow. It was reported that he worked out at a gym every evening and that he was a responsible person. Vlasov was also described as a beautiful 'young Hercules.' '[He has] a wide chest, powerful hands, strong muscular legs, and beautiful proportions. It [was] obvious that it was on such a model that ancient Greek sculptors based their celebrated sculptures.'[7] The reader was told that Vlasov performed his exercises with heavy weights 'easily, beautifully, seemingly without special effort', but that he had achieved such facility only after diligent training. When asked 'What is the secret to [his] unusually quick athletic development?', Vlasov's trainer affirmed the importance of a work ethic and well-rounded development:

> There are no secrets here. . . . Iurii has great physical gifts. He has participated regularly in sports since childhood. But, the most important [reason] certainly lies with his exceptionally serious relationship to any sports activities. . . . He is a multi-talented sportsman. He plays basketball . . . and he throws a shotput almost 14 meters.[8]

Lest any reader persist in believing that Vlasov's success was due to talent alone, *Sovetskii sport* published a piece in May 1959 called 'Now This is Mastery! Iurii Vlasov Trains'. The article argued that Vlasov's intelligence, discipline, and dedication had made it possible for him to develop his extraordinary physical abilities. The author began by asking how the weight-lifter had been able to perform feats of strength that no one (even the great American *bogatyr* Paul Anderson) had ever before accomplished. The key, according to *Sovetskii sport*, was Vlasov's careful planning, both of daily workouts and of long-term preparation for competition. This article put great emphasis on Vlasov's training diary and his careful daily assessment of his performance. In addition, it followed Vlasov during a three-and-a-half-hour Sunday workout (one of his four workouts during a typical week). The reporter noted the athlete's punctuality (Vlasov arrived more than 15 minutes early), his good relationship with his trainer (they went over his plans together), and his well-rounded approach to his body (he cross-trained). 'Everything about this sportsman pleases,' wrote another commentator in *Sovetskii sport*, 'everything provokes sympathy: his powerful exterior appearance, his unhurried way of stepping up to the platform, and even how he adjusts his eyeglasses.'[9]

Male athletes involved in individual strength events included in the Olympic program became favorite subjects for sports writers seeking to promote the athlete as a model of *kul'turnost'*, There was much more to Soviet sport than boxing or weightlifting, however. How were female athletes presented to the public? And what were the expectations and difficulties in cultivating 'cultured' masculinity in the popular, 'working-class' sport of soccer?

Females did figure in the pages of *Sovetskii sport*, both as audience for the magazine and as athletes. Girls and women were among the readers encouraged to participate in sports and to cultivate heroic virtues of self-discipline and dedication. In 1959 *Sovetskii sport* published another poster of a male athlete addressing the youth, but this time the next generation was represented by a girl. The athlete stands above her, holding weights in his hands. She imitates his gesture, looking up admiringly. The caption proclaims: 'To Exercises!'[10]

As models of character and deportment, female athletes bore strong similarities to their male counterparts. They too were portrayed as being blessed with natural talent that had been developed through working hard and following the instruction of fatherly mentors. A typical example is the sketch of Nina Dumbadze, a world-class discus thrower from Tbilisi, that ran in *Krasnyi sport* in 1945.[11] It began with a very lyrical description of her body. Comparing the young Georgian to a Greek statue, the author extolled her power and speed and the strength of her hands. He reported that her talent and potential had been evident even in childhood when, as a 'thin, long legged' young girl, Nina showed the same gift for sport as young Vlasov. She participated in swimming, pistol shooting, tennis, and track. This all changed when as a teenager Nina was injured in a high-jump and doctors advised her to give up competitive sports. The author of the story was convinced that it was these difficult times that formed her 'purposeful will'. Needing to compete, Dumbadze turned to a long-forgotten talent – throwing the discus.

Not only does this article report that the star athlete trained diligently, but it also claims that she poured over books and articles written by foreign trainers, watched the technique of the world's best throwers on film, and studied the principles of mechanics and biomechanics to improve her performance. Nina Dumbadze was not just performing in an athletic event; she was immersing herself in an athletic 'culture'. Her hard work and intelligent reliance on trainers, the latest techniques, and up-to-date Soviet equipment made it possible for her to rise to the top of her sport. In the words of the biographer, 'the victory of the young champion was brought about by her balanced, many-sided development, and, most of all, by the high level of her sport culture'.[12]

In many ways, Iurii Vlasov and Nina Dumbadze were measured by the same standards of athletic heroism. They were both active, talented children. They worked assiduously within the Soviet sports establishment, following the direction of trainers and other authorities and developing their own intellectual and physical mastery of their specialty. At the same time, they became well-rounded adults of good character, diligent, self-disciplined, and patriotic. That is, they were both cultured and Soviet. They also became winners, at home and abroad. But there was a difference, a muted but quite significant one, between the weightlifter and the discus thrower.

Female athletes often were held up as model mothers. Dumbadze, for example, was billed in public-relations campaigns as a sports great, a patriot, a mother, and a wife.[13] Zoia Mironova, a champion speed-skater and veteran of the Second World War, and Kamenskaia, an elite gymnast from the Ukraine, were praised for living cultured lives as mothers, wives, and educated professionals.[14] By contrast, the domestic arrangements of Vlasov, Korolev, and other prominent male athletes were rarely mentioned as among their achievements. In Stalinist and post-Stalinist Soviet discourse, a woman who was not a wife and mother was judged incomplete, whatever else she might have achieved, and so even an Olympic champion had to have babies and a husband as well as medals to qualify as a model of female *kul'turnost'*.

The responsibilities of male athletes to the younger generation did appear as a theme in *Sovetskii sport*. Men were portrayed as examples of strength and as teachers of skills, whether to their younger proteges or to children. A particularly vivid example is a 1955 poster entitled 'Steel' that features a bare-chested, well muscled man holding an infant aloft (Fig. 6). The caption below reads, '[You] will not fear either heat or cold. Temper yourself like steel.'[15] This advice reflected the same beliefs in the importance of physical toughening that Catriona Kelly analyzed in an earlier chapter in this book. Soviet sport magazines regularly encouraged parents to teach discipline and hardiness early in a child's life through a regular routine of feeding, playing, and rest.[16] A child's sleeping area was to be well ventilated and sunny. Regular time outdoors was considered part of the process of 'tempering' the body to make it more resistant to childhood illnesses. Various cartoons and photographs printed in *Sovetskii sport* suggest that this aspect of a child's development should be the father's responsibility. In another example, a heavily muscled man in a suit and hat is pictured walking his infant in a stroller that sports barbells for wheels. The caption reads, 'Today's *bogatyr* and a future *bogatyr* out for a walk.'[17] Another cartoon tells the story of a father and son in six panels. The father packs for a camping trip, says goodbye to his wife, and sets out. Once in the woods, he dumps his heavy pack, only to discover that his son, anxious to share the expedition with him, has stowed away inside it. In the last panel father and son tramp off joyously together.[18]

The process of transforming raw youths into cultured athletes was in reality far more difficult than the celebratory 'success stories' suggested. In many cultures – and the 1950s Soviet Union was obviously no exception – athletes are admired for their exceptional physical talents. They are feted and made over by the press, by political leaders,

Figure 6 'Don't be afraid of hot or cold, temper yourself like STEEL!' Physical culture poster, 1955

and by an adoring public. But they are also tightly controlled, prohibited from indulging their appetites and enjoying their celebrity because they must observe rigid training schedules and health regimes. The stars who receive the most publicity are also expected to live up to the images of them as fine fellows created by their teams and the press. Male athletes seem to chafe at these controls more than do females, for reasons suggested by R. W. Connell in an analysis of Australian sportsmen:

> S., the exemplar of masculine toughness, finds his own exemplary status prevents him from doing exactly what his peer group defines as thoroughly masculine behavior: going wild, showing off, drunk driving, getting into fights, defending his own prestige.[19]

Daily newspapers in today's North America and Europe are full of stories of male athletes who break out of the confines of training and 'culturedness'. Soviet sports magazines in the 1950s were not permitted to report the escapades of their superstars, but those escapades occurred nonetheless, and the Soviet athletic establishment had problems with unruly champions that are very similar to those that plague team owners in today's world. The propagandists and the politicians saw it as a battle between *kul'turnost'* and *nekul'turnost'*, between the self-discipline of the true athletic hero and the crude machismo of an uneducated brute.

Korolev the champion boxer and war hero was a case in point. Although they lauded him in the press, party officials, journalists, and of course, people in boxing knew that Korolev was a drinker and a womanizer. In 1949, ten days before the European boxing championships in Oslo, the Soviet Union's strongest heavyweight contender was denied the right to travel abroad.[20] It is not clear what the reasons were, but it is possible that he was being disciplined. In July rumors surfaced that Korolev was politically and morally suspect because he had spent time eating and getting drunk in restaurants in the company of women (not including, we can presume, his wife).[21] Perhaps the boxer promised to reform, for he continued to compete for the USSR. Probably Soviet officials decided to look the other way and the press kept its silence, much as American reporters at the same time were conspiring with the management of the New York Yankees to cover up the alcoholism of media-darling Mickey Mantle.

For the actual treatment of *nekul'turnyi* superstars in the USSR in the 1940s and 1950s was very little different from that in western Europe or North America then and now. An athlete who won competitions could get away with a lot of shabby behavior in his private life, as long as he kept on winning. This was especially true in the period 1948–52 when the USSR was developing its first Olympic team. Soviet sports management seems to have been particularly forgiving with team sports such as soccer and hockey.

One of the most infamous players in Soviet soccer was Eduard Strel'tsov. By all accounts he was an exceptional performer who consistently set records in goal-scoring. He was also one of the USSR's 'most difficult personalities', according to Robert Edelman.[22] Strel'tsov had a reputation for fighting, drunkenness, and carousing that caused considerable tension between a rival team, the Moscow Dinamo organization, and the All-Union Committee on Physical Culture and Sport (VKFKiS), the body charged with overseeing Soviet sports. Dinamo, which had as one of its sponsors the Moscow city police, knew about Strel'tsov's behavior and claimed to have reported him to the chair of the VKFKiS as well as to the Moscow Party Committee and even the Party Central Committee. Apparently no action was taken immediately despite recommendations from Dinamo that the star be arrested or sent to the army for a year. These same Dinamo officials blamed the VKFKiS for enabling Strel'tsov's continued drunkenness. Finally the soccer player was arrested for rape in 1958 and sentenced to six years in prison.[23]

Strel'tsov's experience was extreme, but problems with alcohol and violence were common among athletes, especially soccer and hockey players. Various committees in the Party and sports apparatus were convened over the years to come up with solutions. In 1949 and 1959 there were campaigns to educate athletes and the press did weigh in from time to time to censure public behavior that reflected poorly on the cultural level of Soviet sport and on the USSR in general. By far the most frequently cited lapses in discipline involved alcohol: an athlete had appeared drunk in public and caused a disruption that could not easily be ignored or explained. The more politically sensitive the audience for this behavior, the more insistent the calls for censure. When there were serious lapses in front of groups of children, other athletes at sporting events, or the international media, the issue was very likely to be discussed in the press and in sports management.[24] The Moscow Committee for Physical Culture and Sport was also called in to investigate reports of athletes staggering around in public places such as the zoo, sports stadiums, and restaurants.[25] Although drunkenness in private was not necessarily considered acceptable, it became a disciplinary matter only in cases where it led to more serious crimes, such as assaults on women.[26]

Sovetskii sport inveighed against such dissipation to its male readers. In 1959 it ran a series of articles criticizing alcohol and tobacco consumption among athletes and sports fans. In March, a physician suggested that there was a need to distinguish real athleticism from the male soccer culture of nicotine, alcohol, rough play, and raw strength. She called for the development of the higher, cultured, Soviet masculinity to counter the crudeness on display at soccer matches.[27] The author declared that as a woman she was 'incompetent' to comment on the specifics of play, but she felt that she could stand up to the 'skeptical smiles of some men' when discussing the issue of 'athleticism' from a medical perspective.

After excusing herself for presuming to comment on the male domain of soccer, the author observed that the ancient Greek sports ideals could still be found among weightlifters, gymnasts (male) and discus throwers, but not among soccer players as a rule. Many soccer players are 'real athletes', she conceded, who possessed strength, speed, precision, and endurance. Players, trainers, coaches and fans should not, however, confuse raw strength with real mastery of a sport. There should be less rough play on the pitch and less alcohol and tobacco consumption off it. Drink and smoking, she argued, were leading to declining levels of physical fitness among soccer players and among Soviet men in general. The doctor concluded by apologizing again for her gender; that is, she urged her readers to consider her pleas the advice of a physician, not the nagging of a spouse.[28]

Although this tension between 'cultured' and 'uncultured' behavior was particularly acute in soccer, it was in no means limited to that sport. One skier complained to Moscow officials:

> If for example, I have a bunch of good competitions, and after each competition I get drunk, what can come of it? Isn't it ok? For example, my birthday is in the winter, so can I never go and drink some wine because training or competitions are coming up. . . . Comrades, sometimes it happens this way: they ask you, 'Let's go have a smoke!' You answer, 'No, I don't smoke.' And they say, 'What kind of a man are you?'[29]

Sovetskii sport frequently published cartoons and articles which attempted to make alcohol and nicotine less attractive to men. One portrayed a Russian man's day in four panels.[30] The reader was shown an office worker lying around in bed smoking, eating, and drinking until he passed out, or playing cards into the night with friends, and then finally wondering why his head hurt at work in the morning. Another cartoon featured a weak, drunk man struggling under the weight of an empty wine glass.[31] This image was accompanied by a poem entitled 'A Difficult Case', the subject of which was a weightlifter who lifted 100 grams (that is, shots of vodka) more often than weights in a gym and ended up following a 'strict regimen' in prison instead of a strict training regimen (*strogii rezhim*).

The USSR in the 1950s was hardly unique in its efforts to use sports to teach proper behavior. That athletic competition is valuable for the ideals it imparts as well as for the physical skills it builds is a principle widely accepted across the European world. Sports stars are routinely held up as examples of healthy minds in healthy bodies and just as routinely they fall from grace. In the year 2000 alone, two prominent players in the National Football League of the United States, Ray Caruth and Ray Lewis, were indicted for murder in separate cases, and Caruth was found guilty in early 2001. Nor were Soviet observers unusual in their concerns about the rowdiness that seemed a part of soccer culture. The hooliganism that plagues European matches is legendary and every year around the world fans die in soccer riots.

It is the ways in which Soviet commentators defined their sports enterprise and linked it with larger projects of instructing the citizenry that make their case interesting. The Communist Party had sought to teach *kul'turnost'* to a rough-hewn working class and peasantry, whose wild sides it feared, long before 1917, but the first generation of the party had thought competitive sports were corrupt and bourgeois. They preferred group calisthenics and long walks. By the postwar period those Bolshevik prejudices were long gone, and the Soviet government was well on its way to building an international reputation for sports excellence. Now the argument for sports as a means to cultured citizens was easily made. Commentators asserted strenuously that the natural talent of a potential champion had to be developed through the system, which they personalized in the figure of an avuncular but highly skilled coach. Long years of diligent work with this mentor and within the sports establishment would grind away the rough edges, teach an athlete his craft, and also impart self-control, loyalty to the system, even abstemiousness. A star so trained could be an example to the nation, selling not the products of capitalism as western athletes did, but the Soviet system itself in widely publicized media events at home and major competitions around the world.

There were female and male athletes in the Soviet pantheon. Influenced by its much qualified commitments to women's equality, the government provided far more support for women's sports than did any western nation in the 1940s and 1950s, and made more of its female athletes. Although they were praised for many of the same virtues as men, women were under the additional obligation of being model mothers. The resultant ideal – talented, disciplined athlete, good comrade, patriot, and mom – was simply another variant on the New Soviet Superwoman who had been a central player in the Soviet cast of ideal types since the 1930s.

The masculine values promulgated by *Sovetskii sport* came just as directly out of Stalinist ideas and the Bolshevik Marxism that gave birth to Stalinism. Self-control, hard work, study, submission to superiors, patriotism, and the individual success that all this dutiful behavior brought were the defining characteristics of the New Soviet Man. Indeed they also figured importantly in the hegemonic masculinity prevalent throughout the European world in the twentieth century. *Sovetskii sport* added a concern with the male as father-figure that was relatively new, a product of the attention to domestic life that became possible in the more relaxed political and social atmosphere of the post-Stalin decades. It is a delicious irony that even in the 1950s, while American red-baiters were excoriating the Soviets as enemies of civilization, Soviet opinion-makers were earnestly attempting to create'responsible,' 'respectable', 'cultured' men and were doing it, at least in part, through sports. Long before highly paid advertising executives in the US had crafted their 'Be Like Mike' campaign, an artist working away in the dingy offices of *Sovetskii sport* had dreamed up the slogan, 'If you want to be like me, train!'

Notes

1. *Sovetskii sport,* 20 July 1950, 4.
2. It is worth noting that these athletic biographies have much in common with the life histories analyzed by R. W. Connell in 'An Iron Man: the Body and Some Contradictions of Hegemonic Masculinity', *Sport, Men, and the Gender Order: Critical Feminist Perspectives,* ed. Michael A. Messner and Donald F. Sabo (Champaign, Ill., 1990). Note especially the relationship between the development of heroes and the development of a particular style of masculinity as 'hegemonic'. Many American sports movies (for example, *The Karate Kid* series, *Hoosiers,* even *Bull Durham*) have similar plots. Differences arise in the ways in which particular ideologies shape the narrative structure of these biographies.
3. *Sovetskii sport,* 28 September 1946, 4.
4. *Bol'shaia sovetskaia entsiklopediia* (Moscow, 1950), 5, 339–40.
5. *Sovetskii sport,* 22 January 1955, 3.
6. Ibid.,16 March 1957, 1.
7. Ibid.
8. Ibid.
9. Ibid., 18 August 1959, 5.
10. In fact, there is a photograph of a little boy imitating this same gesture with his grandfather in ibid., 22 May 1958, 6, and another of a little boy lifting weights in this way in ibid., 17 October 1958, 3. The caption with this last article reads 'If you want to be healthy – temper yourself!'

11. *Krasnyi sport,* 7 August 1945, 4.
12. Ibid.
13. For examples of the use of Nina Dumbadze's image to promote various Party themes see *Sovetskii sport,* 15 June 1946, 4, and 21 July 1946, 5. See also ibid., 9 August 1952, 17 July 1954, and 2 April 1955.
14. Ibid., 7 August 1945, 4, and 6 September 1951, 4.
15. Ibid., 22 January 1955, 3.
16. Ibid., 6 September 1951, 4.
17. Ibid., 14 September 1958, 8.
18. Ibid., 7 July 1956, 4.
19. Connell, 'An Iron Man: the Body and Some Contradictions of Hegemonic Masculinity', 86.
20. Rossiiskii Tsentr Khraneniia i Izucheniia Dokumentov Noveishei Istorii (RTsKhIDNI), f. 17, op. 132, d. 267, l. 40.
21. Ibid., d. 264, l. 59.
22. See Robert Edelman, *Serious Fun* (Oxford, 1993), 132, for more on Strel'tsov and the effects of his behavior on the performance of Soviet elite soccer teams.
23. Tsentral'nyi Gosudarstvennyi Arkhiv Organizatsii Rossiiskii i Sovetskii Sport goroda Moskvy (TsGAORSS g. Moskvy), f. 1067, op. 1, d. 170, ll. 59–60, 1958. Recently debate has arisen over whether Strel'tsov was indeed guilty.
24. Ibid., f. 758, op. 1, d. 13, l. 166, 28 June, 1957; d. 24, 25 June, 1959; f. 1967, op. 1, d. 68, ll. 134–8, 21 November 1949; f. 1067, op. 1, d. 170, l. 16–18, 25 June, 1958, and f. 457, op. 1, d. 88, l. 2–7, 27 November 1950.
25. Ibid., f. 758, op. 1, d. 4, l. 21, 1949; d. 24, l. 97–8, 1959.
26. Ibid., f. 1067, op. 1, d. 170, l. 58, 1958.
27. In 1959, *Sovetskii sport* published a letter from a female volleyball player who asked whether women could be true soccer fans. As an answer to her question, the editors published an article by a female medical doctor entitled 'Soccer – it's a male thing!' 8 March 1959, 5.
28. Ibid.
29. TsGAORSS g. Moskvy, f. 1067, op. 1, d. 170, l. 66–7, 1958.
30. *Sovetskii sport,* 21 September 1957, 8.
31. Ibid., 6 October 1957, 8.

13
Conclusions

Rebecca Friedman and Dan Healey

We know what trembles on the scales,
and what we must steel ourselves to face.
The bravest hour strikes on our clocks:
may courage not abandon us!
Let bullets kill us – we are not afraid,
nor are we bitter, though our housetops fall.
We will preserve you, Russian speech,
from servitude in foreign chains,
keep you alive, great Russian word,
fit for the songs of our children's children
pure on their tongues, and free.

'Courage' (*Muzhestvo*), translated by
Stanley Kunitz with Max Hayward

On International Women's Day in 1942, Anna Akhmatova's famous poem appeared in the pages of *Pravda*.[1] It was, of course, part of the increasingly traditional call to all Russians to the defense of their homeland, here imagined not as a territory or a population, but as a language, the 'great Russian word'. Akhmatova's appeal, published on the day in the Soviet calendar devoted to the celebration of women, addressed both women and men, evoking in its few short lines the awesome disasters threatening those on the battlefield and those in the rear. Yet this poem (perhaps especially in this translation) can potentially be misconstrued if the masculine is not read back into it. The title, of course, relies on that Russian word for 'courage' derived from the root for 'man' ('muzh-') and in the poem itself *muzhestvo* beats solemnly not once (as in this version) but twice, in its third and fourth lines.[2] If this English rendering conveys the sacrifice of life at both the front and the domestic rear with its falling 'housetops', the original was more ambiguous, referring not at all to houses under siege but only to those Russians 'lying dead under bullets . . . [and] left drained of blood'.[3] While Akhmatova's intention was no doubt to include women here as victims of a merciless total war, one might ask if some readers would have imagined soldiers at the front as the chief sacrifice hailed in these lines. Finally, the 'children's children' who will inherit the 'great Russian word' in the original poem were male grandchildren (*i vnukam dadim*, literally, 'And we will give [the great Russian word] to our grandsons').[4] From its nod to the paternalistic role of the Great Russian nation in the Soviet Union's struggle with the invader and its imagery glorifying the ultimate masculine sacrifice, to its suggestion that the nation's spirit was in hands of (and on the lips of) Russia's sons, Akhmatova's poem could be read as an appeal to men to assume their traditional and politically resonant duties as warriors and fathers. In Russia's bleakest hour, its greatest poet, a woman speaking on International Women's Day, called upon men to be manly. What, though, did it mean to be a manly Russian man? How have the expectations that Akhmatova implied changed over time?

The essays in this volume suggest that Russian masculinity has been made and remade, as has much else in Russian history, through the complex interactions of home-grown and imported ideas, values and practices. The relationship between Russia and western Europe as seen from an exploration of masculinity is far from straightforward. On the one hand, the essays in this collection reveal that as a Eurasian polity striving to emulate European partners and rivals, the evolution of Russian masculinities followed much the same path as those observed in nations further west. From the reign of Peter the Great, elite manhood began to shed its patron–client structure as the ideals of the self-directed man of action were admired, rewarded, and inculcated. By the nineteenth century an elite Russian man was in many respects meant to conduct himself like his bourgeois counterparts in Germany or France. Emotional voluntarism and responsible fatherhood were part of this equation: love in marriage and, increasingly, a domesticated and gentler husband figure were regarded as desirable. Elite family life was meant to be ruled by a measured mutuality rather than unbridled patriarchal authority. Self-discipline, rational self-fashioning and vigorous participation (if not coarsening 'excessive' success) in the emerging market became traits that members of the Russian middling classes sought to encourage in their male children. Later at the end of the Imperial era as sexual conduct became the focus for a burgeoning public debate, certain sexual behaviors acquired the status of the pathological. An incipient division between homosexual and heterosexual sexualities appeared, with an emphasis, as elsewhere, on redefining the masculine. By the time of the First World War some Russian men displayed most of the attributes of a range of recognizably 'modern' masculinities based on or in reaction to Europe's dominant bourgeois ideal of manhood.

Yet the Russian story is far from being just a footnote of confirmation in the gender history of Europe. The social complexion of Russia generated tensions and discontinuities in the western European models of manliness even as they were imported, tailored, and tried out. Peasant patterns of socialization into manhood included an expectation of balancing the norms of the village and the models for the city-dwelling proletarian. Russia's middling classes were far from hegemonic, and older styles of aristocratic manhood that emphasized service, order, and rank retained influence and power. A second factor that demonstrates the unique nature of masculine gender in Russia is the role of the state in shaping men and manliness. To an extent seldom experienced in Europe, state intervention and sometimes tutelage had long been a determinant in the formation of important masculine identities. Yet, even here, men created their own rights and rituals outside the official state arena. The central role of intense emotions between men also sets Russia apart from current understandings of European manliness. In the final volume of his semi-fictional memoir *A Russian Schoolboy* Sergei Aksakov describes the intimate attachment he formed with a young student in the first years of the nineteenth century: 'My friendship with Alexander Panaev . . . grew by leaps and bounds, and soon there was such an intimacy between us as can only exist in early manhood.'[5] Russia's patterns of social status and class, the role of the Muscovite, Imperial, and Soviet state and the culture of masculine intimacy are themes in the essays that set Russian manliness apart from European versions.

Until well into the twentieth century peasants constituted Russia's largest if not its most powerful social group, and their ideals and practices of masculinity were an inescapable reference point whenever the formation of new types of manhood was envisioned or undertaken. Village men were not mere 'children' or a tabula rasa upon which 'civilized' values could be written. Peasants *had* masculinity, as Christine Worobec shows, a constructed performance of gender scripted by rituals and social convention. Officials and educated observers were repulsed by peasant men's violence. Yet such violence was governed by an 'ethics of honor' that structured relations within the village and between villagers and outsiders. Urban-dwelling elites hoped that one day peasants could acquire 'culture' or 'civilized' values. Yet peasant men were socialized to respect and honor fatherhood, to nurture and mentor sons and young men, and to aspire to form stable and productive households. Their apparently prodigious and ruinous vodka consumption was structured around community rituals and homosocial spaces that reinforced primary masculine traits.

Peasant manhood proved to be adaptable when migrants left for the workshops, construction sites, and factories of Russia's industrializing towns. In many respects it retained the same communal ethic (in the *artel'* and in the homosocial spaces of apprentice-lodgings, worker-barracks, and the tavern) as well as the same structuring through camaraderie, violence, and alcohol. Russian industry would only develop if it could harness this particularly robust and resilient human capital. As Stephen Smith argues the transition to a 'modern' urban proletarian masculinity was far from complete by 1914. Indeed, some of the change he discerns may have in fact been driven by peasant values. The new emphasis on skill over brute force as an aspiration felt by workers came perhaps from recognition that in new circumstances, the peasant admiration of productive toil and the manly provider role inspired a new respect for smarter work. The new worth placed by migrant workers on wit or cleverness could adhere to the same realization. If urban workers drank more regularly and recreationally than their peasant cousins, it was still in the homosocial environment of the tavern where they continued to seek mentorship, establish their reputations, and learn about the world beyond the factory gate.

On some level, however, other aspects of urban life challenged these reassuring similarities with the masculinity of the village, and evidently contributed to the anxieties experienced by Russia's urban workforce of the late nineteenth and early twentieth centuries. The authority of the peasant patriarch did not extend to the town, and young migrant laborers eagerly sought new leaders to guide them. Some turned to the intelligentsia as a model, to refashion themselves into what would be dubbed a 'conscious' proletariat. In this ascetic framework love was based on emotionally intimate relations with women and tempered by sexual probity. Many other men found the seductions and pleasures of consumerism attractive: here were amusements (the music hall, the cinema, fashion, sports, the brothel) that promised distraction, gratification, and consolation, and offered pleasurable ways to remake oneself. For some peasant migrants earning cash wages for the first time, city life brought the 'narcissistic' pursuit of 'consciously crafted sexual attractiveness,' an attempt to emulate the fashion-plates they saw on the boulevard and the cinema screen. They found admirers for their dandified appearance among both urban and rural women. Yet these consumers also endured merciless teasing and resentment from fellow men if they paraded their new manners and outfits in their home villages; their masculinity was insecure in this environment for they repudiated the vestimentary codes of rural life and degraded their personal reputations by appearing to elevate pleasure above other values.

The evolution of working-class masculinity proceeded with little direction from the autocracy, but the same could not be said for the middling sort and its men. Russia's governors and administrators had long been the subjects of projects to refashion them. As Nancy Shields Kollmann reminds us, Peter the Great shaped generations of new men to transform Russia into a European polity, by drawing on the spectrum of European and elite masculinities he admired. However critical that the acquisition of new technology and new skills were to the success of Peter's transformational ambitions, state tutelage did not end there. It also brought with it determined and sometimes impatient attempts to transform gender identity at the intimate levels of private life and the body. The *Domostroi* model of marriage and relations between the sexes was overturned, but the prescriptive impulse was not. Peter's decree on 'assemblies' inaugurated new public spaces, the salon and the pleasure garden, where men and women of the elite strata were compelled and exhorted to perform according to new gender scripts. His marriage and divorce legislation sanctioned 'emotional voluntarism' in love, while attempting to retain the sanctity of lifelong monogamy. In the reactionary last years of the Imperial period, as Barbara Engel shows, tsarism was still engaged in the micromanagement of marital life, although now its creaking separation and divorce regime barely held back a tide of family disintegration. The state's unwillingness to implement a legal framework that reflected contemporary realities apparently encouraged some recalcitrant husbands to resurrect the *Domostroi* as their ideal of domestic manliness.[6]

The body too was recruited to realize Peter's project: beards were taxed or shaved off, and mannequins on street corners modeled the French and German apparel that was mandatory for city dwellers. From the evidence presented by Olga Vainshtein, the body and its adornment became a key focus for self-fashioning during the eighteenth and early nineteenth centuries among aristocratic and gentry servitor men, even serving as a means of demonstrating one's sympathies or dismay with westernization. In the universities of Nicholas I, the petty regulations of the student uniform and public comportment that were imposed on Russia's future administrators imparted another kind of masculinity-by-fiat. Under the surveillance of a network of inspectors, students acted out a series of roles required by the Nicholaevan state's obsession with *nravy* (morals) and *pokornost'* (pious duty). As it strengthened its bureaucratic networks, the autocracy required men to do its bidding in the far reaches of the empire; it officially mandated a set of values and behaviors that neatly uniformed students were to bring with them to the far reaches of the empire after graduation.

Yet as the flamboyance of the Russian dandy and the rebellions of Nicholaevan students suggest, the Imperial man was not constructed from ukases alone. What these essays assert is that Russian men were indeed agents in their own history, sometimes struggling with state-dictated notions of manhood, other times complicit in their own creation. Outside the purview of the state – whether Imperial or Soviet – rowdy students, muscular athletes, aging *tetki*, courageous soldiers, and disciplined workers carved out niches for themselves in formal and informal arenas of daily social life. This autonomy took numerous forms, from tavern brawls and illicit sexual encounters to experiments with dress. The increasing wealth of aristocrats, gentry servitors, and (later in the nineteenth century) the middle strata allowed conscious self-fashioning and conspicuous consumption to flourish. Items of clothing and fashions such as dandyism were enthusiastically imported from abroad. Indigenous conditions (a harsh winter climate) and geographic factors (the lag in the transmission of new fashions from Paris and London) as well as the unusually strict and occasionally arbitrary regulatory environment transformed aspects of these imports. The transformations could render the Russian variant almost unrecognizable next to his western analogue, as in the case of the slavish fashion-consciousness and the ostentatious display of some dandies (instead of the internalized self-discipline and 'good taste' exercised by British originators of the trend). Another local peculiarity of this type was the military dandy obsessed with pouring himself into his tight-fitting uniforms, if necessary with a girdle. The plethora of ranks, hierarchies, and uniforms in official Imperial Russia offered men an extensive discursive field upon which to rewrite themselves in their service clothing.[7] In eighteenth- and nineteenth-century Russia, dandies exploited the possibilities presented by their circumscribed circumstances to push the boundaries of acceptable manhood outward.

Similarly, university students under Nicholas I found that manliness was a delicate balancing act between the reality of intense moral supervision and the aspiration to enjoy the 'comradely society' of their peers. To avoid becoming a mere 'simple chinovnik' the Nicholaevan student sought sociability with his classmates in rituals of alcohol consumption and rowdiness and, less frequently, outright violence or sexual distractions. Manliness consisted in knowing how to combine respectable comportment before one's betters with indulgence in the disreputable activities that raised a man's reputation in the eyes of his peers. Paradoxically it was the representative of the state that helped to mentor these young men in this balancing act, in the person of the university inspector.

This balancing act was not unique to the Nicholaevan student. One theme that weaves its way through the collection is the ongoing tension between a traditional masculinity – marked by qualities including drunkenness and toughness – and a 'new' more refined manliness defined by self-restraint and *kulturnost'* in the later period. Rather than imagining a single moment of crisis where traditional models were overtaken by more 'modern' ones, these essays – taken together – emphasize how becoming a proper Russian man involved a constant negotiation between official and unofficial, long present and newly emerging models of masculinity.

The sons and grandsons of the university students discussed by Friedman faced the industrial 'take-off' of the 1880s and 1890s. Now the state's prescriptive masculinities with their emphasis on emphatic hierarchy (the Table of Ranks) and *pokornost'* were, as Catriona Kelly notes, unsuited to the requirements of capitalist organizations. The late Imperial government failed to sponsor or encourage masculine gender roles that adequately met the demands of industrialization and urbanization.[8] Instead, the construction of new forms of manhood took place in the negotiations between peasant-migrants and factory foremen, between the sons of *chinovniki* and venture capitalists (many of them foreign), and in a new wave of ideological imports from western Europe. Advice manuals and medical tracts, whether they promoted the virtues of *zakal* or laid out the dire consequences of 'sexual perversion', represented a new stage in the old story of foreign influence on Russian masculinity. Again there were divergences from the original western application of these ideologies, especially when Russian translations of western advice manuals soft-peddled the rigidities of gender present in the originals. The cult of *zakal* began its career perhaps less focused on the banishing the feminine (or effeminate), although with the proliferation of moral tracts and advice manuals translated more-or-less literally from European languages, such subtleties declined by the twentieth century. Equally, the medicalization of sexual love between men (transforming a sin, sodomy, into a symptom of a psychiatric illness, homosexuality) found fewer and later converts among doctors in Russia than in France and Germany, despite the prompt translation of most of the key texts of forensic medicine and psychopathology.

There were moments, however, when rigid prescriptions were paramount. By the end of the Imperial era the cult of the iron will, the tempering of the body, and the denigration of passivity and effeminacy were well-established. Russian memoirists of the 1890s reflected the new value placed on toughness when they adopted an incredulous and hostile tone to describe the 'effeminate' hairstyles or make-up sported by dandies of earlier generations.[9] Effeminacy and the dandy's obsession with his personal aesthetic were now more explicitly devalued through an association with 'sinful' sexual practices, especially sodomy. Even if little was said in public about the circumstances leading to Oscar Wilde's downfall (reported in the Russian press and avidly, often sympathetically, discussed), the shadow of his particular formula of illicit sexuality and dandyism cast its pall from the opposite end of Europe.[10]

Underlying the anxiety that eros between men began to evoke was the increasingly visible presence in Russia's cities of a homosexual subculture, with its market in male desire and male sex. Incredulity and hostility marked social critics' views of the *tetki* and the men who sold them sexual favors, much of it based on the premise that one partner in these transactions was 'passive' and therefore feminized by this sexual posture. It is hardly surprising that the effeminate figure of the *tetka* appears more frequently in late Imperial discussions of homosexuality than the culturally less intelligible 'woman-hater'. The latter's manly external appearance and narcissistic desire for an equally manly lover apparently confused observers, and perhaps even participants, who preferred to leave their desires and practices unnamed. Meanwhile the gender inversion assigned to (and intermittently practiced by) the *tetka* conformed to the script that taking the receptive sexual role was a submissive and therefore 'feminine' act. It certainly appeared to be an abuse of the male body, the reversal of all the aspirations embodied in the cult of *zakal*; yet the explicit opposition of 'tempered' 'normal' manhood to an effeminate male homosexuality seems to have been relatively weak in Russia. 'Normal' masculine sexual desire (from 1900 in Russia increasingly dubbed 'heterosexuality') underwent a kind of slow clarification by default, as around it various 'sexual perversions' were discerned by a modest (by western standards) number of doctors.[11] Nevertheless, the view that sexual desire in Russia was naturally and essentially 'innocent', untainted by depravities cultivated in the Orient or created by neurasthenia as a result of 'civilization' in the West, was an enduring and appealing national myth.[12] As a story of Russian sexual 'innocence', it significantly truncated the reception of western sexology's crucial binarism of homosexuality/heterosexuality.

The myth of sexually innocent Russia allowed – and perhaps continued to allow until very recently – forms of male homosociability and mutual physicality to flourish without the taint of deviant sexuality that arose in the more heavily medicalized West.[13] As we have seen, in Russia, homosocial spaces and rituals that cemented bonds between young men, whether students, apprentices, or soldiers, were not as intensely freighted with fears of illicit desire.[14] Men's romantic friendship including expressions of love (as noted by Karen Petrone in Soviet war literature) and occasionally intimate physical proximity were valued as transformative experiences well into the twentieth century.[15] The revolutionary and later Soviet impulse to build 'male community' among soldiers traced by Petrone was replicated in the predominantly male Communist Party, where intimacy was amplified by the observance of the practices of 'conspiracy'. The 'revolutionary romanticism' discerned by Catriona Kelly in the Soviet intellectuals' pursuit of self-tempering was a kind of politically acceptable homosocial bonding agent. In wartime it counselled emotional self-control, tight loyalty to one's fighting group, ferocious aggression in battle and stoicism afterwards. In peacetime political life it romanticized war experience by importing the metaphors of the battleground into ideological debates.

A key aspect of this romantic, militarized revolutionary masculinity was its misogyny. The contempt for the feminine, documented in Bolshevik ideology by Tom Schrand, was of necessity a concealed current in a Party overtly committed to the emancipation of women. Yet the revolutionary bonds forged between Russian men were in part constructed by feminizing what was Other, whether it was an internal junior comrade like the Caucasian or Central Asian soldier, an entire social stratum such as the peasantry, or an external military enemy. The peacetime indulgence in military rhetoric peppered Soviet political speech with nervous chest-thumping claims of political virility and triumphant domination of 'castrated' enemies. Meanwhile in the Soviet imagination Russia's men were presumed to be in possession of a spontaneous, natural virility that (unlike female sexuality) was in little or no need of medicalization. Men who acted like women (homosexuals) were thus probably class enemies, not biological 'anomalies'. One of the regime's most vividly masculine figures, Nikolai Krylenko, claimed in 1936 that 'little gentlemen of this type' were 'from the remnants of the exploiting classes'. Bewildered by the triumph of a workers' society, they supposedly turned to 'pederasty' to sow demoralization.[16] In reality, however, the blanket ban on male same-sex love turned up plenty of worker and white-collar homosexuals; these men had to be concealed in a closet of closed-door justice, and if possible, rehabilitated through the prison camp.

To what extent did the Soviet experience create a 'new Soviet masculinity'? With research only beginning on the question (not only in the Soviet period, but in the Muscovite, Imperial, and post-Soviet as well), it is too soon to make any claims, but from the essays in this collection we can propose some points for consideration. First, rather than conceive of the Russian Revolution as a culminating moment in the creation of a new masculine identity, the authors in this collection suggest that Russian and Soviet masculinity were always in the making, influenced by official (state) and unofficial (social life) prescriptions. Second, it would be more prudent to think in terms of several competing or coincidental masculine identities rather than a single Soviet manhood. Manliness as an ideal in Soviet propaganda may have seemed monolithically proletarian, but the realities of political and social status, nationality, location, occupation, and so on impinged on gender roles for men just as they did for women. As many of our essayists demonstrate, manhood was divided internally by hierarchies that expressed often-unwritten expectations about, for example, ethnicity or class.

A third point is that the revolutionary experimentation and later the so-called conservative 'retreat' in family life and heterosexual relations affected men's behavior and expectations of marriage and fatherhood in ways that deserve further investigation. It appears that the abandonment of wives and mothers increased during the 1920s and 1930s to proportions most observers found critical. We still have little idea of why such an apparent surge in men's flight from marital and parental responsibility should have taken place. The suggestion that the intrusion of the state into the domestic realm demoralized men who hankered after traditional patriarchal power, by offering women alternative means of support, may be a partial explanation. Yet as an explanation it rather unsatisfactorily blames women for demanding recognition for motherhood, and the state for trying to 'emancipate' women.[17] Another causal factor could have been the disruptive economic conditions that led many workers in the 1930s into a nomadic search for better pay, work, and living conditions. Men's aspirations and disappointments in marriage as experienced after the Revolution need to be probed more fully, from diaries and personal papers as well as divorce and alimony records, to produce a clearer picture of their sense of appropriate revolutionary values in husbands and fathers. Another productive way to consider this question could be to examine how fatherhood acquired new social meanings during the Soviet era, as Gilmour's descriptions of sports propaganda suggest. Just as university students looked up to their inspector-mentors with filial emotion, and migrant-laborers turned to experienced peers to 'teach them to work', during the Soviet era the metaphorical fatherhood of military officers, sports trainers, and the Party itself apparently satisfied many men in search of validation of their masculinity.

A final point about the validity of the new Soviet masculinity is the striking persistence of alternative forms of manliness despite the 'total' claims of the state. As we have seen throughout the nineteenth and early twentieth centuries, alcohol, sexuality, and homosociability continued to present men with opportunities to establish their manhood in ways inimical to state control. Disruptive and disreputable masculine styles, such as the bonding through drink and womanizing that continued to mark Soviet team sports of the 1950s, were scarcely suppressed despite the state's resort to hectoring, medicalization, and, less frequently by this time, coercion. Similarly the survival of a male homosexual subculture continued to offer a sharp alternative to the prevailing sex/gender system. The Party's ideal of a cultured, healthy, and 'normal' Soviet man, like the nineteenth-century university's notion of administrative, self-controlled manhood, was far from hegemonic. It is now the task of historians of Russian gender to look past the mask of Communism's idealized manhood to see what lay behind.

Notes

1. See Anna Akhmatova, *Sochineniia v dvukh tomakh* (Moscow, 1986), 1: 199, 422. This translation is from Anna Akhmatova, *Selected Poems*, trans. Stanley Kunitz with Max Hayward (London, 1989), 125.
2. 'Chas muzhestva probil na nashikh chasakh. / I muzhestvo nas ne pokinet.'
3. 'Ne strashno pod puliami mertvymi lech', / Ne gor'ko ostat'sia bez krova' – literally, 'It is not terrifying to lie dead under bullets / It is not bitter to be left without blood.'
4. Another ambiguity in these lines stressed the Soviet Union's leading nationality. As the 'great Russian word' appears in the original isolated as *Velikoe*

russkoe slovo, on its own line, attentive readers would have heard an echo of traditional claims to 'Great Russian' (*velikorusskii*) paternalism over the subject nations of the Soviet Empire.

5. Sergei Aksakov, *A Russian Schoolboy* (Oxford, 1983), 128.
6. For an argument that the extreme dysfunctionality of the old regime's divorce and separation system 'fueled widespread disenchantment and alienation, even among believers', see Gregory L. Freeze, 'Krylov vs. Krylova: "Sexual Incapacity" and Divorce in Tsarist Russia', *The Human Tradition in Modern Russia*, ed. William B. Husband (Wilmington, Del., 2000), 16–17.
7. Not that Russians were the only men who preened themselves over their uniforms, or sought to join a particular regiment because they found its uniform flattering. See Joanna Bourke, *Dismembering the Male: Men's Bodies, Britain and the Great War* (London, 1996), 171–209.
8. Its bid to revive duelling in the officer class as a way of imbuing recruits from non-aristocratic backgrounds with 'noble' values was emblematic of this failure of vision.
9. M. I. Pyliaev's descriptions of military dandies, discussed by Olga Vainshtein, are particularly good examples of this anxiety.
10. On the 'fortuitous political expediency' that facilitated the mythologization of Wilde as 'a saintly sufferer', see Evgenii Bershtein, 'The Russian Myth of Oscar Wilde', *Self and Story in Russian History*, ed. Laura Engelstein and Stephanie Sandler (Ithaca & London, 2000).
11. On the resistance of Russia's doctors to the pathologization of sexual 'perversion' see Laura Engelstein, *The Keys to Happiness: Sex and the Search for Modernity in Fin-de-Siècle Russia* (Ithaca & London, 1992), 152–64. For a discussion of the structural reasons for Russian medicine's resistance to this western trend, see Dan Healey, *Homosexual Desire in Revolutionary Russia: the Regulation of Sexual and Gender Dissent* (Chicago, 2001).
12. For an expression of this tripartite geography of perversion positing Russia's natural sexual innocence, see G. S. Novopolin, *Pornograficheskii element v russkoi literature* (St Petersburg, 1909), 169. The failure of sexological discourses of perversion to operate as in the West when introduced in Russia has been ascribed to their quick politicization by left and right; see Evgenii Bershtein, '"Psychopathia sexualis" v Rossii nachala veka: politika i zhanr', *Eros i pornografiia v russkoi kul'ture/Eros and Pornography in Russian Culture*, ed. M. Levitt and A. Toporkov (Moscow, 1999), 436.
13. In American YMCA clubs between 1900 and the 1920s 'all physical touch between men . . . was being sexualized to some extent' and thus was increasingly fiercely policed; John D. Gustav-Wrathall, *Take the Young Stranger by the Hand: Same-Sex Relations and the YMCA* (Chicago, 1998), 140–57.
14. One of the better known instances of the expression of homosocial desire within the context of the Russian intelligentsia is the oath on Sparrow Hill between Alexander Herzen and Nicholas Ogarev. On this see, Rebecca Friedman, 'In the Company of Men: Student Life and Russian Masculinity' (Ph.D. diss., University of Michigan, 2000), ch. 4.
15. For physical intimacy, see e.g. the short story 'My First Goose' by Isaac Babel (1920), in which soldiers sleep with their legs intertwined.

16. Nikolai Krylenko, 'Ob izmeneniiakh i dopolneniiakh kodeksov RSFSR', *Sovetskaia iustitsiia*, 15, no. 7 (1936), 3–4; Krylenko was an avid promoter of *zakal*, sponsoring the development of Soviet mountaineering and hunting; see Donald D. Barry, 'Nikolai Vasil'evich Krylenko: a Re-evaluation', *Review of Socialist Law*, no. 2 (1989), 131–47.
17. For this line of reasoning, see Sergei Kukhterin, 'Fathers and Patriarchs', *Gender, State and Society in Soviet and Post-Soviet Russia*, ed. Sarah Ashwin (New York, 2000).

Index